TRANSATLANTIC

PATTERNS

TRANSATLANTIC
PATTERNS

Cultural Comparisons of England

with America

MARTIN BURGESS GREEN, 1927

Basic Books, Inc., Publishers

NEW YORK

Library of Congress Cataloging in Publication Data

Green, Martin Burgess, 1927–
   Transatlantic patterns.

   1. Literature, Comparative—English and
American—Addresses, essays, lectures.   2. Liter-
ature, Comparative—American and English—Addresses,
essays, lectures.   3.   English fiction—20th
century—History and criticism—Addresses, essays,
lectures.   4.   American fiction—20th century—
History and criticism—Addresses, essays, lectures.
I.   Title.
PR129.U5G7   820'.9'0091   74–78305
ISBN: 0–465–08688–8

Contents

v

Contents

Contents

TRANSATLANTIC
PATTERNS

Chapter 1

TWO CAMBRIDGE
EPIPHANIES

Cambridge, England, 1950

I went for a walk early one Sunday morning—long before breakfast could be got—and saw a couple of young men, presumably undergraduates, standing beside a car with the engine running. They were smoking and talking quietly. No one and nothing else was stirring. It was a sports car, and one of them was in evening dress, the other wore one of those stiff-skirted, white, riding-coat macs. They seemed to have been up all night and were about to leave town. Clearly they belonged to a different world from mine. More privileged, no doubt, but that was not the point. More strenuous. They had just freshened up. Their hair was newly and flatly combed; their cheeks were newly and shinily shaved. And it was the harshness of the discipline they had imposed on themselves which struck me—the rasping of the razor and the dragging of the comb—that each had treated his face as if it was just another part of his body. They had both stocky, strong-looking, hard-muscled bodies, but that their faces should be the same struck me as a revelation. They were not just tough; they were toughs. For this was not discipline in preparation for work—that I was familiar with—but discipline in preparation for pleasure. They did not mean to participate in some occasion of pleasure or to please; they had not soft-

3

ened and opened themselves, quite the contrary. They had prepared themselves to be efficient in taking—also in giving, perhaps, but that was not the point. As I loitered on the other side of King's Parade to watch them—their car was parked outside the Senate House—two girls in evening dress hurried up and they all got into the car and roared away.

What I thought, as I watched its saucy rear zooming out of sight, was that Cambridge belonged to them. Not to me. I belonged to Cambridge. I tunneled through its book-rooms as through cheese. But the Senate House and the colonnade at King's made more reference to them than to me. That marble fancifulness was a celebration of their pleasures, not mine. Theirs was the poetry of action. They were Yeats's hard-riding squires. And the poetry of Cambridge, too, offered no early morning incense to the poet. The glamor of King's Parade was the glamor of the picture papers. It let itself all be sucked in the wake of that noisy exhaust pipe. The whole place was a fraud. It was a temple in pawn, in bondage to other men's values. All of us, dons as well as undergraduates, all were mousy in our own eyes, shabby, second-rate human types, scurrying with our books from library to study, while our minds were mortgaged to those louts in the car. That was the poison in the poetry of Cambridge. Amis's poison.

Now you could hear nothing but the cooing of pigeons in the infinite hollowness. Yeats of course was an eager traitor. He advised the would-be poet to assimilate their toughness himself. And Cambridge . . . failed us. Lacked faith. Thrust up no stable launchpad for our rockets. Left us soft and worm-like naked. Allowed these bric-a-brac erotica their depth charge. The cheap poetry of college and lawn, gilded by that May dawn sunlight, shimmered across a drowning pool.

Cambridge, Massachusetts, 1970

From a window of the Widener Reading Room I saw three boys bring their parents up to the flight of steps outside and start them mounting it. One of the mothers, trim and taut as to the shoulders, delayed progress by swinging round to view the Appleton Chapel, gesturing. It was full eleven o'clock May sunshine. The fathers were an undistinguished lot. Though one in blue looked as if he were a man of power in other circumstances. His air of shambling shame looked rather definite and formed, a weapon. He was a hulking man, a Magwitch.

But what I noticed when they showed in the Reading Room doorway was the boys. Two of them had that straight lank buttercup hair, which only grows out of gold, but buried gold, deep hidden under rich black loam. They were giants, and both wore that baggy and colorless tweed and corduroy which is like the sacking round a young tree or a just unearthed Apollo. That was their rich black loam. But their gold was not buried; it lay in the grime under those painted fingernails and in the pouches under the man's eyes. Both the trimness of the wife's shoulders and the sag of his betrayed that recent mining, while the boys' high blank Viking brows looked away to other shores.

It was Spring Reading Period and the Reading Room was full. In the parents' presence, its tense nervous membrane shimmered and shivered. With those brains all plugged into the books in front of them, those bodies twitched and stirred continually, their imaginations coiled and caressed and intertwined. Girls coiled their hair ceaselessly around their hands, tossed it back, piled it in shining masses on top of their heads, still reading. Boys flexed their shoulders unconsciously, sauntered across the room, hitching their jeans. It was Fellini again, a fantasy brothel in which everyone exaggerated his own sensual style, and swerved away from striptease only at the last moment. A boy trudged in between the parents, unshaven and pale, swung his book bag down onto the nearest table and stared stupidly around for an empty chair, his eyes still closed with sleep. Unostentatiously, he gave his body its first stretch of the day. He had rolled out of bed into this crowded hall in one motion. The room's languor stirred like a counterpane with the bodies beneath. Every five minutes someone shifted lower into his chair and swung his legs up from the floor onto the table, placing them delicately in the public domain, an offering to the general eros. Of course, some were brisk. They rose from their note-taking without a pause and glided or charged across to a book. But theirs was just as much a sensual performance. Their muttering lips and bushy hair and slapdash eyeline promised a hysteria of license.

The parents turned and went. I followed them out and found them being shown one of the display cases on the landing. But two of them were covertly watching instead a conversation nearby, where a very large young man was sitting on the marble balustrade and haranguing two Indians, a girl and a man. He bounced up and down on his hands to make his points, wearing theatrically old and tattered jeans, slit along the thighs so that his legs showed through. He was discussing some point of Cambridge politics, but his interest was high-ideological. He wore silver-rimmed fanatic's glasses and an Afro. The girl, swathed in a raspberry silk sari with the scarlet caste-mark between her eyes, put her hand on his knee, trying to interrupt, and poked her pointed painted nail inside a slit.

The parents went down the staircase and I followed down the other flight. Going so slowly, as to music, the madness of power flushes the brain at each step. There is a royalism in stepping down a broad marble staircase, a palace-psychology takes over—servitors, applause, deference, decisions, graciousness, authority. And so along the hallway, under arches, paintings, vaults, with perspectives into throne rooms. Beyond there must be lawns and bridges, pergolas and ha-has. At the door, they stood again at the top of the outside steps, discussing and descending a little awkwardly, crab-wise. Where next? To some underground cafe, to see Madison style conspirators, cruel buccaneers of revolution, mustachioed and black-avised, silent and severe. I stood at the top of the steps, and gazed out and down across the Yard, across our domain.

Chapter 2

OUR IDEA OF MARRIAGE I:
MARRIAGE IN HOWELLS
AND LAWRENCE

The cultural image of marriage, as the central institution of Anglo-Saxon life, as the source and end and focus of love and life and law, seems to have tarnished and cracked at the end of the nineteenth century. Marriages formed the triumphant climaxes of the novels of Dickens, Thackeray, George Eliot, and the American novelists did not dare in public, or even in conscious privacy, to attack it. But at the end of the century it became impossible to celebrate marriage sincerely, in anything like the traditional terms. In Butler and Hardy, in Crane and Norris, there are various kinds of emotional shift away from it. But it is in the novels of William Dean Howells, the dean of American literature, that the sacred image of marriage is most desecrated.

This desecration is so effective partly because it is unintentional—in some sense unconscious. The author is revealing against his own will what he feels. Howells was himself a notably married man, and he wrote for a notably married audience, and represented his own point of view in his novels via an exemplary married pair. Basil and Isabel March appear as *raisonneurs* in seven of his novels, David and Lucy Sewell in several others. David Sewell is an enlightened minister, Basil March a magazine editor, but they are essentially the same, and essentially Howells himself. This identity is especially striking in the pattern of their relations with their wives. This is a mutually destructive pattern, and Howells's way of presenting it breeds a fever of repudiation in the reader's mind, because he reveals all that is wrong with the relationship and then offers palpably inadequate palliations and justifications, jokes, and sentimentalities. After the Anglo-Saxon imagination had absorbed Howells, it had nothing to do but renounce marriage.

The reaction was so strong because Howells was a highly gifted writer, very intelligent, very responsive and responsible, very honest. He fully deserved to be the dean of American letters, to direct the American literary sensibility, as he did for forty years, from 1880 on. He "understood," in some sense encompassed, both James and Twain, those two poles of literary imagination for Americans. He was close friends with both. He taught all the talented writers of that period, his influence was immense, and his testimony authoritative.

The novel from which I will take my examples of his treatment of marriage, *A Hazard of New Fortunes*, 1889, is a novel which I admire a great deal. It deserves comparison with *The Princess Casamassima*, James's treatment of the same political themes, and the comparison works to the advantage of Howells. His treatment of the political themes (of a metropolis and its extremes of wealth and poverty, of the threat of revolution, of the change in national consciousness over the second half of the nineteenth century) has the authority of genuine experience, of openness, limpidity, readiness for conviction; and to turn to technique, the disturbingly wide thematic focus, which takes in so many facets of its subject without "placing" them till much later in the novel, gives the reader something of the same conversion experience as the hero. Basil and Isabel March come to New York from Boston, and gradually become convinced—at least, Basil does

—that they are living in a radically unjust society, which is not to be "accepted."

The descriptions of city scenes (taken straight from Howells's own journal) and the scenes bringing into confrontation men who represent different parts of the system, are all very vividly done, and more substantial than anything equivalent in the James novel. But most to be admired is the theme represented by the Dryfoos. This German family, who belong to an evangelical sect called the Dunkards, have come to New York City rich with the proceeds of selling their Ohio farm when oil was struck there. The father becomes a speculator in stocks, and gradually loses all those activities, interests, relationships, which gave him moral substance before. All are supplanted by a cruel rapacity and cynicism only potential in his former life. His son reacts the opposite way to their new situation, becoming even more fervently religious and unworldly than he had been. (This character owes something to Prince Mishkin, and the influence of both Dostoevski and Tolstoy is strongly to be felt in the treatment of all Howells's political themes.) They are convincing enough as naturalistic portraits, but their virtue is even more that they dramatically represent the West and the new wealth, and the disastrous change coming over American life. Fulkerson, who also represents the West, admires Dryfoos for his luck and for his forcefulness. He compares him with Bismarck, and the comparison is significant. Howells is employing large ideas, and making naturalistic details substantiate them.

But all this bears on Howells's treatment of marriage because his artistic authority *there* undermines his statements, his intentions. There his naked-eye observation and limpid readiness for conviction work to the opposite effect. They contradict the value judgments he offers, instead of substantiating them. The truth-telling virtues are those for which he was praised by his contemporaries, and they operated on much more than visual objects and surfaces. Howells was a very sensitive observer of the moral and psychological life, and he conscientiously recorded his observations even while composing a portrait of charm and winsomeness like the

9

Marches. He arranged the facts to make them more attractive, but he would not alter them.

The Marches are our guides and companions through *Hazard*, and we are asked to love and admire them, to laugh and sigh with them; though of course also to laugh at them a little, shake our heads at them. recognize their little weaknesses, for this is affection not hero-worship, the most humane kind of admiration. They are just two gifted, privileged, responsible people, who make as much as one can reasonably expect *anyone* to make out of being married to each other and being middle-class citizens of the world's greatest democracy. Howells persuades us to accept them as our representatives, to assume that nobody else would be *more* to the purpose. If another couple were richer, sharper, more passionate, or even had finer talents, or even greater moral intensity, they could only represent us and marriage and America worse. They would most probably *be* worse; and if better, then they would be less representative.

So we accept them as having as good a chance at life as one can reasonably expect or want. But we notice that we are told that "they had been very happy together. That is, they made up their quarrels or ignored them." And again . . . "They liked to play with the romantic, from the safe vantage ground of their real practicality, and to divine the poetry of the commonplace." And again . . . "Then they had travelled and seen much of the world, and they had formed tastes which they had not always been able to indulge, but of which they felt that the possession reflected distinction on them. It enabled them to look down upon those who were without such tastes; but they were not ill-natured, and so they did not look down so much with contempt as with amusement. . . ." Such sentences set the tone, or unsettle it, and the constant play of such irony, plus the constant recording of their mutual friction, erodes all that happy sympathy with them which the writer otherwise labors to arouse in us. "Neither he nor his wife supposed that they were selfish persons. On the contrary, they were very sympathetic; there was no good cause that they did not wish well; they had a generous scorn of all kinds of narrow-heartedness; if it had ever come into their

way to sacrifice themselves for others, they thought they
would have done so, but they never asked why it had not
come in their way." Obviously that last irony prepares for
the theme of that social conscience which the Marches learn
to cultivate. But the main thrust of the irony about them
goes, or ought to go, in quite a different direction. It refers
to their relations with each other, and it demands the culti-
vation of what one might call an erotic conscience.

Thus they quarrel over whether Basil shall go to New York,
when Fulkerson offers him a literary job there. He wants to
go, she not.

> "Basil," she appealed solemnly, "have I ever interfered with your
> career?"
> "I never had any for you to interfere with, my dear."
> "Basil! Haven't I always had faith in you? And don't you sup-
> pose that if I thought it would really be for your advancement, I
> would go to New York or anywhere with you?"
> "No, my dear, I don't," he teased, "I. . . ."

It is that last word, "teased," the intimation from Howells
that he is not going to take the disagreement seriously,
which makes it all so disturbing to the reader. In themselves,
the quarrels are not so bad, even in an exemplary couple.
But they call for a keener concern from Howells than he is
willing to give them.

Later, Basil and Isabel "lunch silently together in the presence of their children," and take up the discussion after the
latter pair have disappeared. "He would have liked to take it
up at the point from which it wandered into hostilities, for
he felt it lamentable that a matter which so seriously concerned them should be confused in the fumes of senseless
anger; and he was willing to make a tacit acknowledgement
of his own error by recurring to the question, but she would
not be content with this, and he had to concede explicitly
to her weakness that she really meant it when she had asked
him to accept Fulkerson's offer." (Of course, Isabel *hadn't*
really meant it, and Howells insists on our seeing that.) He
then says something about what New York would be like to
live in. "Oh, I see you are going," she twitted.

"I'm going to stay," he answered, "and let them turn me

out of my agency here." And later, "he figured with bitter pleasure the pain she would feel when he came home some day and told her he had been supplanted, after it was too late to close with Fulkerson." Thus, subtly and relentlessly, the points are made that demonstrate the mutual destructiveness of this pair, and yet we are asked to continue treating them as exemplary, and to travel on in the Marches' company, sharing their jokes and their experiences, full of ease and interest.

The story is told from Basil's point of view, and so it is Isabel who is, in this half-hearted way, blamed for what goes wrong. She has all the power of initiative between them, and stands between him and full manhood, as well as between him and New York, and later between him and social activism. Thus we are told that "Mrs. March was one of those wives who exact a more rigid adherence to their ideals from their husbands than from themselves. Early in their married life she had taken charge of him in all matters which she considered practical. She did not consider the business of bread-winning in these; that was an affair that might safely be left to his absent-minded, dreamy ineffi-ciency. . . ." This is of course a joke. Isabel is only being like so many wives. But just *as* a joke, just *because* of its tone, the idea corrodes all faith in marriage; even tolerance of marriage. Mrs. March as wife represents (speaks for and takes the blame for) all the inhibiting forces of society in her husband's mind.

This attack on Isabel is balanced by generous tributes, but these remain ineffective because irrelevant. Thus, in the prep-arations for moving to New York, "She kept up with tireless energy, and in the moments of dejection and misgiving which harrassed her husband, she remained dauntless and put heart into him when he had lost it altogether." But this is only a conscientious acknowledgement, which cannot prevent us from feeling that she does him more harm than good.

Isabel quite calamitously fails to measure up to the chal-lenges that New York offers them both. The main incident occurs during the strike of the transport workers of the city; Conrad Dryfoos is shot dead by a policeman during a riot, and Lindau, a German socialist who had been March's friend in his youth, is badly injured; both within view of March. Isabel, we are told, was mainly concerned with Basil's having been there, even though only as a bystander. "To her mind, March was the principal actor in the whole affair, and much more important in having seen it than those who had suffered in it. In fact he had suffered incomparably." This goes beyond the limits of the usual joke, and seems just excessive and unbelievable about Isabel—motivated apparently by spite against her.

As always, the indictment of Isabel's stupidity is followed by an even worse indictment of Basil's ineffectuality.

> "I think Conrad had no business there, or you either, Basil," said his wife.
> "Oh I don't defend myself," said March. "I was there in the cause of literary curiosity and conjugal disobedience."

In the context of his friends' vigorous action and heroic death, his joke leaves a very sour taste in the reader's mouth.

March is a portrait of self-pity. He takes one effective action in the book. He quarrels (minimally) with both Dryfoos and Fulkerson, when they want to fire Lindau from the magazine for his socialist opinions. But after, and during, both effective moments, we are told, Basil feels sorry for the man he has defeated. "He was sorry to have got the better of that old man for the moment." Clearly this is a pity indistinguishable from fear of action—indistinguishable from self-pity. When his wife reproaches him for risking his job that way, "every word was a stab in March's heart, so weakly tender to his own; his wife's tears, after so much experience of the comparative lightness of the griefs that weep themselves out in women, always seemed wrung from his own soul; if his children suffered in the least through him, he felt like a murderer." Again Howells hopes we will like his character for having these feelings; he is copying one of the designs that call for pity and liking in the Victorian novelist's collection; but the honesty and precision of his own drawing make us see the things—the weakness, the resentment—that prevent our responding that way.

It makes us see, above all, the *fusion* of husband and wife, and the consequent susceptibility of the husband to the wife's feelings, an indecent, an immoral, susceptibility. Basil has Isabel's feelings. He feels them, but against his will, repudiating them as they happen inside him—except that he *doesn't* finally repudiate them. He finally accepts them as his own, and repudiates his own integrity instead, betrays his own authenticity of being, sins against his erotic conscience.

Thus the final indictment is not of Isabel, nor of Basil, but of the pair of them. When he finally has learned to see New York "not as a spectacle but as life," when he has learned to feel "complicity" in it, the two of them argue the question in a way which is the worst half-conscious condemnation of all.

> She lamented the literary peace, the intellectual refinement of the life they had left behind them; and he owned it was very pretty, but he said it was not life—it was death in life. She liked to hear him talk in that strain of virtuous self-denunciation, but she asked him, "Which of your prophets are you going to follow?" And he answered, "All—all! And a fresh one every Sunday." And so they got their laugh out of it at last, but with some sadness at heart and with a dim consciousness that they had got their laugh out of too many things in life.

It is the two of them *together* who are condemned. It is their relationship that betrays both of them. And that clearly derives from the institution, marriage.

The interest of Howells's failure is that it was so representative. If he thought Basil and Isabel March the best that the Anglo-Saxon middle class could offer, he had the backing not only of his audience but also of his colleagues. Basil and Isabel's qualities were those of all the heroes and heroines of the nineteenth-century Anglo-Saxon novel—the qualities that guaranteed the married happiness of David and Agnes Copperfield, for instance. The difference was only that Dickens stopped his novel when the marriage took place. One may say that Howells took upon himself the ungrateful task of asking what the later life of David and Agnes would be like— and that of Pip and Estella, and that of Herbert Pocket and Clara; and the same goes for exemplary Thackeray heroes and heroines, like Dobbin and Amelia; and would Dorothea and Ladislaw be so different? Of course, if these were real people, we could not properly ask such a question, because they have different personal qualities. But as novel-characters they are all alike in that they all represent different aspects of the same large idea of a successful marriage—different moments in the same dialectical movement. Each one's individual qualities and his relations to his partner are all conceived within the same general outline as belonging to the same idea.

The relations between men and women in the novels of Tolstoy belong to a different idea, and in the novels of Dostoevski; and it is no doubt just because Howells was sensitized to those possibilities that he so insistently though maladroitly draws our attention to his own characters' failures in those ways. One can almost see Kitty and Levin overshadowing Basil and Isabel. It is a failure characteristic of the Erasmian artist—Howells was too aware of other people's strengths, strengths he himself could not appropriate; he was insufficiently insistent on his own virtues. He also had the kind of success characteristic of that kind of writer. He made something of the challenge which Tolstoy and Dostoevski offered him in their treatment of political and religious themes. His novel is not, like theirs, a great imaginative adventure, but it is moving, intelligent, educative. But he could make nothing of—deeply as he felt it—their challenge to redefine norms of personal relations.

That challenge was taken up, for the Anglo-Saxon world, by D. H. Lawrence. Tolstoy and Dostoevski represented to him too the great alternative to marriage, not so much marriage the social institution, but marriage as he believed in it, the religious union of man and woman. Tolstoy meant to Lawrence that puritanical and political direction of man's energies which I have called Calvinist. Dostoevski meant a spiritual and mystical religion, which was equally anti-erotic. Clearly, Lawrence started from Hardy and with the ideas of the erotic movement, which he interpreted in a morally conservative way. What gave him his prophetic flair was his conviction that he could complete the work that Hardy had begun, and so redefine and celebrate the life-giving relations of man and woman (and of both to the earth) that men could again have faith in life. That life-giving relationship he called marriage, and it constituted a return to patterns of the long-gone past. In this sense he defended traditional ideas—such as the idea of marriage—against the different radicalisms of Tolstoy and Dostoevski.

Lawrence was not, so far as is known, conscious of Howells. In *Studies in Classic American Literature* it is Hawthorne he treats in rather the way I have treated Howells here—as the great unconscious betrayer of the conventional values of love and marriage. And he ignored the Russians' social and political challenge, which Howells had taken up. Lawrence dismissed the social conscience as a trap, a distraction, a *pis aller*—men needed to devote all their energies to their erotic lives. So we could not expect him to have had any patience with Howells.

But he was very conscious of all those treatments of marriage, in books and in actual living, which gave it the same character as Howells gave it. Basil and Isabel March represent that middle-class mode of being which he repudiated so often: in *Sons and Lovers*; in Paul Morel's late conversations with his mother, in *Kangaroo*; and in some of Mellors's diatribes in *Lady Chatterley's Lover*. Lawrence did not need to attack Howells' idea in detail, or Howells himself, because in his day it and Howells had been discredited, and *every* serious artist was attacking them. Howells's Collected Edition, which began to come out in the first decade of this century, had to be discontinued for lack of demand after six of his novels had been reissued. His long period of success ended suddenly and finally. He died in 1919, only just before the publication of *Women in Love*, that greatest example of the art that had displaced his art. Ursula Brangwen's experience, her whole nature, her relation to Rupert Birkin, all are imagined in a mode that defies one to assimilate her to the Marches. The polarity of their relationship, on which Lawrence insists, is designed to save them from that fusion of the Marches. The quarrels between her and Birkin are bitter and destructive, but they are overt; they are opposite in style to the Marches' quarrels, and their style is designed to save them from the other's subtle self-corrosion. The answers she and Birkin make to the claims of society on their privacy are no more heroic by political standards than those of the Marches; but their answers *are* full of pride in their own identities and their relationship to each other; they *are* justified by their erotic consciences.

In some sense everybody nowadays lives, in his imagination at least, by his erotic conscience. It is because Howells's characters do not that they seem so remote to us. Students often indignantly object that Basil and Isabel never seem to make love to each other, and that they can't be imagined doing so. It is easy enough, of course, to defend Howells against this charge if one takes it literally. But clearly his imagination *was* less sexual than that of most twentieth-century writers. It had not been changed by the erotic movement. In *Memoirs of a Catholic Girlhood* Mary McCarthy tells us of her own bafflement before her Jewish grandmother's way of estimating success in marriage. She claimed to have chosen her husband because "I thought he would be good to me," and she asks about Mary's new husband, "Is he good to you?" "This archaic view of the function of a husband astonished me. . . . I had to stop and think, because marriage had never presented itself to me in this light. . . . Love, evidently, was as foreign a concept to her as this 'goodness' was to me." The grandmother was no Isabel March, being a gross materialist, but the gap between her and Mary McCarthy is the same as that between the latter and Isabel March. It is a gap between generations, and it exists because the younger idea of marriage is so much more erotic.

The ideas of marriage that have established themselves in England and America in this century have both been erotic, but they were not of course the same ideas. As we shall see, the British idea has been much more Demetrian, the American much more Promethean or Faustian. The two are profoundly opposed and constitute a kind of antithesis between the minds of the two countries, but they are equally importantly alike in being both the work of the erotic movement.

Chapter 3

OUR IDEA OF MARRIAGE II:
OUR EROTICISM

The great erotic movement, which changed the Western imagination at the end of the nineteenth century, broke with very different effects on the shores of the two Anglo-Saxon countries. Surprisingly enough, it achieved more artistic success, at the level of significant literature, in England, while in America it established itself only in very fragmented and deflected forms.

At least this is true if eroticism is discussed from a Lawrentian point of view. For seen thus, the movement came in two waves, and it was the second that triumphed in England and failed in America. Lawrence said that the work of Hardy in England, that of Tolstoy in Russia, and that of Verga in Italy, were the successes of the first wave, or, to use his terms, were what he had to start from. All three of those writers were able to celebrate the erotic relations of men and women with full dignity, Lawrence thought, and at the same time to set them in their relation to the equally creative affiliation of man to Nature. By virtue of this achievement, they were all erotic artists. But they all fell short of full realization of that vocation, Lawrence felt, because they took a tragic view of man's fate, and after celebrating the sexual passion with moral and religious fervor, they warned men against it. They associated it with defeat, death, and evil. They made the earth and Nature pitiless and harsh enemies of man. Consequently they devised melodramatic plots for their novels, full of theatrical moments of sin and retribution, which he found trashy, and with Hamlet-heroes, full of self-conscious doubts and self-doubts. They became obsessed with either "tragedy" or "salvation," both of which Lawrence despised as mares' nests. He started his career as a major novelist with the calling to complete the task they had only begun, as he says in *A Study of Thomas Hardy*, and one can perhaps see early parts of *The Rainbow* as a rewriting of scenes in *Far From the Madding Crowd*.

Of course, art of the type of this first tragic eroticism was written in many European countries at the time. France was thought of by many then as its peculiar home, and one can point to the work of Flaubert as an example of the French achievement in this genre. And Germany, which was to be the source of the second wave of eroticism, had Wagner as its artist of the first. *Tristan und Isolde* and *Madame Bovary* were great achievements of tragic eroticism.

The ideas of the movement's second wave were formulated well enough in both England and America before Lawrence began to write. Many of them can be found in Edward Carpenter's essays, as M. Delavenay has pointed out, and in more distinguished form they are sketched in Samuel Butler's novel, *The Way of all Flesh*. The Pontifex family live by a non-erotic idea of marriage—of the relations of husband and wife, of the roles of father and mother—that ruins Ernest's chances of happiness. Having learned the lessons of his unhappiness, he resolves to study, and instruct the world in, marriage and the family system. So he sets out to travel among the most comely and lovable nations of his own day, the Italians and the South Sea Islanders, and to study the records of such nations of the past, the Greeks and the Romans. He is in search of the erotic mode of being.

E. M. Forster acknowledged a great debt to Butler, and his

own attempts to "create" these ideas imaginatively shares not only Butler's distinction of mind but also his fatal ironical-playful epigrammaticism. Butler kept the manner of a French moralist while propagating a message of passion and blood-knowledge, and Forster suffered from the same imaginative paradox, which is in effect imaginative timidity. It was not Butler but Hardy who took the plunge of subduing his mind and its workings to these new nonrational experiences which they both believed in, and it was Hardy from whom Lawrence learned. Butler's vitalism found its natural heir in Shaw, the man of wit.

In America the major proponent I know who formulated these ideas was Henry Adams. The famous chapter of his *Education* entitled "The Virgin and the Dynamo," is an eccentric and paradoxical statement of most of the key ideas of eroticism. (This chapter is dated 1900, the book 1906; Butler's book was published 1903, but written twenty years earlier.) Adams apostrophizes the Virgin of Chartres as a version of Aphrodite and Artemis; as the power of sexuality idolized; and as a force which in the past moved society and material forces via men's imaginations. He warned the West against losing touch with that great force of sexuality, and depicted America in particular as crippled by sexual withering. "The force of the Virgin was still felt at Lourdes, and seemed to be as potent as X-rays; but in America neither Venus nor Virgin had ever had value as force—at most as sentiment. No American had ever been truly afraid of either." America was ashamed of woman, and thought that sex was sin. "In any previous age, sex was strength." Diana of the Ephesians was goddess not for her beauty but for her force. She was an animated dynamo; she was reproduction—all she needed was to be fecund. "An American Virgin would never dare command; an American Venus would never dare exist." Only Whitman among American artists had ever dared insist on the power of sex. "All the rest had used sex for sentiment, never for force; to them, Eve was a tender flower, Herodias an unfeminine horror."

Adams is interestingly precise about the times and places of eroticism. Only since 1895, he says, has he begun to feel the Virgin or Venus as force, and not everywhere; at Chartres, at Lourdes, in Indian mythology; "the idea died out long ago in the German and English stock."

Adams's way of expressing these ideas might be compared with that of Aldous Huxley later among English thinkers; and obviously both are as far from being authentic prophets of blood consciousness as Butler and Shaw. They play with the idea, with all ideas. Adams is all the time comparing the power of Woman with that of the dynamo. The dynamo and the X-rays are occult, supersensual, irrational—a revelation of mysterious energy like that of the Cross, a force one can only measure, as one can measure the force of Woman, by their attraction on one's own mind. He saw the dynamo as representing—while transcending—all those great mechanical forces which had supplanted the Virgin in men's imaginations and consequently in society. He warned the West, and America in particular, against its religious worship of the machines and against their proliferation and self-generation. These are all crucial erotic movement ideas, but Adams is juggling with them. America's erotic movement had its Butler and Shaw, but lacked its Hardy and Lawrence. The same was true of other countries besides America.

All over the world intellectuals then were interested in these ideas, but, in various ways, personally defense against them. A representative case is that of Max Weber, who discussed eroticism with great understanding and some sympathy, but from a point of view totally alien to it, and irreconcilable with it. He could, one guesses, have appreciated Butler's, and perhaps Adams's, formulation of the ideas, but Lawrence's would have bored or offended him.

It was in Lawrence's work that the second wave of the movement came to triumphant expression. This was the worship of Demeter, treated so beautifully in *The Rainbow* and *Women in Love*. The soil is a living and female power, and only by living in relation to it can men live healthily and fruitfully. Only by reenacting in their own unconscious lives its profound and immemorial rhythms can they achieve natural love. In such a life lies their only guarantee against the falsifying and perverting effects of self-consciousness, idealism, and that modern supplanting of the blood's "knowledge" by that of the nervous fluid; their only guarantee of fulfillment, fertility, fruitfulness, the triumph of Demeter. Within the cycle of life rooted in the earth, there is no tragedy —at worst only such natural death as Tom Brangwen's in *The Rainbow*, drowned in the flood—and no need for supernatural salvation. And the major human institution and sacrament of this cycle of life is marriage—marriage not socially but erotically understood.

Now although a great deal of nonsense was written in England about Lawrence's ideas, they were not ignored by British intellectuals, nor totally misunderstood. Quite apart from discipular figures like John Middleton Murry, there have been two groups who have taken up those ideas and re-expounded them. The Christian moralists have done so directly; I happen to know of Roman Catholic and High Anglican examples, like Brian Wicker, "Father Tiverton," and Father Gerald Vann. And the literary critics who follow Leavis have done so indirectly, making marriage, "an adequate image of marriage," an important criterion by which to judge a writer. Leavis even turns this criterion against Lawrence himself in his essays on *Lady Chatterley's Lover* and *Anna Karenina*. By means of such writings as these, and by means of Leavis's whole personality and career, this Demetrian eroticism has been a presence in the British imagination all through this century.

This sounds a surprising thing to say because the worship of Demeter has not been overtly celebrated. This eroticism's prime characteristic has not been any "positive" image of fruitfulness and flowering, but a negative criterion of authenticity of being; authors have been measured by the erotic version of that criterion. And when tested by that standard, most authors—most people—have been found not to "live on the spot where they are," to use that phrase of Lawrence's which Leavis so often quotes. T. S. Eliot, notably, has been found to fail in life-energy, life-courage, life-faith. It is a moralistic and Erasmian version of Demeter that Leavis worships, as it was a moralistic and in some ways Puritan image of Demeter that Lawrence constructed—but it was still Demeter.

When we turn to America, we find no Demetrian imagination to set beside Lawrence. Sherwood Anderson, for instance, is just not sizable enough. The American who welcomed Lawrence most effusively was Mabel Dodge Luhan, and may we not say that she was the one who finally understood and appreciated him best? This would mark the contrast with England vividly. Luhan was far from being the fool most critics seem to think, but she was not to be compared with Leavis, or with Murry, among the English admirers of Lawrence.

The man she turned to after Lawrence died was Robinson Jeffers. It was to him she wrote her *Lorenzo in Taos,* because she felt that he represented somewhat the same things as Lawrence. But like Anderson he represented them with very much less size of intelligence than Lawrence.

If we look instead to the novelists who *have* had an effect on the American imagination which can be compared with Lawrence's effect on the British, I think we shall have to take Hemingway and Faulkner. Neither of them was a devotee of Demeter, obviously. The imaginations of both were dominated by images of *men,* Promethean men struggling against overwhelming odds and refusing to cry out in pain or self-pity. Of course, they render sexual relations with great explicitness and fervor, and they have a strong sense of man's relation to the soil, to Nature, to the primitive past. Thus both show themselves to be, like just about every twentieth-century imagination, members of the *first* wave of the erotic movement. But they locate their ultimate moral values in acts of individual male virtue, directed against the sky; not in moments of male-and-female union in the lap of the earth. They are only tragically erotic. Marriage is for them a social institution, and though not always attacked in their works, is never celebrated as *the* source of value.

In fact, these American novelists confirm Lawrence's intuition about the essential American soul. He says, in *Studies in Classic American Literature,* that the American soul is "hard, isolate, stoic, and a killer. It has never yet melted. . . . [The American hero is] a man who turns his back on white society. A man who keeps his moral integrity hard and intact.

An isolate, almost selfless, stoic, enduring man, who lives by death, by killing, but it is pure white. This is the very intrinsic-most American." This is the Promethean sensibility that has been the functional equivalent in America to Lawrence's in England.

Neither, of course, is the only sensibility inspiring writers in that country, but each characterizes a group of writers important enough to characterize their national culture. More than the great and brilliant writers, the secondary authors in each case show the influence of the national idea. The celebrants of country pleasures in England, like Laurie Lee and H. E. Bates, feel themselves close to the English idea. While in America the tough guy, in fiction and film, has still a representative national quality. Two recent books happen to illustrate vividly the way the Promethean temperament functions in American culture and literature. John Bowers's *The Colony*, and Francis Steegmuller's *Stories and True Stories*, by their differentness, and their different virtues, demonstrate the pressures on the American writer to try to be "Promethean."

Bowers's book is a breezy narrative of his year or so at the writers' colony in Southern Illinois run by Lowney Handy, the woman who "taught" James Jones to write *From Here to Eternity*, and who was convinced that she could train a whole new breed of writers to produce more "American-tough" novels just as good. (She dictated their reading, their work-hours, their diet, their recreations, as well as directing all they wrote.) It is a book full of fights, obscenities, whore-houses, sexual brutalities, eyeball-to-eyeball tests of strength. Steegmuller's is a collection of fiction and nonfiction deriving from his long career as translator and biographer of French writers for Americans. It is full of art auctions, Paris hotels, *apéritifs* with Cocteau, stories about ladies in doubt over whether to buy a doubtful *objet d'art*. One tells of the infinitely gracious decline into death of an infinitely gracious American lady during a visit to Paris, sustained by her charming son and daughter and the devotion of the entire hotel staff. It is entitled "Soirée à la Chandelle." One can imagine the barrack-room harshness of Lowney Handy's judgment of it.

She trained her literary stable to create aggressively opposite images of life.

The interest of making the two books confront each other is not in choosing between them. That *was* a choice, in the 1940's and 1950's, for many American writers—even so large a talent as Norman Mailer had to choose one or the other, and he in fact visited Handy's colony. He made the same choice as Jones, though he did not stay at the colony. The place was an exaggeration by his and even its own standards, but symbolically he chose that way of being a writer, Bowers's way, and had to give up Steegmuller's virtues once and for all. Perhaps all through the century most American novelists have had to choose between some such options. But for us here and now the interest lies just in the fact that it *is* a confrontation, that there is such a polarity in American life.

It is of course a familiar, a widespread, even an institutionalized polarity. Handy's colony was set up in opposition to such genteel writers' colonies as Mrs. Ames's Yaddo, where books like Steegmuller's get written. We have most often heard this polarity labelled Redskin vs. Paleface. It is embodied, to go no further back, in the opposing figures of Mark Twain and Henry James, those poles of American literary possibility. We are not surprised to hear that at the Colony no one was allowed to read T. S. Eliot or Wallace Stevens, Proust or Camus. Everyone *had* to read, indeed to copy out, Hemingway, Erskine Caldwell, Faulkner, Dos Passos. Everyone lived in hopes of emulating Jones or Mailer.

The two dominant figures at the Colony were James Jones and Lowney Handy, and between them they filled out the Redskin image very fully. It was Jones who introduced the successive dangerous sports, the boxing, the shooting, the diving, the trampolining, at which the men tested each other out. The series climaxed in motorcycling, that most coarsely sexual of masculine exhibitionisms. Lowney seems to have deplored the dangers of these sports in a quite orthodoxly feminine way and to have been rather prudish about obscenities from other people. Obscenity was of course a big part of the Colony's speech-style, and her own speech was full of it, but she did not relish it from others; just as she did not join them in their whoring trips to Terre Haute on their days off from writing. But her protests against such things were without hope of effect, and she was with them in the spirit. She was the harsh-tempered sergeant back in the barracks to whom the troops remain sullenly loyal through it all. (Sociologically, she was building an army unit out of them, not the more natural gang—that was the exaggeration of the colony, its grotesqueness, its self-destroying mechanism.) What she herself contributed was the very rough discipline, and a Southern populist ideology, with a radical antifeminism. Women are all out to trap men, she taught her writers, to fill their wombs, and then get a good provider for themselves and their child.

Bowers offers to tell this story from a critical distance. He left the Colony early, and eventually became a successful editor of men's adventure magazines. He criticizes Lowney Handy's regime by two criteria, two crimes it committed; that of his spoiled love for the girl he left behind him, a love Handy derided and opposed, and that of her and Jones's "exploitation" of the others. But the striking thing is that he is not really distanced from them. He still writes just as the Colony taught men to write, as polar opposites to Steegmuller. His attempt at critical distance doesn't work, though he does give one a sense of the effort in the Colony's spontaneity, the dishonesties within its honesty, and the timidities within its toughness—a strong sense of a society pretending to be free from all social rules.

Handy taught her writers that America is a matriarchy, that its men are all emasculated by their mothers, etc. Bowers drew attention to the obvious irony that she herself ruled her colony with a rod of iron. But her spirit really *was* antifeminist, antimatriarchal, if matriarchy is to be associated with Demeter, the goddess of fruitful marriage, of milk and corn and fertility. Of course sex remained an important force in her world, a powerful drive, but it was one hostile to creativity of every kind. Sexual relations could be clean only with whores. The Colony's prime emotional emphasis was on anal experience, on farting and anal obscenities, and on enemas, which Handy recommended as a cure for every kind of problem, including artistic ones. Its nightmare was homosexuality—that a man should have to take the female role. (Though it is interesting that one man did this, and was forgiven, because he accepted the fact that he was humanly crippled.) It was an all-male world that she created and that the Redskin sensibility always implies.

Meanwhile Steegmuller is a very different sort of man and writer. He has written biographies of Cocteau and Apollinaire and la Grande Madamoiselle, a double portrait of Madame Bovary and Flaubert, and many pieces about French painters and American art-collectors. Much of his fiction appeared in the *New Yorker* and *Harpers Bazarr*, and another piece in *The Magazine of Art*. One story, "The Fair Singer," evokes the same themes as Bowers. Steegmuller's narrator-representative is a young man visiting California from the East during the Depression. He is a college teacher who goes to stay with Mrs. Ives, a friend's aunt, to get something written. In the same house is June Ebbets, the niece of this lady's servants, and the fair singer of the title. But her voice is the only brilliant or beautiful thing about her. Otherwise she is a nice but very ordinary girl. An attraction springs up between her and the narrator, but she is too much "of the people" for him to marry. She comes from a small town in Indiana, and has no culture and no manners. He remembers a Frenchman's comment on another American girl, "Elle est très drugstore," and he conscientiously rejects all June's sexual invitations. It is a Jamesian drama of reluctant renunciation. He sends June back to her Midwestern fate, and gives his own loyalty to Mrs. Ives, the old lady of his own class.

The story stands in vivid contrast with everything the Colony taught. The sexual feeling between June and the narrator is not inauthentic, but it is so gentle and so mildly rendered, and it is transcended by moral and social loyalties so gently and easily. In the Redskin world such renunciation would have to be violent, and above all sexuality could never be *transcended*; because on the polarization of men and women all identity hinges. This is not because life in the Colony was erotic, although some of the books written there participate in the tragic erotic mode. The Redskin world is not categorically erotic. Can one say that Twain is any more erotic than James? What one can say is that the Redskin world exalts men; even Lowney Handy exemplified that; and that the Paleface world is emblemized by women; Steegmuller's stories most often center on a woman. That is the basic polarity. Then one can add that this particular world of men is somewhat Dionysian, and this particular world of women somewhat Apollonian. The emotional range celebrated by Jones and Mailer has some elements of the irrational and the emotionally excessive, the dark and the death-directed. The emotional range of James and Wharton is dominated by reason and wit and moderation. That is one aspect, perhaps the root, of that polarity in the American imagination we spoke of.

Neither book is great writing. There is something pallid and genteel about Steegmuller's Apollo, just as there is something brash and vulgar about Bowers's Dionysus. Indeed, the former is more palpably on the wrong track. He is trying harder, and what betrays him is the vein he has chosen to work. The Apollonian, in America, is not a rich lode. Bower's vein is rich, and it can be purified and worked up into beautiful art. We might compare it with that of Laurie Lee in England. *Cider with Rosie* is the sort of autobiographical writing which stands in the same relation to English Demetrianism and English significant art as *The Colony* does to American Prometheanism and American significant art. Man and woman are much less sharply polarized and opposed in the English book and the English imagination. What happens between them is play, and play in the lap of that great fecund mother, the earth.

It is characteristic that both American books contain contrasting episodes involving a transvestite. Steegmuller describes going to visit Barbette, a transvestite acrobat who inspired Cocteau to a remarkable essay on the deceitful nature of all art. Bowers describes being fooled into propositioning a transvestite strip-dancer in a Juarez nightclub, and being humiliated when she revealed to the audience that she was a man. The first anecdote is very discreetly told and impersonally informative; all the attention is given to Barbette, who is made to engage our curiosity in a hundred ways. In the second, the spotlight is all on Bowers, and on the disastrous and classical nature of his sexual humiliation. Taking a man for a woman is taking black for white. There is no way to blend those two or transcend them both, or see the transvestite as representing all art.

One of the really cardinal facts about America, and particularly about its imaginative life, is that the Redskin polarization of the sexes is always stronger than the Paleface transcendence of them or any Demetrian play between them. The Apollonian mode in America (seen in Trilling and Emerson) is always uneasy and self-deprecating. Steegmuller, like James and Wharton, has to go to France to find examples of a *proud* clarity of mind, to nourish his Apollonian compatriots. One cannot perhaps say that the Redskin mind always triumphs in American art, but the Paleface victories seem to remain superficial, because at a slightly lower cultural level this sexual polarization is so strong. It is certainly much stronger than in England, where Demetrian ideals of marriage have found a validation in the most adventurous of modern art (that of D. H. Lawrence) and also in the lives of intellectuals. To find an equivalent for this American polarization of the sexes one must perhaps go back to Wilhelmine Germany.

The great emblem of Demetrian union is that rainbow which Lawrence evoked so beautifully, time and time again. The iridescent fusion of sunlight and raindrops creates the beautiful arch of union between man and woman, which must remain always an illusion, and yet more real than prosaic actuality. The great emblem of the Promethean union is that laboring and threshing effort at orgasm which Mailer has rendered with such sardonic enthusiasm; often—in *An American Dream* and in "The Time of Her Time"—in the act of anal rape. That Lawrence's image has the advantage in beauty is irrelevant; both are equally vivid and authentic images of our eroticism.

Chapter 4

OUR IDEA OF MARRIAGE III: ANNA WULF AND SAUL GREEN

In the 1960's, we had a remarkable fictional treatment of marriage that brought together the British and the American versions of eroticism into a kind of union. Doris Lessing's heroine in *The Golden Notebook* believes in the Demetrian idea of marriage, and her career throughout the book is a broken arch, an incomplete rainbow, which stretches out yearningly toward the husband whom the men she knows refuse to be. But the book is larger than Anna Wulf's own mind, and it accepts Saul Green's Promethean eroticism as being as authentic as the other. The book says that neither is to be blamed for their failure to make a lasting relationship; rather both are to be praised for solving each other's problems as much as they do. *The Golden Notebook* accommodates both kinds of eroticism—after all, Anna Wulf is herself a Free Woman as well as a wife—though it does not soar above them in any perfected Apollonian arch; it just desperately manages to hold the two together. To see how much is implied by this, we must start by considering each character separately.

Megalomaniacs, that's what our lot are. You say I am what I am because the United States is such and such politically. I am the United States. And I say, I am the position of woman in our time.   Anna to Saul

English woman! Fair! Everyone makes use of each other. You make use of me to create a Hollywood dream of happiness, and in return I'm going to use your experience of the witch-doctors.
                                                                Saul to Anna

The confrontation of Saul Green and Anna Wulf is the climax and culmination of *The Golden Notebook*. Each enters into the world projected by the other's sickness, *becomes* the Other who is needed in order to be hated, feared, destroyed; but each does so voluntarily, consciously, and in such a way as to help the other to emerge. Anna becomes the Woman whom Saul always must flee; he becomes that Joy-in-Destruction which threatens to take over her psyche. Their interaction is thus the resolution (as far as the novel goes) of all the many conflicts of Anna's life, which otherwise have shown themselves to be unresolvable: the problems within each of her political, erotic, and aesthetic lives; and the extra problems which derive from the conflicts between those.

As we see from the quotations above, one aspect of their confrontation is their naming of each other as "American" and "English"; more precisely, as American man and English woman. It is my argument that we legitimately can develop this aspect of the confrontation beyond the point at which Doris Lessing left it, and learn something about both British and American cultural life by so doing.

In thinking of Saul as "the American man," we are only following out Doris Lessing's intention, not going beyond it.

I was looking at him, from the safety of his having forgotten me, and I saw his pose, standing with his back to the window in a way that was like a caricature of that young American we see in the films—sexy he-man, all balls and strenuous erection. He stood lounging, his thumbs hitched through his belt, fingers loose, but pointing as it were to his genitals—the pose that always amuses me when I see it on the films, because it goes with the young, unused, boyish American face—the boyish, disarming face, and the he-man's pose.

She is assimilating him to Brando in *Streetcar Named Desire*, and through him to dozens of other actors, and films, and through them to Americans in general. His sexual style (in that persona) she describes as "the violent young male animal," and her theory of him is essentially that "like all Americans you've got mother-trouble,"—something Anna shouts at him. He declares himself against the world as "I I I I I," but it is predominantly a defiance of women. "I I I I I, but I against women. Women the jailors, the consciences, the voice of society. . . ." And Anna Wulf writes a literary satire, which she means to be a satire on Saul's emotional "set," against all that American fiction which celebrates (in what she calls the Romantic-tough style) the sentimental anti-marriage loyalty of young men to their gang.

To all this, Doris Lessing herself calls our attention. But equally striking is something that is merely implicit; the likeness between Saul Green and various heroes of Mailer's and Bellow's novels. When Saul shouts "I am I, Saul Green, I am what I am what I am. I. . . ." we are bound to think of Stephen Rojack in *An American Dream*, and of Henderson in *Henderson, the Rain King*. They are identified by and with an equally naked egotism. And in his relations to politics, to sex, to marriage, to madness, to magic, to social law and order, Saul Green enacts the persona explored by Mailer and Bellow—and many others. It is an extremely ambitious persona, greedy for every sort of experience, risking its psychic and moral integrity anew every day. "What do you think this thing is that makes people like us have to experience everything? We're driven by something to be as many different things or people as possible," Anna Wulf asks Saul Green; and he says, "I I I I I I, I'm going to show you all with your morality and your love and your laws, I I I I." Like Mailer, he says, "I went to a headshrinker once and decided I could do better for myself." Like Mailer, he has spent all his life until recently, preparing himself for the moment when someone says, "Pick up that rifle." (In *Armies of the Night*, Mailer says that for years he has envisioned himself "in some final cataclysm, as an underground leader in the city, or a guerrilla with a gun in the hills.") Again like Mailer, "Well, I'm not a potential suicide. I would say I'm more of a feeder on women, a sucker of other people's vitality, but I'm not a suicide." This is the fully Faustian or Promethean persona, which entitles us, I think, to describe him as representing America in a much fuller sense than at first appears.

The character Anna Wulf does not represent England in anything like so full a sense as Saul Green represents America. She is a much larger character, not primarily a representative at all, and if she represents anything, it is not England but, as she says, the position of women in our time. She is in some ways positively un-English—to be identified with Rhodesia—and even anti-English, her point of view that of an alien.

So at this point our reading of their confrontation must become more of an interpretation. But it is surely a legitimate interpretation to say that Anna Wulf's attitudes to love and marriage and the male-female conflicts remind one of Ursula Brangwen's, that one can see the character as a further development of Lawrence's themes, as another aspect of his erotic idea, just as Saul Green is another aspect of the Mailer-Bellow idea. In describing the Ella-Paul relationship in *The Golden Notebook*, Doris Lessing uses very Lawrentian concepts. "What Ella lost during those five years was the power to create through naiveté. . . . From the moment Ella meets Paul and loves him, from the moment she uses the word love, there is the birth of naiveté. . . . He destroyed in her the knowing, doubting, sophisticated Ella, and again and again he put her intelligence to sleep, and with her willing connivance, so that she floated darkly on her love for him, on her naiveté, which is another word for a spontaneous creative faith." The Joy-in-Destruction that haunts and threatens Anna is the very opposite of that spontaneous creative faith, so that the two together can be said to be the major theme of the novel. In the relationship with Saul Green, too, Anna Wulf is looking for a stable love-relationship, a marriage, because that alone will bring her naiveté. This is a very Lawrentian idea.

Moreover, Anna Wulf belongs to a novelistic tradition of heroines that has taken the problems of women much more seriously than has the American novel. She can be compared with the Dorothea Brooke of *Middlemarch*, and with the heroines of the Bronte sisters and Jane Austen; for the human size and dignity given her by her creator, and for the link between her and the theme of marriage, also given size and dignity. In typical American novels the women are either lightweight, as in Mailer, or out of relation to marriage, as in Hemingway. Clearly Anna Wulf belongs with Lawrence's Ursula Brangwen and George Eliot's Dorothea Brooke rather than with the Cherry of *An American Dream* or the Brett of *The Sun Also Rises*.

The main thematic values of the British novel seem to have been vested in its heroines. There is first that sequence of pure snowdrops, Richardson's Pamela, Fielding's Amelia, Jane Austen's Fanny Price, Charlotte Bronte's Jane Eyre, Dickens's Esther, Thackeray's Amelia, and so forth. With them the reader is required to tremble and weep, for they will be violated, one way or another, and must be consoled. But that figure gradually became too blatant for serious writers to use. She became equivocal as Sue Bridehead (in *Jude the Obscure*), and is condemned as Miriam Leivers (in *Sons and Lovers*); by the standards of the erotic movement she was a disgrace to womanhood; she was Gretchen, woman as man would like to think of her. She was gradually supplanted by a larger and more vigorous figure, often superior in social station to the snowdrop, Dorothea Brooke, Margaret Schlegel (in *Howard's End* by E. M. Forster), and Ursula Brangwen. This figure often had a younger, more 'feminine,' less interesting sister, just as the snowdrop characteristically had older and coarser ones.

In this later phase of the British tradition a wider range of society's aspects and of emotional patterns is consulted, but always the fate of a woman in relation to these themes is supreme; above all, her fate in marriage. In one aspect or another, the theme of marriage—what are its advantages and disadvantages, what is its essence and what its accidents, what are its relations to love and to law—is the British novel's prime concern.

Of course the number and variety of novels written in England is so large that to speak of a "main line" of concern they all share, is only possible by assuming some preliminary selection. My assumption has been that of Leavis's Great Tradition (though also that of Raymond Williams's system of preference, and that of the standard histories of the novel). This is more than an arbitrary assumption, because it is demonstrable that the Leavis tradition has been one of the two or three that could be called dominant in the general mind—the English imagination—over the last twenty years. Most important, it is the one that has been dominant in the intellectual and imaginative world of Doris Lessing. She herself refers most often to Thomas Mann as the archetypal "great novelist," but her work seems to show as much if not more influence by D. H. Lawrence. By us, at least, Anna Wulf legitimately can be seen as representing the theme of marriage and woman, and many other of the themes of the British novel.

Clearly, Saul Green sees Anna as representing marriage and society; he sees, as we see, that all her rebellions against that institution derive from special problems in herself and in others. Just as clearly, she sees him as representing Promethean eroticism. He says, "In fact I enjoy a society where women are second class citizens, I enjoy being boss and being flattered." And she replies. "Good. Because in a society where not one man in ten thousand begins to understand the ways in which women are second class citizens, we have to rely for company on the men who are at least not hypocrites." But, just by virtue of all they represent, they love each other. "I'd forgotten what making love with a real man is like. And I'd forgotten what it was to lie in the arms of a man one loves. I'd forgotten what it was like to be in love like this, so that a step on the stair makes one's heart beat, and the warmth of his shoulder against my palm is all the joy there is in life." They confront each other, then, as individuals *and* as representatives of the imaginative styles of their own cultures, and the good they do each other is representative too.

Saul Green is the first American hero to come to the aid of an English heroine in an English novel of high imaginative and intellectual level. But it is notable how many Promethean heroes there have been in American novels of this century; in Hemingway and Faulkner before Mailer and Bellow. The American literary imagination has been dominated by the image of the young man, at war with society, and preserving his honor by intransigence in that relationship, while the British novel is as lacking in such men as the American is in Demetrian women. Lawrence's and Hardy's women are more powerful than their men; Forster's are at least more convincing than his men; and none of the men are heroes. The national imaginations that express themselves in these men and these women are in some sense complementary, but only in the same sense as Doris Lessing's two characters are, which is a very incomplete complementarity. There is a strong hostility between Anna Wulf and Saul Green, and they come together only to go apart again. The Faustian phallicist and the Demetrian *magna mater* do not belong together, because they worship different principles of life.

But the character of the two countries, not only their literary character, is vividly illuminated by this confrontation and in turn illuminates it. The political and economic career of the two nations over the last two generations has paralleled the development of these representative figures. America has been the land of power and of violence both abroad and at home. England has been the land of peace and continuance, the land of domesticity. Thus the confrontation of Saul Green and Anna Wulf brings into focus a great deal of our experience of our current situation and reminds us of one of the great functions of art.

Chapter 5

OUR SENSE OF HUMOR I: MARK TWAIN AND EVELYN WAUGH

Wherefore, being a practical Connecticut man, I now shoved this whole problem clear out of my mind till its appointed day and hour should come, in order that I might turn all my attention to the circumstances of the present moment, and be alert and ready to make the most out of them that could be made. One thing at a time, is my motto—and just play that thing for all it is worth, even if it's only two pair and a jack. I made up my mind to two things; if it was still the nineteenth century and I was among lunatics and couldn't get away, I would presently boss that asylum or know the reason why; and if on the other hand it was really the sixth century, all right, I didn't want any softer thing; I would boss the whole country inside of three months; for I judged I would have the start of the best-educated man in the kingdom by a matter of thirteen hundred years and upwards. I'm not a man to waste time after my mind's made up and there's work on hand; so I said to the page . . . Mark Twain, *A Connecticut Yankee in King Arthur's Court.*

There is a very characteristic line of Anglo-Saxon humor that reaches its culmination in *A Connecticut Yankee* and whose dominant note resounds in that passage. It is a humor struck off by the contrast between the practical, skeptical, down-to-earth voice, and the more elaborate, fantastic, or resplendent things it "deals with." Primarily, the reader is asked to feel along with, to identify with, the "practical Connecticut man," and to gaze from his point of view at the other things (Arthurian splendors, in this case) with confident mockery. But the contrast includes some secondary satire of the first and sympathy with the second. The word boss in this passage—and it is a central word in the book as a whole—crystallizes this secondary satire.

The novel can be called a culmination in the tradition of this humor because of the many ways Twain works it out. Within the limits of what one might call the tactics of humor, his most effective device is travesty. He finds innumerable ways of humiliating the Arthurian knights, by making them wear stove-pipe hats and smoke pipes, by hanging advertisements or baskets of sandwiches on their spears, by turning them into commercial travelers or into a Saturday suburban cavalry, by mounting five hundred of them on bicycles, pedaling desperately to Arthur's rescue. There are many such devices besides travesty, and the skill with which Twain makes each one recur without merely repeating itself is a very important part of what makes him a great humorist. (Like Evelyn Waugh, like perhaps all satirical humorists, Twain seems to mentally tickle the reader the way an adult may physically tickle a child, by the forceful, all-controlling skill with which he sets up such expectations of aggressive mockery, and then fulfills, frustrates, overfulfills them. The *power* they exert over us—what makes us call them "outrageous"—is a part of their humor.) But when I say, "the ways Twain works out this humor," I think of its strategies rather than its tactics. And by "strategy" I mean Twain's deciding to make his hero not only a technologist and indeed a technocrat and also a practitioner of all the techniques of vaudeville entertainment, but also a master and minister of the faith in Progress, and so forth. (His choice of Arthurian England as his locale, with all its wonderful Tennysonian perspectives of "romance," is not to be called strategy—that is politics, *Realpolitik*, the choice of which country one will go to war with.)

It was by giving his hero these characteristics and not others that Twain determined what would happen in his book. Its developments all follow from Hank Morgan's character (with one seeming exception) and the situation, the "stories," are of subordinate interest and importance—they are matters of tactics. The one exception is the carnival of death and blood and destruction at the end of the book. Hank Morgan *causes* this, but it seems positively at odds with the easy amiable personality we met at the beginning of the book. That discrepancy, that seeming exception, we must discuss later. For the moment, I want to argue that it is also by giving his hero these characteristics that Twain makes him embody this kind of humor so fully. This Anglo-Saxon humor, *our* humor, *is* that of a technologist, a progressivist, a vaudeville comedian.

One prime example of the technological humor is the chapter, "The Restoration of the Fountain." A holy well has dried up, and Hank Morgan prepares to work the miracle of restoring the flow of water.

> My boys were experts in all sorts of things, from the stoning up of a well to the constructing of a mathematical instrument. An hour before sunrise we had that leak mended in shipshape fashion, and the water began to rise. Then we stowed our fireworks in the chapel, locked up the place, and went home to bed.
>
> Before the noon mass was over, we were at the well again; for there was a deal to do, yet, and I was determined to spring the miracle before midnight, for business reasons: for whereas a miracle worked for the Church on a weekday is worth a good deal, it is worth six times as much if you get it in on a Sunday. In nine hours the water had risen to its customary level, that is to say, it was within 23 feet of the top. We put in a little iron pump, one of the first turned out by my works near the capital; we bored into a stone reservoir which stood against the outer wall of the well chamber and inserted a section of lead pipe that was long enough to reach to the door of the chapel and project beyond the threshold, where the gushing water would be visible to the 250 acres of people I was intending should be present on the flat plain in front of this little holy hillock at the proper time.

Let me point out the delight in technology and expertise, the precision of planning and devising, the specification of facts and figures, and the subordination of human values to them— the 250 acres of people. "We knocked the head out of an empty hogshead and hoisted this hogshead to the flat roof of the chapel, where we clamped it down fast, poured in the gunpowder till it lay loosely an inch deep on the bottom, then we stood up rockets in the hogshead as thick as they could loosely stand, all the different breeds of rocket there are; and they made a portly and imposing sheaf, I can tell you." This is the glee, directly and naively shared with the reader, which is as important as the manipulation of others. This humor springs obviously and immediately from the possession of a certain kind of superior cleverness, and it is the kind that manifests itself in technological enterprise. It is the cleverness of the technological tricks by which white adventurers dazzled natives in the stories of Kipling, H. Rider Haggard, John Buchan, and so forth. It is the glee of white colonialism.

Twain, however, goes beyond these other writers by making his hero a technocrat as well as a technologist. He institutes a human factory, for turning sixth-century serfs into nineteenth-century men. "I'll book you both for my colony," he says. "You'll like it there; it's a Factory where I'm going to turn groping and grubbing automata into *men*." His other great institution is a military academy, a West Point. But its stress will be on the *science* of war. Morgan always exalts minds over bodies, over prowess, indeed over *men*. He feels himself to be, by virtue of his technological skills, his nineteenth-century education, a Superman. After the restoration of the fountain, "the populace uncovered and fell back reverently to make a wide way for me, as if I had been some kind of a superior being—and I was. I was aware of that." At that early point in the book we are not quite sure what kind of a joke that is, but by the end we know it is a very serious one. Just before the final massacre, he tells the chivalry of England that they, with their 25,000 knights, stand no chance against his 54 trainees. "Reflect: we are well-equipped, well-fortified, we number 54. 54 what? Men?—no, *minds*—the capablest in the world; a force against which mere animal might may no more hope to prevail than may the idle waves of the sea hope to prevail against the granite barriers of England."

Mind triumphs over might all the way through the book; and a strong stress is laid on that fact; note how much Twain makes out of the joke that King Arthur is priced lower than Hank Morgan when they are made slaves, because Hank is cleverer, even though Arthur is bigger, handsomer, braver, morally and naturally royal as well as feudally. And the natural expression of this enthusiasm for *mind* is the ruthless though playful mental competitiveness, the examination or debate competition. There is a chapter called "A Competitive Examination," but those called "Dowley's Humiliation" and "Sixth Century Political Economy" are perhaps even more vivid. Hank Morgan exultantly makes a fool out of a rather pompous opponent in argument, by a debating trick. We are called on to share his exultation, even though the other man's punishment is so savage as to make us uneasy. The interest of this is that it makes explicit something which at other times operates implicitly at the source of the humor. This is one of the attitudes we are induced to adopt in order to share the jokes Twain is making. (All tickling depends on some such cooperation on the part of the victim, the passive partner. The cultural significance of a given sense of humor depends on the nature of the cooperation.)

Incidentally, Twain himself was very conscious of how active the humorist's role was, how passive the audience's. That is made clear in Hank Morgan's talk about jokes that "fetched them," and that "broke them up." In Twain's own life the classic occasion of that was an incident which Justin Kaplan tells in *Mark Twain and Mr. Clemens*. Twain gave a speech at an army dinner to honor General Grant, and made some impudent jokes at the hero's expense, though he allied those jokes with a highly emotional deference. And his account of the occasion to his wife and to Howells is extraordinarily aggressive. He *made* General Grant laugh; he broke up that man of iron; the humorist exerted his power over the soldier. The occasion was a great triumph for Twain, and he saw it and felt it in quite sado-pugilistic terms. Humor was quite consciously for him, as for Evelyn Waugh, a mode of power.

Hank Morgan's progressivist ideology makes itself felt in all his jokes about the dirt and nudity of the past, about superstition and traditionalism, about feudal deference and slavery. But there is also a real poetry (still humorous, of course) about Hank's delight in the telephone, once he reinvents it, and gets it installed, and in the newspaper, once he gets that printed and distributed.

> Well, when the priest had been droning for three hours, and the good king polishing the evidence, and the sick were still pressing forward as plenty as ever, I got to feeling intolerably bored. I was sitting by an open window not far from the canopy of state. For the five hundredth time a patient stood forward to have his repulsivenesses stroked; again those words were being droned out; "they shall lay their hands on the sick"—when outside there rang clear as a clarion a note that enchanted my soul and tumbled thirteen worthless centuries about my ears: "Camelot *Weekly Hosannah and Literary Volcano*—latest irruption—only two cents—all about the big miracle in the Valley of Holiness." One greater than kings had arrived—the newsboy. But I was the only person in all that throng who knew the meaning of this mighty birth and what this imperial magician was come into the world to do.

Life gets cleaner, neater, livelier, simpler, *better*, by means of Progress, and Hank Morgan is a propagandist of that faith.

But he is also a professional entertainer. Much of his very first comment on the life of King Arthur's Court is made from that point of view and with that experience behind him. Merlin puts the knights to sleep by telling them a story out of the Morte d'Arthur, and Sir Dinadan rouses them all by tying some metal mugs to a dog's tail.

> Sir Dinadan was so proud of his exploit that he could not keep from telling over and over again, to weariness, how the immortal idea had occurred to him; and as is the way with humorists of his breed, he was still laughing at it after everybody else had got through. He was so set up that he concluded to make a speech—of course a humorous speech. I think I never heard so many old played out jokes strung together in my life. He was worse than the minstrels, worse than the clown in the circus. It seemed peculiarly sad to sit here, 1300 years before I was born and listen again to poor, flat, worm-eaten jokes that had given me the dry gripes when I was a boy 1300 years afterwards.

These are the tones of Bob Hope and a hundred familiar comedians of his type—the dry flat tone, the rattling speed of delivery, the uneasy overself-confidence. Surely this is still the archetypal humor of the Anglo-Saxon West.

And the miracles of the "Restoration of the Fountain" and of "Merlin's Tower" are vaudeville jokes as much as technological.

> I made about three passes in the air, and then there was an awful crash and that old tower leaped into the sky in chunks, along with a vast volcanic fountain of fire that turned night to noonday, and showed a thousand acres of human beings grovelling on the ground in a general collapse of consternation. Well, it rained mortar and masonry the rest of the week. This was the report; but probably the facts would have modified it.
> It was an effective miracle. The great bothersome temporary population vanished. There were a good many thousand tracks in the mud next morning, but they were all outward bound. If I had advertised another miracle I couldn't have raised an audience with a sheriff.

I have pointed out that Morgan's technological tricks are very like those to be found in the contemporary adventure-fiction of imperialism. This is the humor of the white man confronting the black, of the Western countries confronting the East, of the townsman confronting the country boy, of the present confronting the past, of all new cleverness confronting traditional slowness. But it seems especially appropriate to the cleverness of the late nineteenth century, the Cockney cleverness of Kipling and Wells, the penny press and the Wall Street speculator. This was the moment when the glee of colonialism was at its height, when the technological triumph of the West aroused the most self-congratulation. It was Cecil Rhodes's moment, and I think there is a greater contemporary name to be invoked—that of Bismarck. Sir Boss's relation to Arthurian England must surely remind us of Germany's master manager more than of anyone else. "I was no shadow of the king; I was the substance; the king himself was the shadow." And he names de Montfort, Gaveston, Mortimer, Villiers. "At the same time, there was another power that was a trifle stronger than both of us put together. That was the Church." It was his *Kulturkampf* that defeated Sir Boss. There is plenty of evidence, in other writings of Twain, that the rise of Germany and the rule of Bismarck fascinated his imagination, like the imagination of many Anglo-Saxons of his time. The rise of Germany was the more concentrated and dramatic reenactment of the rise of England itself. Germany's thrusting herself into the group of nations that carved up the colonial world among themselves was a tribute to their triumph, though it was so soon to lead to their destruction.

But perhaps the figure most significantly evoked like a ghost behind Hank Morgan is Defoe's Robinson Crusoe. Twain explicitly compares the situation and the talents of the two men.

> There wasn't even a bell or a speaking tube in the castle. I had a great many servants, and those that were on duty lolled in the anteroom; and when I wanted one of them I had to go and call for him. There was no gas, there were two candles; a bronze dish half full of boardinghouse butter with a blazing rag in it was the thing that produced what was regarded as light. A lot of these hung along the walls and modified the dark, just toned it down enough to make it dismal. If you went out at night, your servants carried torches. There were no books, pens, paper, or ink, and no glass in the openings they believed to be windows. It is a little thing—glass is—until it is absent, then it becomes a big thing. But perhaps the worst of all was, that there wasn't any sugar, coffee, tea, or tobacco. I saw that I was just another Robinson Crusoe cast away on an uninhabited island, with no society but some more or less tame animals, and if I wanted to make life bearable I must do as he did—invent, contrive, create, reorganize things; set brain and hand to work, and keep them busy. Well, that was in my line.

The context into which Crusoe's name is introduced defines his role for Twain. He is the patron saint of invention, of technology, of Progress. He is the hero who starts the process by which we arrive at the comforts and decencies of nineteenth-century life. And one is bound to think of him and other of Defoe's heroes at other moments in the book. The poetry of enumerating property, as we see above, is common to both him and Morgan, and the supreme example here is the bill in "Dowley's Humiliation."

> Then he read off this bill, while those three amazed men listened, and serene waves of satisfaction rolled over my soul and alternate waves of terror and admiration surged over Marco's.
> 2 pounds salt.
> 8 dozen pints beer, in the wood.
> 3 bushels wheat.

2 pounds fish.
3 hens.
1 goose.
3 dozen eggs.
1 roast of beef.   etc.

This is the essential poetry of a commercial civilization, created by and for our children as they play at keeping shop, and collect oddments, arrange them on a stall, and sell them to their parents, which is repeated in those middlebrow novels about the rise and fall of some industrial dynasty. This is the basic myth of Western civilization—you find it in de Crevecoeur's *Letters of an American Farmer*—the story of how men make two blades of grass grow where one grew before, and accumulate stores and stocks of all kinds of goods. Its mythic form is the story of one man rebuilding the world from scratch. It has been carried quite considerably by the innumerable successive editions of *Robinson Crusoe* itself, and then by the numerous progeny of that book, from *The Swiss Family Robinson* to *Coral Island*, which have been absorbed by so many generations of Anglo-Saxon children. There are other myths that Defoe had a hand in shaping, like the piracy myth which began with his *Captain Singleton* and the criminal myth which began with his *Moll Flanders*, and they all, in various ways, carry the same mythic values. They all celebrate the same set of virtues, which amount to the dominant traits in Western man's personality, and Mark Twain is the supreme master of that personality's sense of humor.

What began with Defoe ended with Twain. The great adventure of WASP dominance, the great swarming of WASPS over the whole globe came to a horrified halt with the slaughter of the Arthurian knights—once that was confirmed by the battle of the Somme. Twain's sense of humor became distasteful to the sensitive. In the 1920's a new sense of humor was devised, applying the narrow dandyism of the 1890's—"aestheticism"—to twentieth-century situations of all kinds. Of course, the old humor survived at lower cultural levels, and sporadically revived at higher ones, but a revolution had occurred. The old Anglo-Saxon humor and the old Anglo-Saxon personality had lost confidence in itself.

Both the humor and the personality were by 1900 characteristically American rather than English. There were plenty of British versions of the WASP personality as culture hero, of course. They are to be found in the stories of Kipling and Stevenson, Haggard and Buchan. (And Conrad examines the type from a deeply admiring though alien point of view. Lawrence analyzes it, from the erotic movement's point of view, in Gerald Crich of *Women in Love*.) But it seems that the most potent image has always been American. America always has been the homeland of the egalitarian, practical-man half of the Anglo-Saxon race, even those born in Britain and even before the War of Independence. Benjamin Franklin was an emblematic figure of all the practical-man virtues. And at the end of the nineteenth century there was a significant outburst of celebratory writing about the type. (Lawrence's attack on Franklin in *Studies in Classic American Literature* expresses the reaction against that.) Exactly the same type as Hank Morgan was drawn, from a different perspective, by Howells as Fulkerson in *A Hazard of New Fortunes*. And first cousin to the type is Henry James's Christopher Newman in *The American*. "The gentleman on the divan was the superlative American; to which affirmation of character he was partly helped by the general easy magnificence of his manhood. He appeared to possess that kind of health and strength which, when found in perfection, are the most impressive— the physical tone which the owner does nothing to 'keep up'." We have been told before that he was "long, lean, and muscular," that he sat reclined at his ease, with "his head thrown back and his legs outstretched."

His eye was of a clear, cold grey, and save for the abundant droop of his moustache he spoke, as to the cheek and chin, of the joy of the matutinal steel. He had the flat jaw and the firm, dry neck which are frequent in the American type; but the betrayal of native conditions is a matter of expression even more than of feature, and it was in this respect that our traveller's countenance was supremely eloquent. The observer we have been supposing might, however, perfectly have measured its expressiveness and yet been at a loss for names and terms to fit it. It had that paucity of detail which is yet not emptiness, that blankness which is not simplicity, that look of being committed to nothing in particular, of standing in a posture of general hospitality to the chances of life, of being very much at one's own disposal, characteristic of American faces of the clear strain. It was the eye, in this case, that chiefly told the story; an eye in which the unacquainted and the expert were singularly blended. It was full of contradictory suggestions; and though it was by no means the glowing orb of a hero of romance you could find in it almost anything you looked for. Frigid and yet friendly, frank and yet cautious, shrewd and yet credulous, positive yet sceptical, confident yet shy, extremely intelligent and extremely good-humoured, there was something vaguely defiant in its concessions and something profoundly reassuring in its reserve. . . . Neither in this nor in any other respect had he a high sense of responsibility; it was his prime conviction that a man's life should be a man's ease and that no privilege was really great enough to take his breath away. The world, to his vision, was a great bazaar where one might stroll about and purchase handsome things; but he was no more conscious, individually, of social pressure than he admitted the claims of the obligatory purchase.

James here both catches a certain American type, and realizes its potential as a novel-hero. Newman has not "the glowing orb of a hero of romance," but he has the eye that catches the novelist's attention. Though, like Crusoe and Morgan, he treats the whole world as a bazaar, where one primarily buys and sells, he is not merely prosaic. And though, again like Morgan, so skeptical of history, art, and mystery, he is imaginatively alive. It is striking that James could work so well within the Anglo-Saxon myth at that point in his career, since he rebelled so strongly against the West and the money market and all the other things that Newman represents. And the portrait is doubly striking because it holds so exactly true for Gary Cooper. From 1940 to 1960 the image of this Anglo-Saxon hero dominated the imagination of the world via the cinema screen. And Hank Morgan can claim this figure as first cousin on one side, just as, on the other, he can claim Bogart and the detective hero. (Twain was very interested in detectives and detection, as we see in *Pudd'nhead Wilson*—his version of *Moll Flanders*.) In the world of popular culture, the twentieth century has been his.

But in the finer imaginative world, including humor, Hank Morgan was a culmination also in the sense of being the last of his line. The main reason for the revulsion against him was presumably that embodied in the book's ending, in Hank Morgan's horrifying slaughter of all the knights. His good-humored impatience with their splendid stupidity is gradually revealed to be continuous with a contempt for human life. His preference for minds over men is revealed to be the smiling face of scientism and mechanicism—of that fatal *mentalism* which modern prophets (Susan Sontag and Norman Mailer among our contemporaries) have pointed to as the original sin of Western man, as ultimately responsible for the horrors of scientific warfare. An earlier expression of the same idea is Lawrence's accusation of Franklin for so complacently accepting the slaughter of the Indians. The sensuality that these modern sensualists preach is to be a guarantee against abstract and righteous efficiency, because it will both center the personality in its erotic experience—something notably absent from Hank Moran—and make sensual realization a crucial criterion of every action. Subsequent events like the Great War and World War II and the atomic and hydrogen bombs have confirmed their theory, which could be called Twain's implicit theory, even though it condemns his hero and his mood, since he does so gratuitously introduce that ending. It is a measure of all that makes Twain a more impressive writer than Defoe that he included this death-lust in his account of the white psychology, while Defoe did not. (Such a death-lust was of course already expressed, in the Southwestern humor tradition on which Twain based himself, but he still chose to use it in this place and in this way.) But this violence clearly breaks the mood of *The Connecticut Yankee*, spoils it as a piece of humor, just as the world wars have broken the mood of the Anglo-Saxon type as a whole, spoiled its faith in its own cultural image and sense of humor.

There has been a revolution in the sensibility of humor, comparable in importance with that revolution in the sensibility of sex which occurred a little earlier. But the two changes were not at all parallel in their tendencies. The erotic movement tended to root all of life deeper in Nature, in the unconscious processes of the seasons and the blood. It aimed to restore naiveté to eros. The revolution in humor was toward a kind of dandyism, of sophistication and alienation from average experience and social faith. It aimed to destroy naiveté in humor.

The humor that now holds the hegemony seems to be best exemplified in the work of Evelyn Waugh. This is a humor that seems to us much more sardonic and anarchic than Twain's; because it is directed against major faiths in our way of life, major naivetés of our society, which *The Connecticut Yankee* confirms and corroborates. But if we looked at the two men from another point of view, we should find it hard to call Twain the simpler, happier, or naiver. Both were deeply sardonic men, deeply divided and self-contradictory, deeply irritable, bored, unhappy, conscious of profound personal guilt and shame. But seen just as humorists, and in relation to their audiences, there is that large and interesting difference between them, and it is emblematic of the difference between two generations of the Anglo-Saxon mind. Mark Twain's is my father's sense of humor, and Evelyn Waugh's is the one I learned at the university. But they also emblemize a difference between the two countries. Waugh's is an English sense of humor, because it derives from England's decline after 1918 and because it is allied with other powerful forces in English cultural life which so derive—for example, the whole religious-aristocratic reaction represented by T. S. Eliot, Dorothy Sayers, C. S. Lewis, and so forth. Such forces had much less power in the America of the 1930's, 1940's, and 1950's. It is only during the 1960's that Waugh's sense of humor became generally palatable to Americans. Only in those years have phenomena and patterns fixed themselves as American which invite Waugh's kind of treatment. (I'm thinking of books and films like *M.A.S.H.*)

Thus there is this parallelism between the two changes in sensibility. In both Britain took the lead. Of course it is not "objectively" clear—and certainly not at the time—which was "the lead." The American sensibility of the 1920's, both in humorous and erotic matters, was in some ways more modern than the British. But from where we stand now it seems that America is "catching up with" both Lawrence and Waugh— not necessarily the books, but the sensibility.

The British sense of humor as a whole demands separate

treatment. Let us take it for granted here that since the Great War that sense of humor has been markedly ironic and defensive and destructive of the more ambitious and expansive phases of life. The interesting thing for our argument here is to note how often Waugh's modes of humor contrast with Twain's in some simple clear black-and-white ways. For instance, Twain's basic stylistic device is to use slightly less dignified language than the subject calls for. Waugh's is to use a slightly elevated style, slightly too dignified—dandified. Then the structural pattern of *Decline and Fall, Vile Bodies,* and so forth, is Twain's pattern inverted. In *A Connecticut Yankee* the young man from "our" middle-class modern world is introduced into the fantastic world of Arthurian England, and we measure that world by its contrast with him, and find it ridiculous. In *Decline and Fall,* Paul Pennyfeather, who is also from "our" middle-class modern world, is introduced into the fantastic world of Margot Beste-Chetwynde, and we measure that world by its contrasts with him, and find it intoxicating. Margot and her friends make Paul and his standards ridiculous to himself and to us. The reader is dazzled by the wit, the dash, the sartorial and moral and intellectual stylishness of the people he meets there.

At the end of each novel, the reader is returned to "our" world, in the company of Paul Pennyfeather and Hank Morgan. (In Twain's novel, it is literally Clarence who survives, but the effect is the same.) At the end of *Put Out More Flags,* the central characters prepare for the real war, and Ambrose retires to Ireland; at the end of *Huckleberry Finn,* Tom prepares for real life, and Huck lights out for the territory.

Huck has the same place in Twain's comic world as Sebastian Flyte has in Waugh's. Sebastian, in *Brideshead Revisited,* represents that pure delight, pure freedom and playfulness, which cannot grow up, just as Huck does. Tom Sawyer represents in Twain's book that coarse, tougher adaptability with which the author identifies himself, just as Charles Ryder does in Waugh's. Many of the differences between the British and American comic sensibilities are locatable in the contrasts between Huck and Sebastian—the naiveté in Huck's social setting, his association with Nature, his misspelled vernacular, as against Sebastian's baroque social setting, his association with Art, his exquisite diction. And it is significant that in *Brideshead Revisited* Waugh makes use of romance, even of Arthurian romance, to define what is wrong with his "modern man," Hooper.

> Hooper was no romantic. He had not as a child ridden with Rupert's horse or sat among the camp-fires at Xanthus-side; at the age when my eyes were dry to all save poetry—that stoic, red-skin interlude which our schools introduce between the fast-flowing tears of the child and the man—Hooper had wept often, but never for Henry's speech on St Crispin's Day, nor for the epitaph at Thermopylae. The history they taught him has had few battles in it but, instead, a profusion of detail about humane legislation and recent industrial change.

(Hooper is of course a Wellsian figure, with a Wellsian view of history, and as such he is a cousin to Hank Morgan.) Hank Morgan says, "With the spirit of prophecy upon me, I could look into the future and see [England] erect statues and monuments to her unspeakable Georges and other royal and noble clotheshorses, and leave unhonored the creators of this world—after God—Gutenberg, Watt, Arkwright, Whitney, Morse, Stephenson, Bell." Charles Ryder continues: "Gallipoli, Balaclava, Quebec, Lepanto, Bannockburn, Roncevales, and Marathon—these, and the battle in the West where Arthur fell, and a hundred such names whose trumpet-notes, even now in my sere and lawless state, called to me irresistibly across the intervening years with all the clarity and strength of boyhood, sounded in vain to Hooper." Waugh implicitly appropriates and identifies himself with that Arthurian England which Twain mocked. Of course, that identification is humorous, but with a humor that is only a mask for sentiment. Thus, in *A Handful of Dust*, Tony Last's house has its bedrooms named after Arthurian heroes, and John Beaver sleeps in Lancelot, Brenda in Guinevere, Tony in Arthur, as they live out their modern, diminished, version of the great betrayal. The irony of diminishment only masks, and intensifies, the warmth of Waugh's feeling.

In his more satirical books, Waugh's reader sympathizes with Margot Beste-Chetwynde and Basil Seale, the most doomed and self-destructive of aristocrats. It is they who pull off the tricks, and deploy the techniques, which make Waugh's comedy, as Hank or Huck or Tom do in Twain. But they are quite different techniques—matters of manners. Typically, there are no technological tricks in Waugh. The antithesis of Twain, again, he takes *no* interest in technology, or he is interested only with disgust, as in the embalming techniques of Mr. Joyboy in *The Loved One*, or in the chromium-plating of rooms by Mrs. Beaver in *A Handful of Dust*. In harmony with that, Waugh's ideology was *anti*-technocratic. The social technicians of the dissolution of the monasteries and the Tudor establishment are the men he blames for the spiritual and cultural aridities of modern England. And all his imaginative response goes to grandeur in decay—its primary image, grandiose mansions.

As for the other two categories that crystallized out of Twain's sensibility, it needs no arguing that Waugh's is anti-progressivist. Not only was he not at all progressive, he was most assertively anti-progressive—that is the major determinant of all his attitudes. He feared the future, hated the modern in all its manifestations, and only loved the past and the defeated.

And though Waugh was of course an entertainer, a professional joke-maker, as much as Twain was, Waugh's sensibility was not that of a vaudeville comedian. Most of Twain's jokes are made to be shared by a large audience, which comes to appreciate them by means of immediate contact with the entertainer and each other. Twain was in fact a lecture-hall spell-binder, and his written work shows it. The comparable English writer is Dickens. Waugh was not. His jokes *are* shared by many readers, and so act finally as uniters of his audience, but their primary function is almost the opposite of that performed by Twain's jokes—they separate off individual readers from a mass audience. The individual is asked to appreciate the awfulness of this or that general habit, the tiresomeness of this or that general piety, to join the joke-maker in repudiation of the commonalty.

Thus Waugh's is an aristocratic sense of humor, in a sense quite different from saying that he writes about people with titles. But the secondary sense also is obviously true and obviously important. He liked aristocrats, and they liked him. It was no accident that Winston Churchill made *Decline and Fall* his Christmas present to his friends in 1928, the year it came out. (Churchill was to Waugh what Ulysses Grant was to Twain; and the difference between the two military leaders—between their prose styles as well as between their social styles—parallels the difference between Sebastian and Huck.) Randolph Churchill became a close friend of Waugh's, and there is much about Basil Seal, Waugh's finest comic hero, that must remind us of Randolph Churchill. The different members of the Churchill family represent in different ways Waugh's sensibility of grandeur-in-decay within the world of action. And 1928, the year of Waugh's first comic novel, may also be taken as significant, as the moment when the post-war British sensibility, so much of it dandified, was firmly established. It was the year of *Point Counterpoint* and *To The Lighthouse*, and of Orwell's decision to drop out of his own class. It was a year of repudiations and alienations. And Waugh's humor expressed all this. His aristophilia, as much as Orwell's prolephilia, expressed a revulsion from his own middle class and all its achievements and ambitions. One loves grandeur-in-decay when one hates average successful prosperity, and one's sense of humor expresses one's attitudes to one's audience as well as to one's subject. Twain *served* his average, prosperous, middle-class reading public. Waugh flouted his. The effects of the two humors may have been much the same. Who knows? But Waugh's *signified* alienation and Twain's the opposite.

In many ways, Twain and Waugh were strikingly similar. Even within the group of great humorists, they belong together. Both anti-erotic imaginations, they stress male comradeships and represent love-relationships most conventionally and sentimentally. They both show society as dominated by fools and bores, and fate as characterized by betrayal and disaster—life as subordinate to death. For that reason, no doubt, both are much interested in militarism and the machinery of death, as well as in the military and manly virtues. Both men tell jokes that belong to the bar where magistrates gather, managers, captains, men who take responsibility for others and responsibility for law and order. Both were quickly irritated by most *real* clubs and bars. One might say that both belonged to the same cultural type. What shaped the two humors into opposite significances was the shift in the configuration of cultural forces between Twain's generation and Waugh's.

If one looks at more contemporary styles of humor, one can see many inheritors of Waugh now, and some of Twain in the intermediate period. But that Twain style gradually petered out. In America, for instance, the post-Twain humor of Will Rogers soon ceased to seem contemporary or exciting. No doubt the dominant humorous style in America over the last twenty years must be said to be that Jewish style of which Malamud is one of the most distinguished practitioners. This is gentle, ironic, masochistic. It resembles Thurber's self-deprecating and self-depreciating sensibility—that is to say, Howells's—more than it resembles either Twain's or Waugh's. It belongs less to the world of men. But the black Jewish humor of *Catch 22* and *Giles Goat-Boy* seems to me to owe and give a lot to a taste for Waugh (though its direct debt is to Nathanael West, and so forth). Not that that humor is dandified, but that the readers of such books are asked to sympathize with the wild and wicked elements within them, not with the normal and admirable. They may help explain the spread of Waugh's humor to America.

In England dandy humor has long been dominant, but the Twain line was carried on for a time by W. W. Jacobs and even more by H. G. Wells. Kipps and Mr. Polly are jauntier and perkier cousins to Huck and Hank Morgan, typical darlings of "democratic" humor, and it is noteworthy that the joke of the little man who is married to the big woman somehow typifies all of them. This is of course the humor of Charlie Chaplin, and—its supreme embodiment in literature—of Leopold Bloom. (Stephen Dedalus can be seen as Joyce's unsuccessful attempt to escape from this "humorous" view of the artist and to give himself a dandy identity.) Bloom might have said, with George Ponderevo in Wells's *Tono-Bungay*, "I'm a spiritual guttersnipe in love with unimaginable goddesses. I've never seen the goddesses nor ever shall. . . . I stumble and flounder, but I know that over all these merry immediate things, there are other things that are great and serene, very high, beautiful things—the reality."

That is the Wellsian formula for uniting humor with poetry —Wellsian humor and Wellsian poetry. And it represents a standard "democratic" attitude which was dominant among Anglo-Saxons at the beginning of this century, until eroded away by the erotic or the aesthetic movements. It is roughly Tom Sawyer's attitude to Becky Thatcher. In Twain's work as a whole, women are supposed to be "unimaginable goddesses," but turn out to be "merry immediate things," and sometimes not so merry. They are harsh and dominating when they are not sweet and soft. Twain often represented his wife, in jest, as a dragon before whom he quailed. The little man and the big woman joke is ever-imminent in Twain, as in Wells and in half of Joyce.

And at this point one can glimpse a likeness, a common tendency, in the two movements hitherto seen as so divergent, the change in erotic sensibility and the change in humor. Both are alien to that joke and to that "democratic" sensibility. For instance, if one grants to the story of Lawrence-and-Frieda a cultural interest quite apart from Lawrence's books, one can perhaps see in *their* eroticism another antithesis to Twain's humor. Lawrence was a little man married to a big woman. And in most people's jokes against Frieda or against the big woman in general, one can surely see a refusal of eroticism and of Mother Earth. (Of course, there are complex cases where the joke is part of a large imaginative preoccupation with eroticism, as in *Ulysses*.) Lawrence's self-commitment to the erotic movement ended, in his own life, the possibility of his developing his Wellsian humorous persona. There are signs of such a potentiality in his early letters, and he remained an excellent Chaplinesque impersonator of others and mocker of himself in acting out anecdotes. But he wrote to Edward Garnett on April 22, 1914, that he was not *really* "clever" or "part Frenchman and part Cockney" (that is to say, Wellsian). He is really "a passionately religious man." Having now Frieda, "my Cockneyism and commonness are only when the deep feeling doesn't find its way out."

Up to the time when Lawrence committed himself to

Frieda, he could perhaps have said what George Ponderevo said. But in the great works he went on to write, there was no polarization of experience between "great and serene things" and "merry and immediate things," and consequently no joke about the little man and the big woman is immanent, much less actual. And it is interesting that it is not immanent or actual in Waugh any more than in Lawrence. It is not a dandy joke any more than an erotic one. It was a pre-1914 joke, part of that "democratic" humor. It belonged to a cultural moment that was past. Both the erotic and the dandy movements went against it. That joke was exiled to the seaside comic postcard stands, to the outer low-tide reaches of staleness, where it still exists in pathetic testimony to the passing of that moment.

Chapter 6

OUR SENSE OF HUMOR II:
BRITISH COMEDY
IN THIS CENTURY*

It has often been said that George Bernard Shaw was England's great comic genius of this century, and (less positively) that Evelyn Waugh was the second greatest; the radical succeeded, paradoxically, by the Tory; and (much less positively) that Kingsley Amis is Waugh's successor, in another reversal of styles. Edmund Wilson has, at one time or another, made that selection. I agree that these are the important names in the history of comedy in England in this century, but I would like to quarrel with the grouping in part, and in part to develop it at more length, in order to bring into focus its most interesting distinctions and brilliancies. Most important, this scheme only half clarifies, half obscures, the nature and development of the national sense of humor, which has been so acutely class conscious, so deeply asexual, or at least anti-erotic, so reactionary and anti-natural in general, in this century.

First of all, I doubt that Shaw was a comic genius; certainly he was not the liberator by laughter, the shatterer of

* This chapter appeared in the *Texas Quarterly*, Autumn 1961, under the title "British Comedy and the British Sense of Humour."

conventions, the all-daring rebel he offered himself as. What he was, in the first twenty years of the century, was the most forceful and original inventor of comic situations and effects; beside him the comic work of Arnold Bennett, H. G. Wells, E. M. Forster, Henry James, and D. H. Lawrence, seems less distinctively itself, much more derivative from either their own serious work or from earlier comic writers, Dickens, Jane Austen, or George Eliot. But the range of those comic situations and effects is narrow. Shaw's comedy is essentially the same as Wilde's, essentially dandified, but he made it his own. He rescued that dandyism from its narrowly "aesthetic" scope, its mere defiance and frivolity, its ninetyish self-destroyingness, its mere titter. Shaw had vigor and aggression, and he had a very pure, sure taste, within its limits, and he gave a shape that is still recognizable to certain comic situations and attitudes that are even now central to the British sense of humor. For instance, there is the wife who so winsomely acquiesces to all her husband's bluster, and then arranges matters her own way behind his back, and loves him not despite, but for his inadequacy to her. This is developed at most length in *Candida*, but it runs through much of Shaw's work and through that of subsequent writers. One meets the type, admired just as fondly by her creator, in Joyce Cary's and Somerset Maugham's novels; our actresses, for instance, Celia Johnson, have been ready to play her whenever the part permitted; and many a British bride has approached the altar in loving expectation of managing her married life in the same way.

Another of Shaw's inventions (whether or not there were predecessors, he in effect patented it) is the well-bred deflation of melodrama that is found in *Captain Brassbound's Conversion* and *The Man of Destiny*. Here the most exciting events and the most excited speeches are dramatically outreached by a polite, practical suggestion or a coolly undisturbed offer of tea. This has been developed since by Evelyn Waugh, among a dozen others, and is one of the effects British undergraduates have tried hardest at. Most important, perhaps, is the duel of the sexes; where a man and a woman talk at, insult, exasperate each other to a pitch of furious mutual fascination that can be satisfactorily resolved only by a clinch and a curtain. This of course you find in Noel Coward and Terence Rattigan, and innumerable plays and stories about clever and artistic people. Shaw's "issues" had long passed into history, but in England these were still current comic situations in the 1950's, and still bore the imprint he left on them.

But Shaw had not the variety, the scope, the social vision, or, except in his pamphlets and prefaces, the richness that great comedy gets from the tension of differing truths. He was too simple an egotist, too much of a dandy; he saw and heard things and people too much in relation to himself; and that self had been so theatricalized, hypertrophied, dehumanized that other people's relations to him were all equally simple and theatrical. There are only two fully realized and vivid personalities in Shaw's world, Shaw and Woman; the other characters are little more than puppets or charlatans that one or other of the two can manipulate or unmask. The roles that both appear in are little more than disguises, whether it be as Andrew Undershaft or Adolphus (both equally Shaw) or as Britomart or Barbara Undershaft (both equally Woman); both offer equally minor variations and enrichments to the basic, unvarying comedy of two brilliant peacocks parading at and pecking at each other. There is only one voice in Shaw's world, Shaw's, and what is being talked about is usually "Shaw," his brilliance, his audacity, his outrageousness.

This impoverishment is especially obvious in his treatment of English society. He can reproduce social gestures, verbal and behavioral, for lower- as well as upper-class types, for Eliza Doolittle as well as for Mrs. Higgins. But how simple and crude this is beside, say, Evelyn Waugh's Margot Beste-Chetwynde, Julia Stitch, Barbara Sothill, Sonia Digby-Vane-Trumpington, all brilliantly distinct versions of one narrowly defined voice and about whom we feel such a blend of admiration, amusement, delight, exasperation. How quickly, moreover, both class accents fade away into the voice of Woman vis-à-vis Shaw. Above all, how conceitedly and simple-mindedly he offers us these scraps of social insight, with as much *empressement* as Professor Higgins himself, so that what one has to respond to, as so often, is not so much Shaw's cleverness as his delight in that cleverness.

The sensibility of his plays, moreover, the sympathy directed to the differing attitudes and emotions discussed, is too simply conservative. Shaw's humor is essentially that of the debating-club maverick, not to be taken seriously as a comment on the subject under discussion. In so far as it *has* social allegiances, they are all to the *status quo* and the upper middle class. This is not because of any insincerity in Shaw's politics, but because of his temperamental need for situations in which good taste could be triumphant, his revulsion from anything embarrassing, death or a sexual problem or a deeply personal emotion. In the end, the best qualities to have in Shaw's world are elegant techniques for keeping other people's emotions under control. For instance, in the Shavian situations described above, the point of the joke each time, the source of the excitement which issues in laughter, is that the disturbing elements have been outmaneuvered by good sense, good manners, and a sense of humor; even in the duel of the sexes, we laugh because the sexual relation has been revealed to be basically an expression of, or under the control of, nerves and high spirits.

The training Shaw gave to the British mind, then, was most importantly in making debating points, about morality, about behavior, about even personal relations—and the atmosphere of debate, an atmosphere that precludes all possibility of inner change, is essential to it. His sense of humor was not directed at any of the bases or sources of life; again in the examples cited above, each situation has a point a good deal more acute than the one Shaw makes about it, which his humor does not include. He does not admit that Candida is importantly *hateful*, which Evelyn Waugh, for instance, fully admits about Margot Beste-Chetwynde. His sense of humor evades such dangerous facts, and is in effect a powerful conservative influence on his audience, guaranteeing, with its glow of intellectual effort, a poise of mind that has outfaced every weighty challenge, withstood every insurgent doubt, assimilated every audacious criticism into itself; when in point of fact it has recognized only drawing-room facsimiles of these. Its effort goes much more into turning real threats into debating-club, drawing-room facsimiles than into facing them in themselves. The proof of this is perhaps to be seen in Shaw's general acceptance by a level of society that never accepted D. H. Lawrence in the same period.

But this falsity, while it detracted from his claim to genius, did not prevent his being socially effective. He had, after all, talent and taste, and he gave a voice to powerful feelings in his audience, feelings of distrust of spontaneous life in themselves and others. But more than that, Shaw was after all a *kind* of comic genius, a very special kind, deriving nine-tenths of his comedy from his audience's relations with him as reputation. His materials were not personal relations or social or intellectual or emotional experience, but his own persona as public figure, and his audience's half-respectful, half-hostile expectations from him. Our delight is in the variety of masks he assumes—the prophetic, the narcissistic, the shocking, the puritanical, the charlatan, the aesthete, the intellectual, and so forth, and in the skill and pace with which he switches from one to the other. One cannot take seriously, in even a comic way, because one cannot find interesting, his understanding of people and society, or manners and morals; but one must be impressed, particularly in his musical and dramatic criticism, by the way he plays with one's varying expectations, arousing, outraging, and outreaching them.

For all these reasons he could invent comic situations that are still striking, if unappealing, and he has been culturally and socially effective. His effect was to make the British sense of humor most keenly sensitive to the mocking and deflating thrust, and to self-parading, eccentric brilliance; to make sexuality seem a form of self-assertion, and deep feeling a form of stupidity; to encourage the British mind to a distrust and dislike of seriously emotional and seriously rebellious and seriously unhappy people.

Obviously Shaw could not have imposed a sense of humor on the nation which the latter was not already in some degree predisposed to; there were other forces working at the same time as Shaw, or even earlier, working in the same direction. In another way, no doubt, his humor was derived *from* the nation, from earlier writers. As I said, his impudence derives from Wilde and the other dandy aesthetes who had formed themselves into obverses of Victorian manliness, living reactions, and who themselves therefore ultimately derived from Britain's material prosperity and moral unease after Darwin. Writers express and employ, as well as create, a national mood. With Waugh and with Amis, I shall try to indicate some of the social forces they enlist, maneuver, and obey. But with Shaw, because his "situation" is no longer urgently contemporary, I want to take all the other factors for granted and assign the responsibility for the change in the British mind crudely to the major writer in the case.

Of the three writers mentioned, it is Evelyn Waugh who has real claims to genius and who is at least one of the most serious and brilliant artists of this century in any language and any genre.

Waugh's point of view was much more dandified than Shaw's. His sympathies were aristocratic and with the past against the present, and even more against that future which Shaw represented. He rejected even the claims of common sense and common decency—his *humor* did—in the name of wit and style and privilege; he rejected the claims of the consensus in the name of the defiant individual. But in one rather special sense Waugh was less the dandy than Shaw. He did not write about himself. There is no glittering figure in Waugh's books who stands for him, no figure of any description until we get to Charles Ryder in *Brideshead Revisited*, who is sheer neutral sensibility and intelligence; and then Gilbert Pinfold, who is both grotesque and pathetic, a much grimmer treatment of the author than Shaw ever devoted to himself. Even in his travel books, Waugh is present only as a discarnate impudence, not as a person. If one compares Robert Byron's books of the same kind, one will be struck by how much Byron writes about himself, how little Waugh does. Waugh had a sadder relation to himself than Byron or Shaw or any true dandy. The style he loved was performed for him by his friends. (Later in life, it is true, he became markedly and defiantly eccentric, but it seems that he was never easy in the dandy role—too rough and angry in some ways, too stiff and exaggerated in others.) Waugh's dandyism was that of his group and ultimately that of his society.

This difference from Shaw is to be explained in large measure by the events of national history. In Shaw's formative years England was still a great empire, and its positive type (the empire-maker and the empire-ruler) was still heavily dominant. With the disasters of the Great War that dominance was broken, and its recessive types, including its dandies, had the chance to establish a hegemony. In Shaw's time the dandy figures among the intellectuals and artists were Wilde and Beardsley, both doomed to early death or disgrace and both marked outsiders in the English establishment. By Waugh's time there were the Sitwells, enacting the dandy role within the aristocracy; and Harold Acton and Brian Howard had been star figures at both Eton and Oxford, where they had made a great success out of cultivating aristocratic acquaintance. Dandies had in some sense dominated the imagination of some great English institutions.

Waugh's sensibility was deeply cloven and self-contradicting. This is no doubt why he became a great humorist. Just as he was both more and less the dandy than Shaw, his point of view was strongly traditionalist, as well as keenly mocking of tradition. Indeed, in his serious thinking, the balance declined to the side of tradition and even reaction. But within his humor, his irresponsible imaginings, the dominance went to the dandies. Exactly what traits expressed themselves in Waugh's sense of humor, we must discuss in another place, but it may be summed up as being deeply distrustful of the simple and general pieties of our society—the simple and general faith in life.

This sense of humor, then, finds and makes funny (with a note of hostility and fear in the laughter) all that is not stylishly aristocratic and British, whether the style be traditional or anti-traditional (Lady Circumference or Margot Beste-Chetwynde). Though the English, like everyone else, are absurd in Waugh, they are never as simply, two-dimensionally absurd as the Welsh (*Decline and Fall*), the French (*Black Mischief*), the Americans (*The Loved One*), or colored people (*Scoop*). Though upper-class manners are caricatured, they are never made as gross or unpleasant as those of the lower or middle classes (the Connollies in *Put Out More Flags* or the Stubbs in *Decline and Fall*.) And all the people who are too serious to be stylish, who are out of sympathy with the aristocratic point of view, serious businessmen like Lord Monomark, serious intellectuals like Poppet Green, serious bureaucrats like Sir Philip Hesketh-Smithers, are merely mocked, while those who perform exactly the same function in a frivolous amoral way, like Geoffrey Bentley in the Ministry of Information in *Put Out More Flags*, are also sympathetically enjoyed. Of course Waugh's sensibility is too complex to be defined by any statement that simple. (He is far more sympathetic to Ambrose, the Jew and the homosexual, than to Freddie Sothill, the country squire and owner of Malfrey, in the same novel.) But on the whole his sympathies are catagorically snobbish, reactionary, anti-intellectual, and anti-serious.

His writing is naturally a powerful reinforcement as well as expression of these preferences and prejudices. He even more than Shaw has been socially effective. During the last thirty years (his ascendancy seems to have been continuous with Shaw's) he has created a national sense of humor that seems to me the most powerful single influence on the British imagination today. The thing that distinguishes the educated from the uneducated man in England, the general formative effect of going to Oxford and Cambridge, seems to me best defined in a single phrase as the acquisition of that sense of humor. There is a habit of satire that you find among educated people, that directs itself against the poor and the underprivileged as roughly as against other groups, and that you can find among people of the most advanced political sympathies, and of the most humble social antecedents. It is just their sense of humor.

Here we must consider the way the writer has cooperated with, and made use of, social-cultural forces; for Basil and Ambrose are protagonists not only of powerful tendencies in Waugh's mind but also of powerful tendencies in British culture. We are told that Basil Seal was for Seth of Azania (in

Black Mischief) "the personification of all that glittering, intangible Western culture to which he aspired." But Waugh as much as Seth, and we as much as he, bow down before a personification in Basil, the personalification of the perfect Oxford undergraduate.

> He played poker for high stakes. His luncheon parties lasted until dusk, his dinner parties dispersed in riot. Lovely young women visited him from London in high powered cars. He went away for weekends without leave, and climbed into College over the tiles at night. He had travelled all over Europe, spoke six languages, called dons by their Christian names and discussed their books with them.
> Seth had met him at breakfast with the Master of the College. Basil had talked to him about Azanian topography, the Nestorian church, Sakuyu dialects, the idiosyncrasies of the chief diplomats of Derba-Dowa. Two days later he invited him to luncheon. There had been two peers present and the President of the Union, the editor of a new undergraduate magazine and a young don.

The ironic tone here expresses self-awareness, not self-criticism; this is quite seriously the image of the brilliant young man at Oxford. It answers pretty exactly to Waugh's friend, Randolph Churchill, and exists in the general undergraduate unconscious, even now, quite independent of the individual's family background or private judgment.

Basil's later career strikes a chord in a wider general unconscious; the greatest figure in England had done the same things and had described himself in some of the same terms. There are twenty exploits in Sir Winston Churchill's autobiography, *A Roving Commission*, which could have been performed by Basil Seal more easily than by most heroes of modern fiction. Not so much Sir Winston's escape from a Boer prison camp, or the novel he wrote (and published) in two months, as the nonchalant way he did those things; and the airy way he advised the general staff of an expeditionary force in the field on official etiquette, while he was himself a second lieutenant orderly officer two weeks at his post. Not so much the unscrupulousness with which he manipulated family and personal connections, and wangled himself quite unjust privileges repeatedly, as the bland, almost innocent delight he took in his own impudence. Not so much his formidable array of energies and talents, even for personal relations, as the apparent lack of all inner life. One can even recognize something Churchillian in Waugh's description of Basil's posture. "He stood in the doorway, a glass of whiskey in one hand, looking insolently round the room, his head back, chin forward, shoulders rounded, dark hair over his forehead, contemptuous grey eyes over grey pouches, a proud rather childish mouth, a scar on one cheek." They have the same kind of supermanship.

The most important difference between Sir Winston and Basil Seal is that in Basil's career the impulse to self-destruction had much more play. In his later years Basil becomes the archetypal romantic failure, the romantically unfulfilled promise, the inexplicably irresponsible rogue, still with far more potential and potency than others. In this phase he reminds us perhaps of *Randolph* Churchill, who is one of Waugh's friends and to whom *Put Out More Flags* is dedicated. The preface to that book speaks glowingly of "the Churchillian Renaissance" of 1940, and there are many interesting connections between Waugh and the Churchill family. Sir Winston was so delighted by *Decline and Fall* when it came out in 1928 that he made it his Christmas present of the year. Randolph parachuted into Yugoslavia with Waugh and another personal friend during the war. The Churchills as a group are a good public example of the kind of real people Waugh started from in creating his Sonia, Basil, Alastair, and Margot. In all these ways, Basil stands for figures and forces in British life, and as we read about him all our experience of them is brought into play.

Ambrose Silk is equally powerfully the image of the fine writer in England in this century. His two disquisitions in the Café Royal (*Put Out More Flags* again) on the superiority of Chinese culture and on the role of fog in English literature are in comic form exactly what highly cultured and brilliant conversation in England traditionally aspires to. The Chinese theme we might associate with Harold Acton, the fog with Cyril Connolly. Other great conversationalists, like Father Martin D'Arcy and Monsignor Ronald Knox (both personal friends of Waugh's) apparently achieved the wit and cogency

Waugh rendered just as spontaneously. Certainly Harold Acton and Brian Howard, on whom Waugh based the character, did. Ambrose's exploits at Oxford define the archetypal idea of the aesthetic undergraduate, outrageously pretentious but genuinely talented, the successor to Wilde and Beardsley. Among Waugh's friends at Oxford one can cite Brian Howard and Peter Quennell as well as those already mentioned. And from what we hear about Ambrose's writing, it must be like Cyril Connolly's in style and form. The *nouvelle* we hear about in *Put Out More Flags*, called "Monument to a Spartan," is described as having just the eloquence, the melancholy, the wit, the ripeness, and elegance, as well as the overripeness and overelegance, of *Palinurus* and *The Unquiet Grave*.

So that the criticism of life which Basil and Ambrose embody and enact, their insolent questioning of established mores, their stylish assertion of man's ultimate anarchy and amorality, though it remains a purely comic one, is one every Englishman must acknowledge as meaningful, because it is corroborated every day by living facts in the national life. It is a real thing. It hits the headlines of not only the gossip columns but—with the exploits of Burgess and Maclean—of the political pages.

As a cultural force, this sense of humor is nearly as destructive as Shaw's. It is of course allied to a serious criticism of the *status quo*, its institutions and manners, and to a serious dissatisfaction with the world and the self, and even to a serious sexual humor. But that seriousness emanates from such a marked and eccentric misanthropy that it scarcely imposes itself on the reader, and does not succeed in mobilizing half Waugh's resources of intelligence and feeling in its service. Men in love, it takes for granted, are either nice lost little boys, humorously managed by their women, or else unscrupulous, unloving, unblamed seducers; they are never, like Amis's heroes, husbands facing the problems of a complex equal relationship. The inner posture this derives from is military, Pyrrhonist, anti-spontaneous. The social technique it encourages is the assumption of a mask of complete assurance, so that whatever is said measures itself against one's own standards and not anybody else's. This is not so simply aggressive as it often seems to Americans meeting Englishmen; the latter may merely wish to outrage expectation for the sake of general entertainment, with the exquisite precision of a Margot or an Ambrose, and in order to do that must control the expectation. But it is likely to lead to, if it did not derive from, a conscious artificiality, an inflexible unresponsiveness to conversation, and ideas, that do not permit of this treatment.

From this point of view, then, Waugh's sense of humor can be taken as a development of Shaw's, more perceptive, more audacious, more romantic, more caustic, but essentially continuous with it, on the same side against spontaneous life. Other writers too have contributed to the power of this same sensibility. Before the First World War there was "Saki." In the 1920's Ronald Firbank and Noel Coward invented idioms and situations of their own for the same kind of insolent amorality. Nowadays, the same kind of misanthropy can be found in Graham Greene and T. S. Eliot, and in as new a writer as William Golding. But all this increases, not diminishes, Waugh's importance. He is the supreme pontiff of a nationwide movement—not so much of those who simply derive from him, like Nancy Mitford, as of those quite unrelated to him as a whole, but who share something of his temperament and tastes, and who therefore respond most keenly to his sense of humor. Anyone who shares Waugh's point of view in political or religious affairs is obviously likely to share his sense of humor; and even those who admire prose like Waugh's, sonorous, Latinate, literary, elaborately balanced, (for instance Churchill's or the Sitwells') are led to him; because the sensibility expressed in that prose (its love of elegance, formality, and all the traditional grandeurs) finds its acutest humorous expression in him.

Moreover, there is no other equally effective sense of humor available to Englishmen, even those quite different in temperament and tastes. The clinching proof of this for me came in Mabel Luhan's book on D. H. Lawrence, where she describes his first visit to her house, which contained the treasures of her years of collecting. "Italian and French furniture, paintings by many hands, books from New York, bronzes from Venice, Chinese paintings, Indian things." There was evidently a good deal of mutual distrust and hostility in the air, and at the first meal Lawrence, we are told, looked around from the candlelit table at the rich gloom, giggled, and said, "It's just like one of those nasty little temples in India." This is obviously in the Waugh idiom, and even more obviously not in Lawrence's usual one. Lawrence is the most powerful representative of all those forces in British life which do not "lead one to" Waugh; the puritan, provincial, democratic, lower middle-class England. He had a prose and a point of view and a sense of humor of his own, radically different from those mentioned above. But his sense of humor was effective in domestic situations (*Kangaroo* has some wonderfully funny domestic comedy), and between intimates, and was lower class, most typically dialect, in vocabulary. It offered him no tone suitable for an encounter with Mabel Luhan, and he had to borrow from his enemies.

It is Kingsley Amis's great claim to our attention that he began to create a sense of humor for the other half, the Lawrencian, relatively inarticulate, half of Britain. His first novels dramatized its point of view, created a voice for its experience. They asked us to admire and love Jim Dixon and John Lewis, men whose whole effort in life is to be average, normal, decent, and to triumph in their triumph over the affected, the brilliant, the polished, the heartless. The bad characters in the early Amis books, the Gruffydd Williams and the Welches, would be like Basil, Ambrose, and Margot in real life, and are real life imitators of them.

Like Shaw, Amis has a narrow range of situations, because, like Shaw, he writes always about himself and things in relation to himself. But his self is much more real, private, complex than Shaw's, his experience much more painful and personal. His humor is much more thoroughly moral than either Shaw's or Waugh's, and in his early books it was a very different kind of morality—essentially concerned with the difficulties of sexual life and with emotional and intellectual sincerity. He showed a great gift for the detail that distinguished the gentleman from his own kind, the decent, lower middle-class man. In all these ways he gave a voice to powerful forces that had long been inarticulate, and tapped untouched resources in British life.

But it was obvious early on that he was in difficulties. Some of these derived from the pressure he felt from left-wing righteousness to which he feared he was conforming and from which thus purchasing too easy a self-respect. Others perhaps were more purely aesthetic. *Lucky Jim* shifted from one aesthetic mode to another, one level of realism to another, quite recklessly and self-destructively; and the later novels were even more uneven. Altogether, he showed symptoms of an uneasiness that was cultural as well as personal.

He was not at ease. His sense of humor was essentially embarrassed and resentful, or revengeful. It was best adapted to narrating after the event to a sympathetic listener one's own humiliation by what occurred, or someone else's attack on the bully; to finding the exact absurd word to describe one's feelings, one's expression, when Margaret Peel said this, or Elizabeth Gruffydd Williams did that. The comic things his heroes *did* were not real; they could come into the real world only as "I should have" or "I wish I had." If they were not narrating something of that kind, if they were with friends, they were quite lumpishly convivial, all cheery insults, bawdy songs, and drunkenness. His people have nothing to replace the poise and style Sonia and Basil had with each other; or their way of asserting themselves in alien social situations. Waugh's readers, if they share his sensibility at all deeply, can approximate to the same stylishness in their own lives. But Amis's readers, those on the other side of the national division, could inherit through him no tradition of general command and control, outside the home; in a café or a theater they could assert themselves only rowdily. Even in their most private moments they were, by their own standards, ungraceful and unsuccessful. Infinitely more sympathetic though it was, Amis's humor remained a rudimentary thing, useful only in retreat and among other retreaters.

Whatever the reasons, Amis changed his ideological loyalties, and with them the cultural loyalties of his humor. In *Take a Girl Like You,* 1960, he portrayed himself as a Cavalier rake, a habitual seducer, and in *One Fat Englishman,* 1963, he was an Evelyn Waugh Englishman in America, a debased and disheveled dandy, guzzling his pleasures, a Brummell in exile. The roles of representing decency, and health, were assigned to the Americans in the book. The Amis-figure accepted the fact that he must stand for moral compromise, for sophistications and sophistries, and his jokes express a defiant, as well as a bitter, assertion of that persona. Since then he has always shown a central figure in the pursuit of fame, fashion, or wealth, as well as sensual gratification, and resistant to the appeals of morality or seriousness. In *The Anti-Death League,* 1966, and *The Green Man,* 1969, both fine funny novels, his hero is a man first defined by the inner laws he breaks, though by the end of the book we are more aware of the laws he will not break. The Amis figure is not fully a dandy, because he does not offer himself as in any sense glittering or admirable. Quite the contrary, the inner structure of both these, as of all Amis's novels, is a very moralistic self-interrogation and self-punishment, which is a process destructive of dandyism. Amis builds his comedy out of that inner conflict which Waugh would not speak of. Nevertheless, the style in which that conflict is reported is a dandy's style; and in the complex phenomenon of Amis's career, the most significant gesture has been his abandonment of Orwell's imaginative style in favor of Waugh's—the abandonment of "decency" for "dandyism." Like Waugh's total sensibility, Amis's humor is compounded of the respect for tradition and the impulse to attack it—the two annealed by the bitterest self-knowledge—knowledge of the failure to get beyond that dilemma. But the bitterness and self-knowledge are concealed. What is paraded is the insolent defiance of the ordinary criteria of self-respect. And from our point of view here, the important thing is that Amis too has finally spoken for the same sensibility as Waugh and Shaw, after a brave attempt to give a voice to the opposite—to the England of Lawrence or the England of Orwell. Consistently in the century, the English sense of humor has spoken out of dandyism, skepticism, or bitterness.

Chapter 7

OUR SENSE OF HUMOR III:
MEANING AND DELIGHT
IN EVELYN WAUGH

I would like to propose the word "delight" as a key to distinguishing between the best of Evelyn Waugh's novels and the rest. Waugh is a major artist when he delights in the people and events he is presenting, when he laughs at them admiringly and lovingly, and at the same time morally rejects them. At other times he asks you to take an interest in his people and events for other reasons. He asks you to like Tony Last in *A Handful of Dust* because he is dully decent, the Empress Helena in *Helena* because she is hearty and unimaginative, Guy Crouchback in *Men at Arms* because he is reliable, and faithful, dim and defeated; and even worse are the zestfully dislikable people, like Lady Marchmain in *Brideshead Revisited*, whom one is asked to accept for their Catholicism. All these reasons are illegitimate in Waugh's fiction, because they go against the grain of the author's more spontaneous feelings and the feelings he arouses in us. He and we under his influence take far more acute, perceptive, wide- and deep-spreading pleasure in the opposite types, the brilliant, the audacious, the unreliable, the elegant, the outrageous, and in the things they do that affront dullness and decency.

From this point of view, then, *A Handful of Dust*, *Brideshead Revisited*, and the post-war military novels may all be grouped together. Delight has not been the dominant principle in Waugh's sensibility as it worked on them. In all of them there are pages of brilliancy, but one is soon returned from these to the central characters and their central problems; where an unwilling sympathy and interest are exacted from one on behalf of people one cannot spontaneously care for or about. All these books have a dull obsessive resentable painfulness, as the good characters fail, the bad ones succeed, vitality diminishes, brilliance fades and tarnishes, gaiety dwindles and cracks—all with a mechanical and masochistic predictability. There is a constant conscientious direction of our interest toward the decent, the dutiful, the orthodox, the dull (types that do not engage Waugh's creativity, or our participation) and away from the brilliant, the beautiful, the amoral, who do. Waugh has built these novels around protagonists whom he respects, or wants to respect, with whom he identifies the part of himself his imagination "officially" approves of. In *Decline and Fall*, *Vile Bodies*, *Black Mischief*, *Scoop*, and *Put Out More Flags*, the heroes are men Waugh does not respect or in that sense approve of, men with whom he identifies the part of himself he officially repudiates.

In *Evelyn Waugh, Portrait of an Artist*, Frederick J. Stopp categorizes these five, along with *Scott-King's Modern Europe*, *The Loved One*, and *Love Among the Ruins*, as entertainments. This is the category of Waugh's work which he treats most summarily, while I would claim that it is the most important. There are similarities enough between the eight pieces to justify this grouping, but the second set of three are inferior for various reasons. *Scott-King's Modern Europe* bears all the marks of having died on its author half way through; as if all his interest in it had collapsed then, quite suddenly and quite completely. One may guess that this happened because Waugh's imagination did not delight in modern Europe; nor did it delight in the California or the socialized state he describes in the last two of these novels. All these things belong to the future, or rather to the future part of the present—an alien and threatening future—and the things Waugh delighted in all belong to the past part of the present. Anything with echoes of the great British past he can treat with perfect touch, affectionate and admiring as well as mocking; and the same is true of the barbaric society of *Black Mischief*, because it does not threaten him. But in *The Loved One* and *Love Among the Ruins*, and to less extent in *Scott-King's Modern Europe*, he has no richness of experience, and his imagination is working theoretically and doctrinairely; he has not delighted in his subject; he has not seen or heard half as many interesting things in it as he has in his proper fields, and above all his feelings about what he has seen are too single and simple and edgy.

There is plenty of circumstantial evidence to support the idea that it is the past, or rather the outmoded, which attracted Waugh's imagination. Waugh's tastes in the art, architecture, furniture of the past, as well as in its literature, were markedly for that which was grandiose, gothic, a little grotesque, even in its own day. (Take for instance the descriptions of Tony Last's house in *A Handful of Dust*.) Among contemporary writers he admired Beerbohm, Osbert Sitwell, Wodehouse, Churchill; among painters practically no one since the Pre-Raphaelites; among styles of furniture, Victoriana. He loved, that is, whatever harks away and back from the specifically contemporary; especially if it does so imposingly and absurdly. The simply contemporary, the fully real, did not engage his best powers. His opinions, about Catholicism and class-structure, about original sin and socialism, all invite us to guess at private griefs and grudges, and an impulse to self-caricature. "I think it is time we made up our minds that poetry is one of the arts which has died in the last eighty years. . . . I believe that the intellectual communists of today have personal, irrelevant grounds for their antagonism to society, which they are trying to exploit . . . I have never gone into public life. Most of the ills we suffer are caused by people going into public life. I have never voted in a public election. I believe a man's chief civil duty consists in fighting for his king when the men in public life have put the realm in danger." This is circumstantial evidence that whenever Waugh's intellectual conscience is seriously engaged, (whenever it is not disengaged by delight) his imaginative experience is drastically impoverished.

But the crucial evidence must of course come from an examination of these successful "entertainments" (which seem to me serious and powerful works of art) because in them the principle of delight is dominant. They are major art first because of the extraordinary richness of social life they render. The army, the church, the press, ministries, embassies, universities, schools, all perfectly caught; and a bewildering variety of intellectual and social sets, both in London and the country (not the provincial cities) particularly rich of course in metropolitan and upper-class types.

All of which is done with an economy of means which becomes an end in itself. Emma Granchester has one line in *Put Out More Flags*, and that is quite lightly characterized, but in its context, in the preternaturally keen, crystalline visibility of Waugh's world, it completely circumscribes her and her group and their way of life.

> "How did you decide?" asked Margot, when Peter told her of his engagement.
> "Well, as a matter of fact, I don't think I did. Molly decided."
> "Yes, that's usually the way. Now I suppose I shall have to do something friendly about that ass Emma Granchester."
> "I really know Lady Metroland very little," said Lady Granchester. "But I suppose now I must invite her to luncheon. I'm afraid she's far too smart for us."

But despite this brilliant economy, which must remind us of Jane Austen, it is of Dickens we are prompted to think most often, because of Waugh's range and richness of social observation. We can see a further technical likeness between the two writers (taking for granted the common exuberance of their tastes for the grotesque) in the variety of their comic situations and ideas. Take, for example, the scenes involving Basil Seal in *Put Out More Flags*, where at first sight the basic device seems most simply unvarying—a frank unscrupulousness outwitting more complicated and hypocritical and socially accepted forms of egotism. When you examine these scenes you find that Basil is put to many other, even opposite, uses and effects. He is himself the one who is outmaneuvered by Mr. Todhunter and Colonel Plum; he is led astray, diverted from his own interests, befuddled, by Susie and the bride of Grantley Green; he is a figure in a static social frieze, with Barbara, Angela, Sonia; he moves blindly, at cross-purposes with his antagonists, equally a puppet for our amusement, with his mother and the colonel of the regiment; he is the bore and the philistine, with Ambrose and Geoffrey at the Café Royal; he is flatly outrageous, in his treatment of Poppet Green and his betrayal of Ambrose. There may well be more uses to which he is put, and these categories are crude beside what Waugh does with them (and this is only character in the book); but put this list beside any analysis of, say, Shaw and Amis, and you will realize that technically he can be compared only with Dickens.

But all Waugh's work is very inventive and accurate and economical. What is special to the entertainments is that the writer's angle of vision and focus, which controls the selection and arrangement and size of these brilliant fragments, is much more clear and consistent in them. This focus is not, in the books themselves (what Waugh may have "thought" is another matter), any attempt to "castigare mores ridendo"; nor is it the mood of "the last mad dance as the ship goes down." Of course passages can be found in these books with one or another of those intentions, but they are all separable from the rest. At his purest Waugh delights in satire for its own sake, if that can be called satire. That is, he and we get our staple pleasure from seeing group after group react to an event in a way that ludicrously accentuates in each person all his special group ways, and eliminates his general humanity. And we get our luxury of delight from the outraging of all social conventions, from the punctilio of privilege to the most elementary moral decency; performed by people whose criticism of life is brilliant and powerful, but perfectly harmless; who are themselves morally absurd, and yet still exciting and dangerous.

We don't, that is, like and dislike the people in these books, approve some and disapprove others, in consequence of their actions. Waugh is involved with them all (all the major characters) romantically as much as satirically and satirically as much as romantically, and the two involvements interpenetrate to form a new poise of interest. The most obvious example of the complementary romantic engagement is Lady Circumference's epiphany of her "herd" in *Vile Bodies*; where we suddenly, surprisedly, become aware of Waugh's warm sympathy with a point of view he has been satirizing.

> People who had represented their country in foreign places and sent their sons to die for her in battle, people of decent and temperate life, uncultured, unaffected, unembarrassed, unassuming, unambitious people, of independent judgment and marked eccentricities, kind people who cared for animals and the deserving poor, brave and rather unreasonable people, that fine phalanx of the passing order, approaching, as one day at the Last Trump they hoped to meet their Maker, with decorous and frank cordiality to shake Lady Anchorage by the hand at the top of her staircase. Lady Circumference saw all this and sniffed the exhalation of her herd.

But this does not mean that Waugh's sympathies were simply or consistently conservative. He was equally engaged by the opposite type. In *Decline and Fall* Margot Beste-Chetwynde, Lady Circumference's enemy and opposite, the ultra-modern and amoral woman of fashion is presented to us as "the first breath of Spring on the Champs Elysees . . . fresh and exquisite as a seventeenth-century lyric. . . ." And one needs no quotation to recall how satirically both women are treated on practically the next pages in both cases. Waugh delights in them both.

It is worth repeating that what we have here is not the satirist deeply drawn to what he mocks, but the comedian sublimating all his impulses to condemn. Not only in the treatment of individuals but in the design of the whole (in the equal involvement with opposite types) the original critical impulses are all transformed into laughter. It is the mode of humor of *The Importance of Being Earnest*, but the material is infinitely richer.

The same thing happens in *Put Out More Flags*, where Ambrose Silk's highly eccentric nostalgias and velleities are celebrated just as richly, as poetically, as the decent conventional lives of the well-to-do people around Malfrey.

> The lawns were close mown, fertilized and weeded, and from their splendid surface rose clumps of pampas grass and yucca; year in, year out, gloved hands grubbed in the rockeries, gloved hands snipped in the herbaceous border; baskets of bass stood beside trays of visiting cards on the hall tables. Now in the dead depths of winter, when ice stood thick on the lily ponds, and kitchen gardens at night were a litter of sacking, these good people fed the birds daily with the crumbs from the dining room table and saw to it that no old person in the village went short of coal.

> Art; this was where Art had brought him, to this studio, to these coarse and tedious youngsters, to that preposterous yellow face among the boiled sweets. It had been a primrose path in the days of Diaghilev; at Eton he had collected Lovat Fraser rhyme sheets; at Oxford he had recited *In Memoriam* through a megaphone to an accompaniment hummed on combs and tissue paper; in Paris he had frequented Jean Cocteau and Gertrude Stein; he had written and published his first book there, a study of Montparnasse Negroes that had been banned in England by Sir William Joynson-Hicks. That way the primrose path led gently downhill to the world of fashionable photographers, stage sets for Cochran, Cedric Lyne and his Neapolitan grottoes.

This is Waugh's writing at its best, richly romantic, astringently satiric, with no conflict between the two and no ultimate moral position, wholly delighted. It is the angle of vision and focus that produces this writing which is dominant in the entertainments. Even in them, when there is insufficient satire, as with Angela Lyne in *Put Out More Flags*, or insufficient romance, as with the Emperor Seth in *Black Mischief*, we feel a thinness, a prosiness, often a falsity. But normally, Waugh is both for and against everyone, or rather no one, in these books, except where the writing lapses, moral and contra-moral feeling fuse in a delighted amorality.

The most doomed people, by external standards, are exactly those most favored by the internal laws of the entertainments. So that when the author suddenly introduces that external morality, and claims to have been "serious" all along, we have no reason to believe him. It is Margot Beste-Chetwynde and Basil Seal and Ambrose Silk, the morally inexcusable, who are the most triumphant in the novels' terms. They are Waugh's protagonists, the dominant tones in his voice, the sharpest focus of his vision, the realizers of his dreams. They don't take things seriously, and they need not themselves be taken seriously. These together are the crucial criterion. In *Put Out More Flags* Lady Seal takes society and its laws seriously, acceptingly; Poppet Green's group seriously wants to change it; but Basil and Ambrose evade it, abuse it, live off it, without taking it seriously either way. Moreover, they pierce and explode every convention without our having to take their action seriously. In them Waugh and we too can be comfortably, exhilaratingly outrageous, acting out impulses we didn't know we had. They remain seriously shocking people; Basil's treachery, Margot's white slavery, still take our breath away; but only to replace it with a purer, more oxygenated atmosphere, only in a way that brings us into a new world of utter release of which they are leading citizens. In this world they are figures of power, not to be pitied or condemned; and if the author for a moment loses his poise, and asks himself if Agatha Runcible is really happy, or will go to heaven when she dies, there is no need for us to do the same.

Structurally, the five novels have a good deal in common. Each marks an important advance from the preceding one, but they all have an extreme compression of the scenes, a preponderance of dialogue, and a great number, range, and compartmentalization of the characters, so great that one passes from one group to another with an effect of complete contrast, even if their respective inhabitants do in fact sometimes intermingle. They all have a great deal of incident; some which attack the reader's conventions from the schoolboy's warning his teacher how to outwit the other teachers (*Decline and Fall*) to Basil Seal's eating his fiancée at a cannibal banquet (*Black Mischief*); others which more importantly evoke the contrasting reactions of different groups, like the bomb-explosions in the War Office in *Put Out More Flags*. Characters and events are connected with others from very remote parts of the same book in ways that affront realism; for instance, the appearance of Mrs. Ape's angel on the battlefield at the end of *Vile Bodies*. Expectations are reversed to the point where the reversal becomes a pattern and then are twisted another way. The wicked triumph over the good, the stupid over the clever, the innocent over the experienced, only to the point of startling us, not to the point of serious meaning; so that the moment innocence seems to generally pay off, for Paul Pennyfeather in *Decline and Fall*, or for William Boot in *Scoop*, they fall into some new inconsequential disaster; and even their innocence is inconsequential, for each will, on occasion, act the sophisticated or selfish part.

All the novels have a central young man whose adventures cut across the different groups and provide a beginning and an end. But the only way we can believe in and care about this hero is a way that makes a happy marriage, reform, and death, equally inappropriate climaxes for him, so all the books are begun and ended very artificially. In *Decline and Fall* Paul Pennyfeather is led into the world of Margot Beste-Chetwynde by a series of accidents, and at the end is led back out again by a series of elaborate frauds, back to a "normal" existence. *Vile Bodies* begins with Adam Fenwick-Symes's entry into the Bright Young Things' circle, and ends with a World War. In *Black Mischief* it is the reign of the preposterous Seth and in *Put Out More Flags* the "unreal" first phase of the war that parenthesize all the action. Especially at the ends, Waugh insists that "such things couldn't happen now." The war has entered a new and more glorious phase, or people have lost money in the Depression and are turning serious, or all the Bright Young Things have died or disappeared. This insistence is loud and elaborate, and its function seems to be to exorcize the reproaches of our conscience for our amoral delight in such people and such doings.

Decline and Fall, Waugh's first published novel, which one must think of as in some degree experimental, is however almost flawless. It shows the influence of other writers; Paul Pennyfeather's adventures are modeled on Candide's, Lady Circumference could have been a Wilde character, and Augustus Fagan and Dingy and Flossy betray their relationship to Mr. Pecksniff and Cherry and Merry. These are legitimate relationships; everything in the book. wherever it was taken from, has been given a new feeling and a new meaning. But there are too many eccentrics and coincidences (particularly to do with Grimes and Prendergast) for this to be the best objective correlative for Waugh's very realistic sense of the absurd. More exactly, these eccentrics and coincidences have too much of Smollett or Dickens about them, are too loosely related to specifically modern absurdity. But the only real weakness in the novel is Paul Pennyfeather, who, as hero, is cast to play a bourgeois Candide in the aristocratically corrupt world of the Beste-Chetwyndes. He does perform this function occasionally, in the trip to Marseilles, but more often talks that Waugh idiom which is so wrong for such a role. When he is brutally treated in prison, "I suppose I shall learn to respect these people in time," he thinks. "They all seem so much less awe-inspiring than anyone I ever met." The inconsistency is not in itself important, but it brings with it a vagueness, an absence, in the centre of the novel. There *is* no central character. Waugh is not really interested in innocent candor, least of all an earnest bourgeois form of it.

Vile Bodies, 1930, took a step forward by making its hero, Adam Fenwick-Symes, one of the fashionable world by birth. He can employ Waugh's idiom as of right. And it took another by introducing scenes in which he does not appear, so that one has the sense, so vivid and right in Waugh, of following a dozen contrasting group lives simultaneously. Moreover, there are fewer eccentrics as nineteenth-century in flavor as Fagan this time, more, like Colonel Blount, representatives of social-intellectual strata. On the other hand, Waugh here is morally self-conscious, and strikes a false prophetic pose, delivering a message. This is a regression from his first novel, where the normality (of Stubbs and Potts) against which corruption was measured, was itself treated satirically. The death of Agatha, the suicide of Balcairn, Adam and Nina's failure in marriage, above all the conclusion of the books, all embody a message and a meaning, a "Waste Land" vision of social decay, which has no essential connection with the best parts of the novel. In the latter (Agatha at the races, Adam as Mr. Chatterbox, Colonel Blount's daily routine), we are not at all concerned with the decline of the West but with a joyfully insolent defiance of all reason and right. In this novel, too, Waugh declares in favor of certain characters and their modes of life—Lady Circumference and the older generation, Father Rothschild and orthodoxy. (Between the first novel and this one came the shattering experience of his wife's infidelity and his marriage's collapse. Waugh reacted against the Bright Young Things and all modernism.) Very often, as in the next-to-last chapter, where the hitherto farcical treatment of Colonel Blount suddenly turns into a romantic Christmasy celebration of the country squire virtues, this affirmative writing is very beautiful and successful. But we feel even then that Waugh really delights in Agatha Runcible just as much, and that this choosing of sides is a violation of the book's deepest truth.

Black Mischief, 1932, abandons the Dickensian kind of character and coincidence completely, in favor of much more pointed shocks to the reader's sensibility as a twentieth-century Englishman. The Birth Control Pageant, the diplomatic intrigues, the visit of the humanitarian spinsters, all these sharpen the edge of their absurdity on specifically post-war problems and attitudes; and Sir Samson Courteney, for instance, is still more different from Mr. Micawber than Colonel Blount was, still more a figure of his official function. The romantic involvement here is most obviously with the natives, whom he makes exotic and barbaric to us fairly consistently. But it is also with the British Legation, so superbly ignoring the wars, revolutions, murders, plots; so insolently imposing its unreal pattern on life and getting away with it. Waugh is on both sides again and on no side. The bits and pieces of Western culture, which in Seth's hands do not even fit together, much less work, are offered to us to be irreverently recognized, not to be solemnly diagnosed. And the often condemned scene in which Prudence is eaten by her lover is not, in its place in the novel, anything more than the perfect climax to a long series of outrages against decency. But this novel is a great advance at least as much for its introduction of Basil Seal. Basil Seal is the perfect Waugh hero, because he translates into action the insolence which in Margot, Adam, Agatha, Nina, and so forth is mostly verbal, and too soon retreated from. Adam and Nina, Paul and Margot, are too soon frightened and made ridiculous; they marry Maltravers, or they turn and run away from trouble. Basil is a much more energetic and unrelenting challenge. His very twentieth-century career, in all its aspects, sexual, financial, political, expresses the same insolence and amorality as the others achieve only in small gestures. At the beginning he is the archetypal brilliant Oxford undergraduate. At the end he is the archetypal mysterious failure, the romantically unrealized promise, still with far more potential and potency than anyone else. And all the time, by the novel's standards, he is never contemptible or ridiculous.

In *Put Out More Flags*, 1942, Basil reappears, complemented by Ambrose Silk, a writer, who acts out the other half of Waugh's "unofficial" imagination; the reckless freebooter of the intellectual and artistic worlds, whose deep misery is all transmuted into "the art of dazzling and confusing those he despises." (The author's relationship with these characters is easy to trace. Seal owes much to Robert Byron, Silk to Harold Acton and Brian Howard. But it is more than that. Waugh said, what would be anyway evident, that he always wanted more than anything else to be a man of action (Basil); while in *The Ordeal of Gilbert Pinfold* his hallucinatory voices accuse him of being a Jew and a homosexual (Ambrose). Ambrose writes a prose very like Waugh's, appreciates elaborate architecture, painting, furniture, writes manifestos in opposition to left-wing writers. Basil is a soldier, a misfit in civilian life, fond of practical jokes, military passwords, and all the paraphernalia of secret service adventure.) This is the most perfect of Waugh's novels, because the careers of these two brilliant, self-defeating marauders against decency cut against so many static lines of group life at so exactly the right angle for Waugh's purposes, and with such thrust and abandon. Ambrose is a really major artist, of a recognizable twentieth-century type, and a really pathetic victim of life; Basil is really tough, talented. and formidable. We have to take them, in an essentially comic way, very seriously. They have weight behind them, they have truth, though it is all consummated and consumed in brilliant explosion. And consequently in this book the ritual distancing of the events from the reader is more daringly artificial and transparent than anywhere else; the book was published only two years after events it describes; England was still engaged in the war effort Waugh makes so ridiculous.

The best in Waugh is therefore not satirical, if by satire we mean making a thing funny by holding it up against some standard the writer fairly consistently recommends, as Amis and John Wain and Shaw and Swift and Pope do. Waugh, in the entertainments, exposes and ridicules those who behave extravagantly and foolishly, but also those who behave prudently and according to tradition; and those he loves and admires are to be found in both camps. The point of this joke swings from due south to due north in a page; in *Black Mischief* one laughs at the British Legation's insouciance, but also at the French Legation's anxiety, at Seth's naïve enthusiasm, but also at William Bland's congenital boredom. The meaning of it all is total laughter; any other message Waugh may pronounce is as loosely attached as a tie-on label.

Of course Waugh's sense of humor is deeply characterized by his prejudices and his temperament. These books could only have been written by someone deeply misanthropic and reactionary about politics, morals, manners, personal relations, and so forth. But there is another meaning we can take from him, more original than his sense of humor. That is the exercise of entering into a wide variety of experiences, feeling the worth and weight of each, but simultaneously, successively, climactically, exploding them all, denying all meaning and all respect, dancing among the fragments. This meaning denies everything but destroys nothing. When you stop dancing, everything is as it was before; only your blood is renewed. This is the feature of his work we discussed earlier from the point of view of the author's craftsmanship: "delight." Only now we are defining it from the point of view of the reader's experience. It is this experience his four great entertainments offer more purely than the rest of his work, and it is one of the most exhilarating experiences in the whole range of modern literature.

Chapter 8

OUR SENSE OF HUMOR IV: EVELYN WAUGH AND THE COMMEDIA DELL' ARTE*

One group of Waugh's novels is hard to deal with critically, because none of the established criteria or modes of scrutiny seem to bear on the interesting questions about them—about what and why and how much they succeed in doing. This group contains *Decline and Fall*, *Vile Bodies*, *Black Mischief*, *Scoop*, and *Put Out More Flags*, the books which are to my mind Waugh's best work. As I have argued, they are superior to Waugh's more serious books, because in them the principle of delight is given much fuller, freer, bolder expression, and because Waugh's talents and attitudes are much clearer, stronger, more authoritative, when organized by the principle of delight.

This best work is of course farcical, in the simple sense that it borrows from and imitates stage farce in many obvious ways. The comic situations are stage-farce situations, in tableau and action, in costume, grouping, pose, gesture, plot connection, and so forth. In *Decline and Fall*, for instance, think of the debagging in the first scene, the pompous hy-

* This chapter appeared in the *New York Arts Journal* (Vol. 1, issues 3 and 4), ed. Richard Burgin. Reprinted by permission.

pocrisy of Paul's guardian in the second, the histrionic eccentricities of Dr. Fagan, and so forth, up to the recurrence of characters like Grimes, Philbrick, and Fagan in absurd disguise. In *Vile Bodies*, think of Colonel Blount popping in and out of his front door when Adam calls, or of the Colonel's series of misidentifications of Adam. In *Black Mischief*, Basil's maneuvers to get the money to go to Azania, the scene in the nightclub there, the nursery inanities of the British Embassy there; in *Scoop*, Mrs. Stitch's levée, her car down the men's lavatory, William's difficulties with his passports. These scenes, it will surely be granted, are closely related to, are derived from, the traditional farce of writers like Feydeau, and of performers like Chaplin and the Marx Brothers. The moving forces of the plots are equally farcical. In *Vile Bodies* nearly all the action derives from Adam's attempts to get the money to marry Nina, and he both gets it and loses it by means that are traditionally farcical, and that mount in monstrosity up to his selling her to his rival. Identities are travestied; ceremonies, which are frequent, are always interrupted; many (vain) attempts are made to do the same thing; action is taken on preposterously inadequate grounds, and motives are preposterously overinterpreted. And "stage farce" here must be understood to include film farce. The motor races in *Vile Bodies*, and especially the scenes in which Agatha joins the race drunk, leaves the track and speeds across the country out of control, crashes and is concussed, staggers wild-eyed to London, and holds her final cocktail party in a nursing home—this sequence must surely remind us of films by the Keystone Cops, the Marx Brothers, and so forth.

We may be surprised, once we begin to count it up, by how much farce material we find in the books. They do not, in one sense, *feel* so farcical, because the farce, especially the more physical elements of it, does not involve the reader. We are conscious of wit more than of farce. The amorous chases of pantomime, the grapplings in the dark, the custard pie in the face, these are not elements of Waugh's comedy. There is more of that in the black humorists—there is more even in Powell. Waugh's comedy does not, as farce often does, primarily reduce minds to bodies. Waugh is not interested in bodies. But neither are some great traditional farceurs, like Chaplin. For them, and for Waugh, the body is a metaphor for indignity. The essential thing in all farce is that dignity is reduced to indignity, but in Waugh's case it is not so much that the mind is reduced to a body, as that the adult is reduced to a child.

Therefore, as Waugh transforms the terms of stage farce into literary terms, he makes them the terms of a refined and "classical" literature. He does this by rather general means, like the elegance of his prose, the moderation of his effects, the severity of his taste, but also by two sets of specific techniques. First, most often he reports the scenes of farce to us, or rather, more complexly, he has them reported by one character to another. For instance, we learn of Paul's debagging in *Decline and Fall* by means of the conversation between the two dons, so that the farcical action itself takes place in the background. The foreground is occupied by the drawing-room comedy—which is also moral satire—of their prim and mean and greedy hypocrisies. Our attention is mostly focused on them, and the farcical action *seems* accidental—though of course it is essential to the total effect. Again, in *Black Mischief*, the Birth Control Pageant is presented to us through the interstices of the exchanges between Dame Mildred Porch and Sarah Tin, which are full of the satiric comedy of their relationship. The skill in complexity of these techniques and the severity of the moral judgments, counteract the grossness of the action, and in a sense intellectualize the farce.

The second technique, or set of techniques, which has the same tendency, is the serialization of farcical action. The most famous example of this is the wounding, the sickening, and the dying of little Lord Tangent in *Decline and Fall*. Because the sequence of events is brought in (and immediately dropped out) time and time again, it never happens for us, it is merely used, and so becomes a device of Waugh's wit and not an event in black humor. The suicide of Lord Balcairn in *Vile Bodies* is presented directly, and so is an event in black humor—and much less successful in establishing Waugh's mood than the other. This serialization occurs unobtrusively all the time, and is a part of Waugh's normal narrative. In *Black Mischief* we don't realize that Basil is stealing his mother's emeralds until long after the scene in which she tells him to stop fiddling with them; and in *Put Out More Flags,* we see Basil paint a moustache on Poppet's Aphrodite long before we hear Ambrose congratulate her on this moustache as a brilliant stroke of satiric burlesque. The effect of serializing these actions is to obviate the grossness and obviousness of the action itself.

Of course Waugh's farce is also intellectualized in the less formal sense that his comedies make such full reference to contemporary events and personalities, and their background in history, politics, and aesthetic taste. They are a kind of history of their times. For instance, the motor races in *Vile Bodies* are described in such a way as to make us see what such events are like, as well as being an occasion for farcical action. The books reduce the history of their times to the dimensions and intensities of farce, but they also give a knowledgeable account of that history. This is a counter-pressure within them, which complicates the form. At moments the ingredient of farce is minimal, because Waugh's eye is on some contemporary phenomenon he wants to record accurately.

These techniques of "intellectualization" which are equally techniques of wit and taste and style, may perhaps be compared with that modification of the ballet that was Diaghilev's most personal contribution to it—that formal and Apollonian control which he imposed on the Dionysiac spontaneity, sensuality, lavishness, of Nijinsky and Bakst. Stravinsky once said that Diaghilev's ballet was "the perfect expression of the Apollonian principle." Because Waugh's aestheticism, like that of all his friends, was so influenced by Diaghilev, I think of the latter when I note these characteristic "exquisite restraints" of the novels; that in *Put Out More Flags* Ambrose does not in fact "tell his beads" when he poses as a priest, nor "contemplate—go into an ecstasy"; it is only that Basil *tells* him to do these things, and it is the merest hint of farce.

But modified farce the form clearly is. Moreover, the conduct of the action seems to me related to the conduct of action in a pantomime. (I shift from "farce" to "pantomime" here because I am now concerned with the art of the mime rather than with plot and stage effect.) Note the accentuation of vivid gestures in Waugh's characterization, the omission of the detail that would make it "realistic," the successive bursts of movement and inertia, the general heightening of each figure's personal style to the verge of caricature. In the dialogue, note the sharply sticho-mythic pattern of the exchanges, the mutual misunderstandings, the mutual deceptions, the invitation to the audience to see "through" both speakers, in both senses of "through." One might surely say that Waugh's dialogue is all mimicry—that, as author, he is imitating the way colonels or bishops or judges or newspapermen talk, and is giving us the same sort of pleasure as a stage mimic gives.

Then Waugh's rogues and dandies—figures like Basil Seal and Ambrose Silk—can remind us of pantomime dancers and acrobats in the "muscularity" of their verbal and behavioral styles, their habitual success in "dazzling and confusing those they despise," their unnatural, one-sided brilliance as personalities. But it is above all, Waugh as author who is the dancer. We see this in the virtuoso quality of his narrative style—those larger-than-life Homeric similes—and in the showy expertise of his plot-management. The narrative prose of *Put Out More Flags* seems to me to bear the same relation to normal narrative prose as a ballerina's walk across stage does to normal walking, or an acrobat's ascent of a ladder to normal ladder climbing—it is a performance that so outdoes the "real thing" in grace and elegance, or power and speed, that it verges on both satire and self-satire. As for expertise, consider the dialogue via which we gather that Adam and Nina are making love, and compare that with the similar dialogues between Jake and Brett in *The Sun Also Rises*. The techniques are much the same, but the responses we make are different; because we laugh in part at Waugh's technique for its showiness, for its trickery. It is said that Henry Woodward, an eighteenth-century Harlequin, would eat imaginary fruit to music, alone on the stage, and so vividly that the audience saw and tasted the different fruits. That audience laughed as it admired, just as we laugh at Waugh for his showy innuendos and ellipses.

Then we are also reminded of pantomime by the latter's use of elaborate sets, which corresponds to Waugh's use of, for instance, the country houses he loves to describe. He spends a good deal of the narrative on Hetton or Brideshead or Boot Magna and on their inhabitants and regimes of life. Often he involves the set in the action by sending into that house some naïve character, whose baffled investigations and adventures there become part of the comedy. Take for instance Paul's exploration of King's Thursday, Adam's of Doubting Hall, Charles Ryder's of Brideshead, Mr. Salter's of Boot Magna. In pantomimes the sets were always elaborate and multiple. Thomas Dibdin's "Harlequin and Mother Goose" of 1806 had nineteen sets, including a village with stone bridge, a cottage, a church, a graveyard, and so forth; a market town; a farmyard; a mermaid's cave; a pavilion by moonlight; St Dunstan's Church; Vauxhall Gardens with gala illuminations; and so forth. And a good deal of the action arose out of Harlequin's arrival in these places, investigations of them, interactions with them.

Finally, we are reminded of pantomime by the passages of improvisation, in which Waugh gives the impression of being so carried away by a comic idea that he develops it "irresponsibly"—out of artistic proportion. For instance, in *Decline and Fall* the verbal extravagance of Dr. Fagan on the Welsh (which could be attributed to the character and not the author) is followed immediately by Waugh's description of the Welsh band, which equally derives its zest from an unmeasured exaggeration, a preposterousness and outrageousness. Thus our attention is drawn away from the action and away from the character to the puppet-master behind them both. Another kind of improvisation occurs when Waugh makes "real" something that had clearly been invented as a mere verbal device, a trope. Thus in developing (in itself an improvisation) his preposterous list of all the invalids, and nurses, and nurses-turned-invalids, in Boot Magna, he includes "Aunt Anne's old governess, Miss Scope." She is clearly no more than a name on the list. But then later we are told that in William's bedroom at home hung a watercolor of the churchyard painted by Miss Scope in her more active days. The joke here is partly the serialization, but partly the improvisation—an impudent testing of the reader's credulity, as it were, an impudent exaggeration of the author's prerogatives. Such effects are surely parallel to the "lazzi" of the great artists of pantomime, the sequences of capers and grimaces with which they impudently interrupted the action when they felt like it, performing tricks of their own, in very loose relation to the plot and very tight relation to their audience. These "lazzi" were unabashed manifestations of virtuoso skill that drew the audience's attention away from the play's "illusion of reality" to the performer's direct claims on their admiration. A modern example might be Chaplin in a tea-party scene, jerkily carrying his cup among the poised and elegant socialites, bumping into tables and apologizing awkwardly, and so forth, until suddenly he sits down on a non-chair, turns head over heels, and comes up still holding his cup still full of tea. Realistic fiction can offer no parallels to such effects, but Waugh's fiction can.

Then beyond both farce and pantomime, the term Commedia dell'Arte suggests traditions and techniques which are quite specifically and deeply related to Waugh's scenarios. "Comedia" suggests above all that central trio of characters, Pierrot, Harlequin, and Colombine, and their inter-relationships—Pierrot's naïve and hopeless yearning for beauty in general and Colombine in particular, Colombine's tenderness for him but weak and treacherous yielding to the brutal importunities of Harlequin, and Harlequin's heartless and unscrupulous aggressions against the other two, which leave him still bound to them for ever, and which never win him any substantial advantage. This complex surely provides the center for the objective correlative to Waugh's sensibility in these novels.

This sensibility might perhaps be described as that of the 1920's as a whole—as one kind of modernism. The figure of Pierrot, in particular, has a distinguished history in the iconography of modernism, quite apart from Waugh. The appreciation of Watteau's "Gilles" and of Deburau's miming had renewed the Commedia figure's meaning for a central configuration of nineteenth-century French writers and painters, notably the group of friends around Baudelaire, so that quite a rich and strong tradition crystallized in the Pierrot of Jules Laforgue. Laforgue identified himself with Pierrot, as a poet *became* Pierrot. He gave the figure its modern reference to the artist isolated among crudely normal Philistines, its modern setting, the waste-land townscape, and its modern idiom, the fragments of lyricism, philosophy, and madness he mutters or sings to himself.

T. S. Eliot brought Laforgue's Pierrot into English verse, and the Sitwells and Peter Quennell and half Waugh's friends among the writers of the 1920's saw themselves in the figure. Cyril Connolly has said that the novelists of the 1920's built their stories around a Petrouchka hero (Petrouchka is the balletic version of Pierrot) and cited *Antic Hay*, *South Wind*, *Vestal Fires*—he could have added his own *Rock Pool*. But perhaps the best fiction of the period needed Harlequin for a hero. Nabokov tried Pnin, a Pierrot, but succeeded with Humbert Humbert, a Harlequin. And Waugh's early works suffer from the nullity of early Pierrot heroes, like Paul Pennyfeather, or from the Pierrot characterization of heroes whose actions are Harlequin's, like Adam Fenwick-Symes. Adam sells Nina to Ginger, and then steals her back and impersonates his friend on their honeymoon visit to her father; but Waugh is unable or unwilling to bring out the full brutality of the character. In *Black Mischief* he does create a Harlequin hero, Basil Seal, who exploits his mother and his mistress quite unscrupulously, and who, having stolen Prudence from her former lover, ends by eating her in a cannibal banquet. And finally in *Put Out More Flags* he created a true Pierrot, Ambrose, who stands in the perfect complementary relation to Basil. The two have maintained "a shadowy and mutually derisive relation" since Oxford, and they are bound to each other as allies and comrades against the ordinary world, and yet Basil betrays Ambrose to the police on a charge he himself invents, and then has Susie (a Colombine figure) unpick the letter "A" from Ambrose's crepe-de-chine underwear to replace it with his own initial "B."

Ambrose is Pierrot by virtue of his "absurd light step and heavy heart," because of his self-caricaturing mannerisms of nodding his head and fluttering his eyelashes as he speaks, because of his hopeless yearning for love, because he is a true artist and a Jew and a homosexual. He is the perfect objective correlative for feelings that, for instance, Balcairn in *Vile Bodies* is supposed to objectify but fails to. Basil is a much better Harlequin than Adam, not only because his brutality—and his boringness—is so frankly brought out but also because his sexual psychology (his narcissism and sadistic phallicissism) is so boldly and yet delicately drawn. And *Put Out More Flags* is the best of the novels because it exploits these *Commedia* characters. It has in fact three Harlequins, Basil, Mr. Todhunter, and Colonel Plum; and two Pierrots, Ambrose and Cedric; and four Colombines, Sonia, Angela, Susie, and the bride of Grantley Green. Waugh's sensibility here finds its objective correlative, in the world of the Commedia.

Around the three main characters, the Commedia deploys Pantaloons, Pedants, Scaramouche-braggarts, Brighella-intriguers, and so forth. Figures like Lady Circumference, Lord Copper, Dr. Fagan, Captain Grimes, and so forth, do not correspond in detail to the former, but they are designed in the same way for the same function. They have as much fictional life, and the same kind; they are plausible and implausible in the same ways and to the same degree. And through some of these contemporary cartoons, these pompous Press lords and shrill interior decorators, the traditional masks of the Commedia may be seen to shine, and this is an effect traditionally employed in the Commedia genres. Ballets and pantomimes often began with young lovers who, in a dream or spell, were transformed into Pierrot and Colombine, and so could express their themes with great aesthetic exuberance. And ballets like *Petrouchka* began with an audience outside a show-booth—an audience already more vivid and lurid than the real one, gypsy women who perform a gypsy dance, a bear-leader who dances with his bear—but when the inner action begins, it is performed by puppets, still more vivid and lurid and aesthetically exuberant yet, quintessences of human life. In the same way the Commedia "archetypes" (not real archetypes because their connotations are purely social and aesthetic) exert a puppetizing pressure on the "contemporary reality" aspects of Basil and Ambrose.

I don't suggest that Waugh was consciously thinking of the Commedia and its traditions. But there were various ways in the early 1920's in which those could have been semiconsciously present to his mind as artistically exciting, besides the interest in Pierrot. Diaghilev's Ballets Russes were England's greatest artistic stimulus during the immediately pre- and post-war years, and they carried the seed of the Commedia with them, particularly in the Stravinsky and Cocteau ballets, like *Petrouchka* and *Parade* and *Polichinelle*; and in 1926 Diaghilev put on *The Triumph of Neptune*, an early Victorian pantomime ballet, with music by Lord Berners and a story by Sacheverell Sitwell, friends of Waugh's. But it would be characteristic of Waugh that he should have imbibed his inspiration not directly from Diaghilev, but from the analogous, but much more British and modestly circumscribed achievement of Lovat Fraser. The Lovat Fraser production of *The Beggars' Opera*, which ran for a long time at the Lyric, Hammersmith, in the early 1920's, was a great favorite among Waugh's group. Fraser brought to theater costume, design, rhyme sheets, book illustrations, and so forth, the bright gay color and crisp line of the Commedia, just as Gay brought the equivalent to the plot and characterization of *The Beggars' Opera*. Moreover, that tradition was brought into modern entertainment by Chaplin and the other stars of the early film comedies. All Waugh's friends loved those comedies, and Osbert Sitwell, for instance, made the connection between Chaplin and the Commedia.

Indeed, something like a Commedia influence could be seen in society as a whole, in the styles of clothes and make-up of the 1920's. The rather doll-like or clown-like make-up was theatrically noticeable, and the clothes worn by young people of both sexes were often transsexual. And the life-style of the beauties of the time had something of Colombine in it—something bold and dashing, but at the same time compromised and self-contemptuous, something expensive but at the same time cheap. This was in the style of, in real life, Nancy Cunard, in literature, Iris Storm and Myra Viveash (figures in popular novels drawn from Nancy Cunard); on the stage, Tallulah Bankhead (who played Iris Storm); and on the screen Garbo and Dietrich. As Waugh admitted about Virginia Troy, most of his heroines are versions of that same idea—though there is a softer, sillier, more girlish type of Colombine also in his work. (Other distinguished fiction which made use of those figures, at the same time, include novels by Hemingway and Fitzgerald; in *The Sun Also Rises*, Brett is another Colombine in the femme fatale style, Cohn is an unsympathetic Pierrot, oppressed by a composite Harlequin; in *The Great Gatsby*, Daisy is clearly a Colombine of the softer kind, Tom a Harlequin, and Gatsby a Pierrot.)

That is why one can suggest that in society as a whole, during the 1920's, there was a kind of imagination at work which corresponded to that of the Commedia. Take for instance the taste for the rococo and the baroque, guided by the Sitwells, and in books which themselves belonged to the same traditions, formally. The Sitwells wrote a mix of history, travel, aesthetics, crossing the frontiers of genre, century, culture, and those between art and life, in ways which had been developed in books about the Commedia characters. The roles in the Commedia transcended the individual players as much as the players transcended the plays, so that the history of the genre could be written in terms of those roles. One example is Cyril Beaumont's *History of Harlequin* of 1926, dedicated to Osbert and Sacheverell Sitwell, and with a long preface by Sacheverell.

These great performers thus came to seem—the characteristic ones—living masks, with neither souls nor nerves. And their art was in some ways brutal, and sensual, and coarse. "All standards of decorum were obliterated by one phallic stroke," Beaumont wrote about Harlequin. This antithesis to the moral style of nineteenth-century humanistic art—the style of George Eliot—also attracted the young aesthetes of the 1920's. After the triumph of realistic drama, with Ibsen and his followers, there came a reaction toward the colorfulness and cruelty, the vigor, the spontaneity, the formal virtuosity, of the earlier style. And this became available just after the war, when young men like Waugh needed an aesthetic style to make their own, untainted by the uses of their fathers.

This way of thinking about Waugh's comedies, this imaginative context for them, should win us practical-critical advantages, by suggesting where we should look to see the artist at work on his design, and also by helping to clarify our sense of which evaluative and interpretive criteria are relevant to his case. Clearly, this is not realistic fiction, in the great tradition of Tolstoy, George Eliot, Lawrence, the dominant artistic tradition that serves the mature and responsible purposes of our culture. Nor does it belong to those other categories of Northrop Frye's, "fiction but not novels," the romance, the confession, the anatomy. Of course, Waugh's comedy combines some features of all of those, and it combines them in complexes for which Dickens provides a major literary precedent. But even Dickens seems less useful than the Commedia as a critical context for Waugh. It is the comic half of Dickens that Waugh resembles, and the other half— Dickens the reformer, the sentimentalist, the moralist, and even more the overarching presence of Dickens the showman who conducts both these enterprises, Dickens the great Victorian figure—with this Dickens Waugh has nothing to do. Waugh's talents and techniques come together under the aegis of the dandy, the defier of established pieties, the mocker of great Victorian figures.

That is why we have to learn new criteria and new modes of scrutiny in order to read Waugh. By apprenticing ourselves to the novelists of the great tradition, we learn criteria of artistic appreciation that relate ultimately to the inner life of the characters—to each author's ability to create that for us, to have something new about it to tell us, to have new freedoms from old rigidities of moral or imaginative convention. Implicitly, we tend to ask ourselves, "Does this new book give us new insights into the inner lives of people who in some way transcend ordinary limitations?"

Obviously, we have to emancipate ourselves from such

criteria in order to be able to take seriously our pleasure in Waugh. His art is irresponsible/immoral in the sense that it challenges or evades all such criteria—not so much by its particular "statements" as by its whole mode of operation. Sometimes it challenges us to deny that life is farce—defies us to deny the pleasures of irresponsibility—pleasures which are after all also truths, and acts of courage. But more essentially it turns its back on life seen any other way, seen morally or seriously. Waugh's characters are phenomena of pure style, and the central ones apprehend each other that way. In *Put Out More Flags* Alastair does not expect Basil to understand or respect his moral sense, and vice versa. They don't, in any obvious sense, take each other seriously; nor are they, in any obvious sense, fond of each other. Yet clearly they are permanently and strongly bonded to each other, like Basil and Ambrose. The bond is this sardonic freedom that each grants the other to perform his own style; this is the positive and life-giving side of something whose more obvious harshness is notable in Basil's betrayal of Ambrose—and even more in John Plant's relations with Roger Simmons in *Work Suspended*. This was the dandy style in life to which the Commedia style in art formed such a natural analogue.

Waugh's style in art reduces our experience (of war, of colonialism, of teaching, of the daily newspapers, of the bright young people) to the proportions and colorings and feelings of farce. The word *reduce* is deceptive, however, insofar as it implies diminishment, for the effect and indeed the motive power of this process is to magnify the subject rather than to diminish the object. We feel enlarged because so many oppressive official realities are exploded for us, and because our own subversive desires, or velleities, to see that happen, have been recognized and given imaginative status. Waugh shows us so much wit, gaiety, courage, freedom, and knowledgeableness combined in seeing the world this way, that we gladly share the vision and claim our share of those qualities.

And once we see Waugh's books this way, and say that he is interested in reducing life to farce, we can expect to see him interested sometimes in the one, sometimes in the other—sometimes exaggerating wildly and recklessly, sometimes describing with scrupulous moderation and truth—and yet giving us essentially the same pleasure both times. So we begin to look for the points at which he subdues the complexity of experience to the dimensions of farce, in characters like Mrs. Ape, and then the points at which he does the opposite, in characters like Angela Lyne. Those are the easiest to identify as extremes, because they are unsuccessful. But Lady Circumference is clearly farcical, and Lady Seal is clearly realistic, and both of them are successful.

We can also get some useful directives in practical criticism by comparing Waugh with other writers. Among those superficially like him, he might be put side by side with satirists like Aldous Huxley and Mary McCarthy. The comparison must surely work to Waugh's advantage. These writers involve the reader in so much of their own pain, and in so much intellectual machinery, that the delight which gives the zest to their work as to Waugh's is dimmed and diminished. Huxley, for instance, insists on our sharing his characters' humiliations, insists on our paying on the spot for every laugh with a contrary reaction of horror or disgust or pity to the same phenomenon. Waugh insists on our noting the price—he rings it up very clearly on the moral register behind his characters' backs—but, except for lapses, he does not insist on our paying. If one compares *Antic Hay* with *Decline and Fall*, one sees how Huxley laboriously points out the difference between a character's feelings and what he says he feels, between his intentions and his effects, between his beliefs and his behavior. Waugh spares us all that, as he spares us the essayistic accounts of the ideological positions of his characters, which are so "impressive" in Huxley and McCarthy.

Among writers rather different from him, Waugh can be compared with Nathanael West. This contrast is not all in Waugh's favor. *The Day of the Locust* has a force and accuracy much superior to *The Loved One*. But if one compares *A Cool Million* with *Decline and Fall*, one is struck by how simple and how crude, comparatively, West's design is. The difference between the two narrative styles is representative of the general difference. Waugh's style is able to combine so many tones, so much romantic appreciation, so much gaiety, so much sympathy with the sardonic wit and the conscious cleverness that both novelists share. Perhaps more important, Waugh's characters have so much more vitality of the kind appropriate to farce than West's do. Among the latter, only the ex-President comes alive in the way that so many of Waugh's do. The rest are palpable constructs, transparent figureheads for ideas. Waugh's characters have all idioms, of behavior, speech, or dress, which are vivid in themselves, in some sense socially authentic, and vividly related to the behavior they perform in the plot.

And when we put him beside West, Waugh appears strikingly British and non-modernist. In West's world, one is always aware of the reading of Dostoevski and Kafka that preceded the writing. In Waugh's world one is aware of Dickens, Wilde, Firbank—very much less challenging presences to both reader and writer. Moreover, Waugh's "classical" style and structure and his "restrained" taste in incidents and effects are full of an implicit faith in order and control, an implicit allegiance to civilization and tradition. Nothing very violent happens, and the reader is shielded from the worst that does happen by Waugh's indirection. On the whole, this contrast works to Waugh's advantage or to West's disadvantage; like so many modernists, his gestures of despair and violence and disgust are so violent and so often repeated that they lose the power to convince. It is representative that the Commedia archetype pressing through Lemuel Pitkin at the end of *A Cool Million* is a Pagliacci clown—something much more blatant than Ambrose-as-Pierrot.

Finally, we can compare these best of Waugh's works with some of his other novels. If we do, I think we shall be struck by the vitality of the Commedia form and the severity of its internal laws. Within the war trilogy, *Officers and Gentlemen* is clearly superior to the other two novels, and it is because in this one Guy Crouchback is allowed to be a dandy, not just a victim, and the action is allowed to be gaily farcical, not just a demonstration of the unfairness of life. That is why the reader can enjoy the book so much more than he can *Men at Arms*. But because *Officers and Gentlemen* is also realistic, is addressed to a responsible and mature and serious sensibility, the vitality and scope of the farce is diminished and circumscribed. The gaiety of the vision is the palest shadow of that communicated by *Put Out More Flags*. We can see how this happens in the first scene on the island of Mugg: an officer lucky enough to have a room in the hotel is injured training, so will have to go on leave, and immediately, panting, one after another, his comrades rush back from their training to claim the room for themselves. They enter the hotel with the decorous haste, the perfunctory grief, the neat repetitiveness, of stage comedy. But because this is a realistic novel, Waugh has to *say* that they enter as in a well-constructed stage comedy. And this fatally limits the point. Instead of our being drawn into the vision of life as farce, we see that *their* lives, for that *moment*, were *like* farce. A space, the space of our realistic sense of what life is usually like, surrounds and isolates and insulates that moment. And when, a little later, Guy and Tommy go to a farcical dinner party in the castle on Mugg, they laugh together about it on the way back, and their laughter replaces ours, diminishes ours; it expresses the judgment on the event of sensible, normal, realistic people, and so isolates and insulates the event again. *Officers and Gentlemen* subdues farce to realism, and that makes it not more but less serious artistically. There is a vitality in the Commedia genre that bleeds away when it is subdued to realism and responsibility. But it is Waugh's achievement that he did capture that vitality in a sequence of novels that are as distinguished as anything written in England after Lawrence.

Chapter 9

OUR DETECTIVE
HEROES

No Orchids is the 1939 version of glamorized
crime, *Raffles* the 1900 version. What I am concerned with here is the immense difference in moral
atmosphere between the two books, and the change
in the popular attitude that this probably implies.
George Orwell,
"Raffles and Miss Blandish", (1944)

The contrast I want to draw, between Lord Peter Wimsey
and Travis McGee, is similar to Orwell's in lots of ways, but
not in its account of "the difference in moral atmosphere"
or of "the change in the popular attitude." Not only is the
moral difference which I see to America's credit, but I would
read some of the signs differently, and change the terms of
the analysis. I don't believe you can read moral values into
cultural signs so simply as Orwell implies. And I differ from
his method by concentrating on the central figure in a series
of novels, instead of whole individual novels.

But more significant than our differences is our similarity—
our common interest in a certain sort of adventure hero, the
sort who stands half way between the rebel and the avenger,
Prometheus and Jupiter, the criminal and the police inspector.
(Of course, Raffles was all criminal. But then he wasn't really,

as Orwell himself admits, because he was a gentleman.) And the private detective, or private investigator, seems to have proved a more successful formula for this cultural stimulant than the gentleman crook, a better way to realize all these excitements of being both for and against society, of working both within and without the law. Orwell declares his interest to be in glamorized crime, and so treats Raffles's loyalties to society and the law as mere blinds, and his criminality as the real thing. But I think that Raffles's ambiguity was real, and that he belongs to the line of Lord Peter Wimsey. By putting him instead in line with Slim of *No Orchids*, a real criminal, Orwell was mismating genres in order to produce a melodramatic moral.

Not *No Orchids for Miss Blandish* but Dorothy Sayers's novels about Wimsey are surely the 1939 descendants of the Raffles stories. The people who read *No Orchids* in 1939 were not the sons of those who had read *Raffles* in 1900, but of those who read stories about Jack the Ripper. However, my difference from Orwell is not so much in opinion about objective fact as in direction of interest. I am interested in reading all the resonances of the Wimsey stories, the way they resound to the England of their times. Orwell was interested in reading resonances of the Chase novel, such as the one he quotes, "It's pure Fascism." The one reading does not make the other false, though it does of course criticize it. It seems to me that Orwell yielded to the temptation to read the more alarmist meter for his own time and a more indulgent one (more likely to give readings of stability, decorum, stability) for the contrasting past period. That was more than a low temptation; being a moralist *means* finding such contrasts. But other contrasts were available.

Wimsey is, from my point of view, linked to both Raffles and McGee. Like Raffles, his social rank is in tension with his "crime" activities, but like McGee, those activities derive from his social conscience, and are professional as much as amateur. All three, of course, are heroes of adventure-within-society, practitioners of frontier or colonial virtues transformed for civilized uses. (The moment when they whip their sword-blade out of their walking-stick, or reluctantly turn their hand-shake into a karate-chop, is the emblematic moment for their whole careers.) The literal frontiersman or imperialist adventurer (of the P. C. Wrenn, E. Phillips Oppenheim, John Buchan kind) seems to have lost his mythic viability after 1914. And of that myth's descendants, the Tarzan-type stories were too crude to carry the sort of interest we are looking for, while the cynical-reporter stories were perhaps too sophisticated—they seem always ambitious of more serious treatment. The subgenre that best carried the same interest as the Buchan books, that paradoxical combination of serious and anti-serious interest, where lively imaginations work at high pressure but low control—deeply involved with their subject in both distinguished and vulgar ways—and so reveal things otherwise hidden, the subgenre that best carried that interest was that built around the private detective.

But Raffles and Wimsey, the British heroes, are in one way like each other and unlike McGee, and that way is crucial to their fictional and cultural vitality as an idea. They are figures of class-feeling. Orwell presents Raffles as being a character expertly constructed to evoke and satisfy all our feelings about class superiority. He presents him as being *essentially* a gentleman, as importantly associated with cricket, for instance, as a figure of the class-code which supplants the Christian conscience-ethic, and as doomed to an expiatory death in the Boer War—"a practiced reader would forsee this from the start." All this is true of Wimsey too, but he is much more elaborately developed. In the place of cricket, one could name a dozen features of British life with which he is identified, but no doubt the most important is Oxford. His moral sense is much more complexly related to the class-code. And he is not doomed to die, because he is not a criminal. The fantasy is bolder than it was in *Raffles*. Wimsey is a hero, a much more generally normal one than, say, Sherlock Holmes, and he can marry and find exemplary happiness. (He even has a child in one of the short stories.) That is one of his interests for us. As the novels about him continued and developed, so did he. As he was involved in more and more situations, he "came alive." He acquired a family, a history, a future, and they all have imaginative life. He remained a snob fantasy, but he became related to all sorts of cultural issues, in artistic and intellectual ways.

Dorothy Sayers was in her way an artist and an intellectual, and she had a real imaginative devotion to certain cultural dilemmas of post-war Britain. She was born in 1893 in Oxford, the daughter of a headmaster who became a country clergyman. She had a French governess, and was taught Latin at seven, which delighted her because it gave her a superiority over her mother, her aunt, her nurse—over mere women. Later she studied at Oxford, took a First Class degree in 1915, and remained passionately in love with the place. Blackwells published a volume of serious poetry by her in 1916, and it is always said that she drew Lord Peter first from one of the Oxford dons of her time. (This is just one case of a general phenomenon, of connection between the British detective and British Toryism. Margery Allingham said she drew her hero, Albert Campion, from the Duke of York, who became George VI.)

Dorothy Sayers then worked for a large advertising agency in London, but there, as in the popular and vulgar fiction she began to write, she yearned back always to Oxford, scholarship, and intellectual integrity. She was thus devoted to one of the great institutions of romantic conservatism in English life, and *Gaudy Night* is a quite extraordinary love-song to it, Oxford's Song of Solomon. Nor did she lack intimate knowledge of, or equality of status with, the object of her love. She was herself a poet, playwright, translator, scholar, working within the circle of those interests common to Oxonian High Churchmen then; like Charles Williams, C. S. Lewis, and T. S. Eliot. She edited *Essays Presented to Charles Williams* in 1947. And if she occasionally worked in their areas, they occasionally worked in hers. Williams wrote thrillers too, Lewis wrote popular propaganda for Christianity too, and Eliot wrote religious plays too. She was their ally, one of their club, and she was so even in writing about Wimsey.

And what degree of talent do we attribute to her? That is not easy to answer, though only because there is no generally acknowledged vocabulary for such ideas. I should say that she shows a fictional talent quite commensurate with her "serious" intelligence. It was not, in either case, the kind of mind or talent to which one applies the terms "great" or "brilliant." But she had more talent than, say, Hawthorne, and maybe as much as Graham Greene. What puts her fiction in another category from theirs is that she let her talent serve her own and other people's day-dream fantasies; and serve not honorably but slavishly; she wrote shameful things.

But she also had an artistic conscience. She *could* not, she tells us, end *Strong Poison* the way she had intended, with Wimsey marrying Harriet, because Harriet was in too dependent a position to accept him with dignity. She went to great lengths, involving several books, before she could achieve that marriage properly. And the books corroborate the author's account. Sayers's shameful fantasies alternated with her serious interests in mastery of her talents, and sometimes shared them equally. Other writers, serious writers, do that occasionally. There are parts of *Brideshead Revisited* that have to be read the way one reads Dorothy Sayers, because in them Waugh let his talents serve his fantasies. But that was a rare lapse on Waugh's part, while she wrote that way half the time, about Wimsey. But to say that is not to say either that she was untalented or that she was unconscientious. One might say that her work relates to Waugh's the way that *No Orchids for Miss Blandish* relates to Faulkner's *Sanctuary*. As Orwell pointed out, those two books have many resemblances—Chase's character, Slim, is also a distant relation of Greene's Pinky in *Brighton Rock*, so his book provides two examples of parallel imaginative designs on different imaginative levels. The *cultural* significance of these images is the same whether they are designed with distinction of imagination or crudely.

As for the cultural *effect*, while the reader is concentrating, the good writer will have a very different effect from the bad writer, but images work in the imagination long after the concentration is relaxed. So there is no impropriety in treating Sayers in some of the same ways as one treats serious writers, and taking Wimsey seriously on occasion.

But primarily Wimsey, like Raffles, is a figure of class-feeling fantasy—only more so. British culture in this century has produced a remarkable series of such figures, in real life and in literature. And, even within popular literature, these figures have evoked an equally remarkable interest from readers, expressed in positive cults, especially among intellectuals—for instance, in humorous fiction, the figure of Bertie Wooster and the cult of P. G. Wodehouse; in detective fiction, the cult of Sherlock Holmes and the figures of Wimsey and Campion and Ngaio Marsh's Roderick Alleyn. All are figures of class-feeling.

Dorothy Sayers was surely one of the world's masters of the pornography of class distinction. She plays around the problem of class-feeling the whole time, exploiting every kind of interest in it; aware, capable of being aware, of our criticisms of what she is doing, capable, at times, of shrewd reflections on it herself, but most of the time herself involved in crudest wish-fulfillment and thus appealing both to very gross and to quite sophisticated appetites.

This, I take it, is the secret of all vivid pornography. The writer has done a lot of thinking about his subject, and is quite able to draw subtle distinctions, and severe moral conclusions within it; is also able to admit the indignity, and even the sheer preposterousness of his fantasies. But he combines that knowledge with a surrender to the crudest temptations of his subject, and so makes his book an anthology, in which you pass from some gross indecency to some quite subtle and moral reflection on his theme. This is what you find in the classics of sexual pornography, like Cleland's *Fanny Hill*. So Lord Peter, who is the Fanny Hill of class-distinctions, sometimes is smirkingly referred to as "his lordship" or "that young sprig of the nobility" or "this younger son of a duke." In the novel *Whose Body?* little Mr. Thipps, a "vulgar little beast" who drops his h's and says "reely," is described as being "touched by this sympathetic interest in the younger son of a duke." This, I take it, is as crass an invitation as you could find to indulge in the pleasures of condescension, and the thrill of being on the ducal side of the great social divide. But in other places Lord Peter is referred to austerely as Wimsey, and his power to patronize and snub others is quite acutely analyzed and moralized on. For instance, a few pages on in *Whose Body?* Lord Peter sharply defeats the forces of ordinary snobbery in the shape of a "highly respectable" woman, who avoids contact with Mr. Thipps. By virtue of his real social superiority, you see, Lord Peter is the enemy of all second-rate, second-hand, imitations. This is, I suggest, the way all high-grade pornography operates.

What we remember first about this snobbery is simply its absurdity, of course. No one who read it can forget the picture of Lord Peter "whistling a complicated passage of Bach under his breath." Whistling *with* his breath, or whistling a simple passage of anything would of course be beneath him. Or take the picture of him sitting in his library, reading a rare fourteenth-century manuscript of Justinian. "It gave him particular pleasure, being embellished with a large number of drawings in sepia, extremely delicate in workmanship, and not always equally so in subject. Beside him on a convenient table stood a long-necked decanter of priceless old port. From time to time he stimulated his interest with a few sips, pursing his lips thoughtfully, and slowly savouring the balmy after-taste." Obviously one is asked to read this all agog, with lips parted, breath bated, murmuring to oneself, "So that's how those people live."

And then there are passages in which the author seems suddenly to betray herself quite startlingly. "Wimsey sat late that night in the black-and-primrose library, with the tall folios looking down at him. They represented the world's accumulated hoard of mellow wisdom and poetical beauty, to say nothing of thousands of pounds in cash." One wonders if that *can* be normal self-betrayal or bluntness of sensibility. Anybody might have ended that sentence "to say nothing of the thousands of pounds they cost," without realizing at first all the implications. But to add "in cash" so completely disposes of the mellow wisdom and the poetical beauty that the phrasing takes on a life of its own. This is the life some fictional *characters'* language has; Mrs. Gamp and Mrs. Malaprop make remarks of that kind.

All this is fairly simply absurd. But take one last example, which comes from *Gaudy Night*. "For a garden, as Bacon observes, is the purest of human pleasures, and the greatest refreshment to the spirit of man, and even idle and ignorant people who cannot distinguish heptosiphon hybridus from Karl-jussian anelloides, and would rather languish away in a wilderness than break their backs with dibbling and weeding, may get a good deal of pleasant conversation out of it, especially if they both know the old-fashioned names of the commoner sorts of flowers, and are both tolerably well-acquainted with the minor Elizabethan lyrists." Here we catch exactly the same lofty intonations as before in phrases like "tolerably well-acquainted," and "minor Elizabethan lyrists," and the throw-away reference to heptosiphon hybridus and the other plant from which *some* people can't distinguish it. But we recognize also that the attitude is a good deal more culturally plausible here, and that a good deal more intellectual effort went into writing this sentence. We are on the outer fringes, in the outer suburbs, of the classical light essay. And the idea that cultured people naturally know the old-fashioned names of flowers, and the minor Elizabethan poets, that this is what you expect from a truly cultured person, that idea is both intensely irritating and undeniably true. That *was* the Oxford idea of a cultured person. Cultured Oxford people *did* know that sort of thing and did not know, for instance, about electricity or modern poetry. This passage is still absurdly snobbish, but it is no longer a simple absurdity.

It is Lord Peter above all who is not simply absurd. He is a genuine creation, who not only possessed his creator's mind but also can in his way possess ours. Dorothy Sayers tells us that his affairs became more real to her than her own, and we can believe it. He has real fictional vitality. He is a created character. His life and personality, his clothes, manners, education, family connections, military service, and love life have all been worked out with real richness and inventiveness of detail. With the result that we can, for instance, predict what he would do in situations his creator did not specify. Moreover, it is interesting for us to imagine him in those situations, because his mode of behavior is significant for all of us. He represents a part of ourselves, a part of the British national personality. And lastly, he engages some range and scope of attention in us, because what he represents

is a mode of power. His field of action is 90 percent just social, of course: class-distinctions, how to recognize them,
how to cross them, how not to. But in that field he is not
just passive; he does not merely *know*; he acts, he manages
awkward situations. He shows us how to deal with every kind
of difficulty: drunken taxi drivers, sullen socialists, exotic
beauties, Bohemian artists, pompous colonels, hysterical women.

Situations of these kinds crop up all the time in the novels.
And they are presented to us as problems—problems of the
investigation, primarily, of course. Often Inspector Parker or
Harriet Vane has failed to solve them, and then Lord Peter
arrives and all is well. He solves some of them by whipping
out his sword-stick or by revealing hidden skills in judo like
Sherlock Holmes. He solves some by rational deduction like
Hercule Poirot. But far more he solves like nobody but himself by his command of the English social structure and his
perfect mastery of English manners. He knows exactly what
to say to each English social class and psychological type to
make them melt into pliancy.

His techniques work, and would work in real life. Of
course, they are also quite absurd, but that is because their
motivation is so transparent and unacceptable, not because
they are ineffective. We don't take them seriously because the
writer has not taken the taxi drivers and so forth seriously. She
has treated them as fictional clichés of the flattest kind. But
Lord Peter's techniques, if applied ruthlessly enough—if you
treated other people as fictional clichés—would work. They do
work, when managerial types apply them, as they do every
day. What Dorothy Sayers offers us is very shrewdly observed and valid enough as social directive.

She was essentially a didactic writer, always giving her
readers hints about their social lives, tips on what to look out
for, techniques of how to behave. When Harriet Vane goes
walking in *Have His Carcase*, "her luggage was not burdened
by skin-creams, insect-lotion, silk frocks, portable electric
irons, or other impedimenta beloved of the 'Hikers Column'.
She was dressed sensibly in a short skirt and thin sweater,
and carried, in addition to a change of linen, and an extra
provision of footwear, little else beyond a pocket edition of

Tristram Shandy, a vest-pocket camera, a small first-aid outfit, and a sandwich lunch." This is the tone of the etiquette book, thinly disguised as a novel. But when she wrote about Lord Peter her romantic excitement saved her from that too "schoolmistressy" note. She could afford, and achieve, quite fine extravagances, inspired by her strong feeling for, and understanding of, her subject. Thus she describes him with a bold stress on his silly, meager, weak looks. "A fair, foolish face, with straw-coloured hair, sleeked back; a monocle clinging incongruously under a ludicrously twitching brow; a chin shaved to perfection, hairless, epicene, a rather high collar, faultlessly starched, a tie elegantly knotted."

Now Dorothy Sayers was, to put it mildly, attracted to Lord Peter. Yet she felt she could afford to deny him all physical glamor and natural dignity quite ruthlessly; nor did she miscalculate; that image had glamor for the English people of that time. The lack of natural power was designed to bring out vividly the intellectual and artificial power of Lord Peter's taste, his brains, his position, his breeding, his learning, his sophistication, his analytical intelligence; all that is symbolized in the monocle. Artificial power seemed to Dorothy Sayers a better quality in a man than natural power, because it was safer, no doubt, but not only for that reason. Above all, she felt it and her readers felt it as *power*.

This blonde, chinless, burbling type was very prominent in English culture between the wars. Dorothy Sayers herself compared Lord Peter to P. G. Wodehouse's Bertie Wooster and to the roles created by Ralph Lynn in the Aldwych farces, and, of course, she surrounded Wimsey with other characters out of those imaginative worlds. Bunter is plainly modeled on Jeeves. He falls short of his original as much as Wimsey transcends his, while the Dowager Duchess of Denver could have come out of one of Ben Travers's farces.

And other writers copied Lord Peter. Margery Allingham's Albert Campion was given a biographical note, too, which had him born in 1900, going to Rugby and Cambridge, marrying Lady Amanda, living in Piccadilly, and belonging to prestigious clubs. But Lord Peter is more interesting, as a cultural image, than any of his rivals or models. Partly because he was put into significant relation to such a range of English reality—social and intellectual. But more because he was a figure of such power. Bertie Wooster and Ralph Lynn were not such fools as they seemed, but the power did finally reside with Tom Walls or Jeeves. Lord Peter seems just as silly, but is masterful. And once we have met him, the other verions of his idea seem lacking in important ways. We feel that Dorothy Sayers had found the true full form of this image. And the reason we feel this is surely that this was a national image of the Englishman.

Dorothy Sayers herself defined Wimsey as "the interpretative artist, the romantic soul at war with the realistic brain." But this was his *intention*, and we are interested only in his *effect*. The effect we all respond to in Wimsey is an ultra-*English* version of the "romantic soul." He is authoritative, in his odd way, because the Englishman then *was* wanting to see himself as a Wimsey. He felt himself to be in implicit contrast with the Australian or the American, both so much richer in natural power and tough experience, so much younger nationally. We identified ourselves with upper-class effete figures because we knew that that was the way we must seem to the rest of the world. We took an interest in the difficulties and triumphs of people born to high estate and low income, because we all of us felt a bit like that when confronted with American or Australian cousins. And even within England educated people felt they made the same contrast with the insurgent lower class. But, we didn't want to seem to ourselves really weak and silly. A weak endowment by nature, but tremendous artificial power—socially and intellectually subtle, sophisticated, ruthless. That was how we saw ourselves, and that was why Lord Peter represented us. (And represented us to other nations too. Lots of Americans, even highly intelligent ones, took him as England, and those who wanted to be dandies themselves came to England as to their natural home.)

This question of representation, however, is a complicated one. In many ways, it is Chief Inspector Parker and later Harriet Vane who represent *us*, and Lord Peter is just a glamorous national ideal, the ark of the British covenant, the heritage that makes life worth living even in the post-war wilderness. For "us," the readers, I take to be dowdy, respectable types of the professional, or would-be professional classes, grammar-school educated, while Lord Peter and his mother are the public-school, upper-class types, who exerted such a fascination over the others during those decades. For it seems that among the English county families, during the post-war twilight, there were born individuals, and a whole way of life, rich in eccentric stylishness, which satisfied the whole nation's craving to turn real life into a kind of fancy dress, eccentric comedy. Evelyn Waugh is the best chronicler of this phenomenon. Life at Boot Magna (or life at Renishaw) was what "upper class" gradually came to mean, although presumably only a small portion of the nobility actually lived that way. The contrast between upper- and middle-class styles was one of idea, and both ideas could be found within the nobility of fact. The contrast is that between the two Duchesses of Denver. Dorothy Sayers felt very little thrill at the title Duchess as worn by the younger woman. She is essentially middle class and is to be detested. Harriet Vane and her creator are only excited when the title carries with it the semi-French airs and graces of the dowager duchess—the airs of an eighteenth-century marquise, we are told, though in fact we are reminded more of Yvonne Arnaud or Jeanne de Casalis. It is upper-class people turning themselves into comic theater whom Dorothy Sayers delights in, whom Harriet and Parker adore, whom, by virtue of their education, Harriet and Parker are able to join in a junior capacity. Harriet, because she has been to Oxford, is even able to marry one.

When she does so, she finds that he has the solid virtues as well as the superficial graces. "Peter, I believe you're a fraud. You may play at being a great detective and a scholar and a cosmopolitan man-about-town, but at bottom you're nothing but an English country gentleman, with his soul in the stables and his mind on the parish pump," she says in *Busman's Honeymoon*. A few pages later she reflects to herself more seriously, "He carried about with him that permanent atmosphere of security. He belonged to an ordered society, and this was it. . . . She was curiously excited. She thought, 'I have married England.' Her fingers tightened on his arm."

Of course, she still insists that we see Lord Peter as wickedly sophisticated, especially in erotic matters. Harriet is credited with "passion," but Lord Peter has all the sexual glamor. (This treatment of sex is the most vulgar thing in Sayers.) Wimsey's power of sexual initiative is connected explicitly with his social rank. In *Clouds of Witness* he sees a farmer's wife with "a shape so wonderful that even in that strenuous moment sixteen generations of feudal privilege stirred in Lord Peter's blood. His hands closed over hers instinctively, but she pulled herself hurriedly away and shrank back." His erotic skills are explained by his French blood and his education in France—the dirty weekend in Paris. When Harriet and Peter awake after their wedding night, she hopes that his first words will be in French, to prove that she has been as good in bed as a Frenchwoman. (They do these things better in France.)

But all this is naughty and insubstantial. The substance of English life into which Peter and Harriet sink as they fade from our sight at the end of *Busman's Honeymoon* is the ordered life of class-responsibility. Thus Superintendent Kirk reflects:

> Rather a pity, in a way, that [Sergeant] Foster was a bachelor and a teetotaller and belonged to a rather strict sect of Plymouth Brethren or something. A most trustworthy officer, but not very easy for a young fellow to confide in. Perhaps one ought to give more attention to these traits of character. Handling men was born in some people—this Lord Peter, for instance. Sellon had never seen him before, yet he was readier to explain himself to *him* than to his own superior officer. One couldn't resent that, of course; it was only natural. What was a gentleman for, except to take your difficulties to.

Kirk is a jolly N.C.O. type, who knows his place, but who can achieve a certain social equality with Lord Peter. He plays quite remarkable games of quotation with both Peter and Harriet, quoting, counter-quoting, identifying each other's quotations. Foster represents the disturbing forces of upward mobility. He represents the cities, the grammar schools, technology, and death to the class system.

> Kirk never found it easy to get on with Foster. There was, to begin with, this air of teetotal virtue; he disliked having his evening pint referred to as 'alcohol.' Then, Foster, though much subordinate to him in rank, was more refined in speech; he had been educated at a bad grammar-school instead of a good elementary school, and never misplaced his h's—though, as for reading good literature or quoting the poets, he couldn't do it and didn't want to. Thirdly, Foster was disappointed. . . . And fourthly, Foster never did anything that was not absolutely correct. . . .

We shall see later that Evelyn Waugh ascribed a certain Sense of the Past to all public school Englishmen, a sense part aesthetic and part historic, and their major cultural equipment; and denied that sense to secondary grammar-school products. In effect he is saying that the second type lacks "imagination" and "culture," and this is what Sayers is saying too. In her work, the polarity of the two types is perfectly clear, and very strong is the current flowing between them and very unambiguous its direction.

It is this aspiration upward, away from their own dull grammar-school type toward the brilliant high comedy public-school class, which Dorothy Sayers awakens and plays with in her readers. And because this aspiration was a powerful force in British social life then, she has something interesting to say. Here she is summing up the contrast.

> Parker was paid to detect and to do nothing else, and neither his natural gifts nor his education (at Barrow-in-Furness grammar school) prompted him to stray into side-tracks at the beck of an ill-regulated imagination. But to Lord Peter the world presented itself as an entertaining labyrinth of side-issues. He was a respectable scholar in five or six languages, a musician of some skill and more understanding, something of an expert in toxicology, a collector of rare editions, an entertaining man-about-town, and a common sensationalist.

And when Harriet gazes up at Lord Peter on horseback, faultlessly dressed, superbly mounted, negligently graceful, wittily self-deprecating, we see the whole professional class of

England adoring their master—we see what they send their children to Oxford for.

Because of Orwell's moral judgment on Raffles, we must add that the Wimsey stories are not merely corrupting morally. Orwell himself said that they show an extremely morbid interest in corpses, but this is surely one of his excesses of suspiciousness. In the matter of violence they are quite inoffensive, and in general the manners which they insist on are all in the service of a responsible culture. The class system is important to Dorothy Sayers for very moral reasons, as well as for others. And that an interest is pornographic does not mean that the object of interest is unhealthy—if it were, we should have to condemn sex itself. Class-feeling was a phenomenon worth study in the England of those years, and for reasons which Dorothy Sayers put her finger on—the connections between class-feeling and the national identity.

In any case, one cannot use the positivist cause-and-effect approach to matters of cultural interpretation as flatly as Orwell tried to. One has to talk more in terms of signs and symbols. When a writer declares his pleasure in violence, exactly what effect that will have on his readers varies a lot with the individual, and is impossible to calculate in the mass. But the importance of the writer's so declaring himself does not depend on these variable and incalculable factors. It is a fact in itself, significant about that culture, just as the religion of that society is. Books are to be discussed as signs rather than causes.

Turning now to the American detective story, we must first acknowledge the difference between the two genres that the shared title conceals. In England the detective novel began from the novel of manners, as Dorothy Sayers said, and in her hands it tended to return to that. It shared the loyalties of the novel of manners, to silver-fork prescriptiveness, to upper-class comedy, to epigram and elegance of style—in short, to the dandy temperament. Sherlock Holmes is recognizably a dandy and decadent of the 1890's, whose activity is reassuringly confined to pure intellectuality. And it is no accident that G. K. Chesterton and Father Ronald Knox both wrote detective stories and wrote about them—Chesterton in fact becoming the first President of the London Detection Club in 1928—because both of those were, like other Catholic converts, dandies in flight from dandyism. They too insist on the "intellectuality" of what they are doing, to exorcise the ghosts of Beardsley and des Esseintes, but the epigrams fizz away under the camouflage. Brilliance still triumphs over established method. One expression of this paradox of feeling is the assertively dowdy figure of Father Brown—a dowdy dandy of the mind—and another is the dowdiness of Sayers's Oxford.

The American detective novel, apart from those writers who imitated the British, began from the novel of action. As Raymond Chandler said, Dashiell Hammett gave murder back to the murderers, and he also pointed out the connections between such writing and Hemingway's. The dandy is nowhere in view, but the tough guy is everywhere. And this difference between the two readerships, or at least between the ways the two sets of readers identify themselves in responding to the books in fan clubs and letters, and so forth. Exactly who John D. MacDonald's readers are socially and intellectually I don't know, but there seems no reason to suppose them as genteel or as academic as Dorothy Sayers's readers. That elaborate accretion of clubs and mock-scholarship around Sherlock Holmes, for instance, the Baker Street Irregulars and *The Private Life of Sherlock Holmes*, written by and for *bookmen*, especially by and for *men of letters*—that seems to have no equivalent among the readers of Chandler and Hammet. The alliances of this taste are not with scholarship, crossword puzzles, or the "light classics" of literature.

In looking for an American equivalent of Wimsey, one thinks first of Philip Marlowe, Nick Charles, Lew Archer, Sam Spade; the fairly similar (similar to each other) heroes of Raymond Chandler, Dashiell Hammett, Ross Macdonald. Their novels, too, are works of imaginative vitality, and with even more claims to be taken seriously as cultural statements. Perhaps for that reason, they do not form good counterparts to the Sayers novels. They are like those newspaperman stories, a genre that belongs to the major tradition, though in a subordinate way. They are concerned with important themes of the modern sensibility—the city, the police, urban decay, corruption—and they follow the rules of their genre quite scrupulously without the continual and extraordinary lapses that help make the Sayers novels so interesting. They have little of her silver-fork interest, and are closer to that other branch of adventure fiction, the police novel. This last kind of novel is decidedly patriarchal in feeling—all Jupiter and no Prometheus. Orwell complained about the bully worship implicit in this genre, when he talked about Edgar Wallace. And we have many examples of it today, in the Simenon novels above all, but also in Nicholas Freeling, and the Swedish couple who write about Martin Beck. These are all millers of the mills of God, grinding slowly in boredom and squalor and grinding exceeding small. This is antithetical in feeling to Dorothy Sayers's work, and although Chandler, Macdonald, and Hammett only play with these feelings, that is enough to make them unassimilable to her.

The one I do think assimilable, John D. MacDonald, is quite a different writer from her in many ways. He is assimilable perhaps mostly because he *is* a silver-fork writer, though the manners he moralizes are those of the male adventurer's life. John D. MacDonald was born in Pennsylvania in 1916, a generation later than Dorothy Sayers, and took his B.S. at Syracuse University in 1938 and his M.B.A. from Harvard in 1939. He has *not* associated himself with Harvard, or any equivalent of Oxford in American life. He came of age in time for the Second World War, not the First, and in the literary generation of Norman Mailer, not T. S. Eliot. He has *not* associated his imagination with an established church or with the class system or with literary or social decorum. He began writing in 1946, and has since produced five hundred pieces of fiction, including sixty-five novels. He lives in Florida and identifies himself with the life of sailing, fishing, outdoor adventure.

The preoccupation with class in Dorothy Sayers's work is replaced by a preoccupation with sex in MacDonald's. This is pornography pure and simple, unless one considers his sadism an impurity within pornography. But both writers are engaged in the same two enterprises, each of which takes up a great deal of their intelligence and feeling. Both are deeply concerned about the lives of their societies, England and America, and are dedicated to representing its varieties exactly, and to approving some and disapproving others. And both build heroes who represent those societies in an idealized way. Wimsey/McGee is not an average Englishman/American. In different ways, each is notably alien, exceptional, abnormal. But each fights for, and even stands for, the normalities of his culture, in the way that heroes do. Both are ideal figures, and the books about them are exercises in literary idealism, like *Pamela* and *Robinson Crusoe*.

The sexual preoccupation is of course something that MacDonald shares with other American novelists of his time, including the really major ones. It is also obvious that the same is true of Dorothy Sayers and her preoccupation with class. But while her intensification of the feeling and elaboration of the theme seem to me an ultimate, he is not so extreme or absurd. Other writers outdo MacDonald. But his books are still filled with the sense of McGee's two-hundred-pound body, his tanned and leathery skin, his scarred and battered hide, his pale eyes and sandy hair, his big knuckly hands and gangling limbs, his physical indolence and ropy toughness. Lord Peter has no body. We hear rather of his exquisitely tailored back and of his shoulders tailored to swooning point, while McGee's clothes, if he has any, are shabbily unnoticeable. And besides McGee himself, everybody else in the novels is rendered in terms of their bodies and centrally in terms of their sexuality. While the only people who have a sexual body or a sexual personality in the Sayers novels are comic, grotesque, or villainous.

Both heroes engage in psychic salvage. That is a central function of their personalities as heroes. We might contrast Lord Peter's salvage of Ann Dorland in *The Unpleasantness at the Bellona Club* with McGee's salvage of Helena Pearson in *The Girl in the Plain Brown Wrapper*.

The story of Ann Dorland is interesting because important details make it clear that she is a first version of Harriet Vane, and so represents Dorothy Sayers herself. Since the identification is so strong, it is quite an extraordinary imaginative transaction, this "saving" by Lord Peter; the portrait Dorothy Sayers has painted comes alive, steps out of his frame, and gives his creator the accolade of sexual and social desirability. For in terms of plot Lord Peter saves both girls from charges of murder. In terms of theme he saves them from being ugly ducklings, wallflowers, social rejects. Ann, like Harriet, is plain and sulky, deeply unhappy and rebellious against her fate, because she lives in Bohemia and has given her love to a man who does not appreciate her. Lord Peter diagnoses her problem from her bookshelf, which features Virginia Woolf, May Sinclair, Dorothy Richardson—all the writers of female rebellion. He notes the absence of Wells, Bennett, and Beresford, the male intelligence. He then remarks, with alerted intelligence, a whole row of D. H. Lawrence. "Dear me, quite a row of D. H. Lawrence. I wonder if she reads him very often." He takes down her copy of *Women in Love*, and finds it well-thumbed. We realize that her soul is unhealthy; she has been trying to be "modern," rebelling against tradition, trying to be erotic. Lord Peter takes her out to dinner, encourages her to develop some expertise about food and wine, and tells her to look out for a man-about-town. A man of sophistication and experience will appreciate her qualities, having sated his senses with obvious prettiness. The bohemian "artist" hasn't enough intelligence or character of his own to appreciate hers. Ann Dorland accepts this advice. Harriet Vane applies it, and is rewarded with Lord Peter Wimsey himself. She is saved from Philip Boyes, a minor modern poet, and enters the old aristocracy of England.

McGee's salvation of Helena Pearson is purely sexual. No bookshelves are involved, only beds. Her problem is that having been happily married, she fears she could never enjoy sexual love with another man, and so tries herself out on McGee—a professional, as it were—before she accepts a proposal from an old friend.

Helena has "class"—for "class" is a theme of MacDonald as well as of Sayers. "Helena came over on a hot July day. She was of that particular breed which has always made me feel inadequate. Tallish, so slender as to be almost, but not quite, gaunt. The bones that happen after a few centuries of careful breeding. Blond-gray hair, sun-streaked, casual, dry-textured, like the face, throat, backs of the hands, by the sun and winds of the games they play . . . no girl-tricks with the eyes and mouth . . . tasteful, mature, elegant, and sensitive." This is class as MacDonald understands it, which is how Hemingway understood it, too, and Faulkner. At first, she is unable to achieve an orgasm. "She would manage to get herself right out to the last grinding panting edge of it and get hung up there and then slowly, slowly fade back and away." So McGee pretends to have a nightmare from which she must console him and pretends that it has its source in an unhappy love affair, so that she actually seems to be the stronger of the two. Oh, the irony of it. "So in her deep sleepy hypnotic giving, it built without her being especially aware of herself, built until suddenly she groaned, tautened, became swollen, and then came across the edge and into the great blind and lasting part of it, building and bursting, building and bursting, peak and then diminuendo, until it had all been spent and she lay slack as butter, breath whistling, heart cantering, secretions a bitter fragrance in the new stillness of the bed." This is Travis's gift to her, and Helena thanks him for it later. "You did some mending, Travis." Some such episode occurs in each of the McGee books, and at its end he sends the woman back to a husband or some other sad comedown. Helena finds the man she married poor stuff after McGee, and has to divorce him for fear of dominating him completely. And every now and then, after some harrowing adventure, McGee accepts a similar service of "mending" from a girl, though that transaction is never quite so condescending.

We might also compare some of the erotic rhetoric devoted to Helena Pearson's lovemaking with Dorothy Sayers's snob rhetoric. It is surprisingly hard to say which is the more "literary." "There was no cloying kittenishness about her, as that was a style that would not have suited her—or me. She was proud of herself and as bold, jaunty, direct, and demanding as a bawdy young boy, chuckling her pleasures, full of a sweet wildness in the afternoon bunk with the heavy rain roaring on the decks over us, so totally unselfconscious about trying this and that and the other, so frankly and uncomplicatedly greedy for joy that, in arrangements that could easily have made another woman look vulgarly grotesque, she never lost her flavor of grace and elegance." There is the same combination of "Elizabethan" literariness with silver-fork didacticism—keep that flavor of grace and elegance, girls—as we found in Sayers.

To look at another contrasted pair of salvages will bring out the differences between the two writers in the kinds of problems each solves for us. These are Wimsey's saving of his sister Mary from communism, and McGee's saving of Dana Holtzer from emotional sterility. In *Clouds of Witness* Lady Mary Wimsey has a romantic attachment to George Goyles, a Communist agitator. She plans to elope with him on the eve of her wedding to a suave diplomat, in rebellion against her overprivileged fate—she is beautiful and ardent as well as rich and titled. Goyles is not worthy of her, being cowardly, petulant, and ineptly violent. He even fires a gun at Lord Peter when the latter accosts him in the Soviet Club in Soho. (Presumably this satirizes the 1917 Club of Gerrard Street founded by Leonard Woolf, Maynard Keynes, and Ramsay MacDonald, to be a place where young Bloomsbury left-wingers could dine, play Ping-Pong, and discuss revolution.) This sleazy establishment serves bad food and has "that curious amateur air which pervades all worldly institutions planned by unworldly people . . . mission teas . . . an air of having a purpose in life . . . sketchily trained staff." Its members talk pretentiously about modern art, cite D. H. Lawrence to each other, and make absurd plans to convert the sailors of the Royal Navy to communism. After Goyles has quite gratuitously wounded Lord Peter, Lady Mary is skillfully persuaded to go to lunch with Mr. Murbles, the Wimseys' family solicitor, who inhabits "a delightful old set of rooms in Staple Inn . . . mahogany . . . Turkish carpet . . . crimson curtains . . . Sheffield plate and decanter . . . Lady Mary felt a sudden gratitude for this discreet and solid Victorianism." Soon after she marries a policeman, Inspector Parker, who is Lord Peter's best friend but a very unaristocratic type. In fact, he too is discreet, solid, and Victorian. Thus she is able to satisfy her foolish preference for a deprived lower-class life-style without running any real risks. Lord Peter has discreetly saved her from Bolshevism, and incidentally conferred upon his rather dull friend a bride from one of England's stateliest homes.

In *The Quick Red Fox* Dana Holtzer is the inhumanly efficient secretary to glamorous film star, Lysa Dean. She has locked herself away from human contacts because she has been too deeply hurt by life. She had married an epileptic, had a child who must be institutionalized, and then had seen her husband shot through the head by a policeman, during one of his seizures. He too must be institutionalized, and she must earn the money to support them both by doing Lysa Dean's dirty work. This is why she is so withdrawn. Travis is very respectful and does not try to seduce her straight off, but gradually induces her to join him in arch verbal games, and thus melts her little by little, till finally she throws herself at him in Las Vegas. There she becomes all girl, cute and giggling and shy, casting all her efficiency aside. She begins to live again, to trust and love and leave responsibility to men. Unfortunately, she gets hit on the head by an oversexed murderess before her new personality is established—a dangerous blow with a primeval stone rabbit from Iceland— and when she recovers she has lost her new-found courage again. But in these books it is always necessary to leave McGee free at the end, because marriage does not have as high an imaginative charge in the American myth as in the British.

But the great difference between the two is that MacDonald's rhetoric is in the service of a physical, a bodily, imagination, while Sayers's serves a "cultural" and mental imagination. The relation of writer to hero is perhaps not so different. Sayers's personal unlikeness to Lord Peter is perhaps no greater than MacDonald's to McGee. On the book jacket photographs, MacDonald appears round-faced, round-fleshed, baby-skinned with wavy white hair and big round glasses. The McGee body, hymned so often in the novels by the hero and others, is the author's obsession rather than possession. It is of course the body of half the WASP heroes of the Hollywood screen and of James's Christopher Newman, and so forth.

Perhaps we might fairly consider McGee's mechanical equipment as extensions of his body: his Rolls Royce pick-up truck, Miss Agnes, his two boats, the Busted Flush, and the Muñequita. Much is made of these, and, as their names indicate, they are emotionally, as well as practically, important to him. If they are seen as extensions of his body, they continue the contrast with Lord Peter. The latter too has a fast car, but his important "equipment" is his title, his family, his position, and so forth. These are properties of his social self, not his physical self. He has acquired physical skills—McGee has acquired social skills—but his abiding identity is located elsewhere. While Wimsey has his Piccadilly flat and his manservant, McGee lives on his boat and is always tinkering with its machinery. He is extremely knowledgeable about money, particularly about land-development corporations but also about trusts and tax-dodges and investment dossiers. Mac-Donald writes about these things with an ostentation of technicality, a bewilderment of jargon that impresses the reader. This is just like Sayers's ostentation about high cultural *objets*, but MacDonald's hero relates to his country's financial and economic system, to the man's interest in the stock exchange, to the making of money, not to its spending.

Then McGee lives much more on the fringe of society than Wimsey, more on the edge of outlawry. He is sometimes in trouble with the police, which Wimsey never is. Wimsey is firmly rooted in the British elite, and cooperates with the police. The inspector he deals with is his brother-in-law, Charles Parker. But both are deeply concerned about the national life, and full of cultural comment. McGee is anti-corporation, anti-drugs, anti-plastics, pro-environment, but pro-Battista refugees. Wimsey is anti-communist, anti-bohemia, anti-modernist, and pro-Oxford and art and scholarship. And in sexual matters McGee is highly moral; his villains are all protagonists of cold or perverse sex, just as Wimsey is moral about class-feelings, and his villains are quite likely to be snobs.

McGee is a sexual aristocrat, by grace of enormous sexual

and fighting energy. He disposes of great power, and so is the object of extraordinary desire by women and envy by other men. He is the focus of as much excitement and attention from the moment he walks in the room as Wimsey is in England. And like Wimsey, his manner is self-deprecating, though in an American idiom. The natural extension of this extraordinary potency is his extraordinary wisdom, which shows itself in a very detailed and severe sense of what one may and may not do sexually and combatively. Different types of women, in their age and class and psychic categories, all have different claims on a man. And this wisdom is not phony, any more than Wimsey's. McGee knows convincingly what textures and materials, cuts and styles, each of his categories wears, exactly how they stand and eat and respond to a kiss, as well as exactly what to say and do to them.

Of course, MacDonald gets mixed up, like all pornographers, and we find ourselves invited to relish the evil as much as the good. He quite often has a villain who stands to McGee as Quilty stands to Humbert Humbert in *Lolita*, the shadow figure, very similar but going too far, and so to be destroyed. Above all, MacDonald is fascinated by the image of the female sexual athlete toward whom he has very strong feelings, both of excitement and admiration, on the one hand, and of reprobation and fear, on the other. In *Dress Her in Indigo* we meet Lady Rebecca Divin-Harrison, a combination of Hemingway's Lady Brett and H. Rider Haggard's She. She is a triumph of preservation and rejuvenation, and totally dedicated to the arts of love. Her husband and brothers all died in the battle of Britain and life lost all meaning for her. "So I vowed solemnly, ducks, to become the jolly best piece of Anglo-Saxon ass in all Christendom." McGee falters and trembles in the sexual contest with Becky. He is even temporarily mastered, and though he takes his revenge another night and reduces her to womanly subjection, he breaks off the relationship immediately thereafter. And at the end of the book, the villain turns out to be another sexual athlete, this time French, called Eva Vitrier. She is a brunette lesbian, but she has buried four husbands, and one is invited to see her as a shadow version of blond Becky—especially because in the meanwhile McGee has found real happiness with a group of sweet, giggly, humble Mexican geishas.

The figure of the sexually enterprising woman is naturally an important focus for this sensibility, and MacDonald's attitude toward it is no different from Mailer's (take Deborah in *An American Dream*) or Bellow's (take Madeline in *Herzog*). But it is notable how often McGee deals with this threat by running away from the woman. He even finds excuses for throwing such women out of his bed literally; this happens to two millionairesses, the Cuban in *A Deadly Shade of Gold* and the New Yorker in *Nightmare in Pink*. And in *Pale Gray for Guilt* there is an extraordinary sequence in which he keeps such a woman in a state of frustrated sexual excitement for a whole weekend by phoning with excuses and promises to be there soon. Naturally his attitude is highly moral.

> This was one of the new breed who assist the manipulators. . . .
> Sex with a particularly skilled and desirable woman who could
> convince you that you were the greatest thing since fried rice
> was a marvellous gadget for one of the manipulators. The be-
> dazzled male is incautious, mazed, thunderstruck. In that condi-
> tion he can provide the maximum benefit and the least problem.
> He will come trundling along in the entourage just to be near his
> brand-new love-light. He will tell her all he knows and all he
> hopes, and in a frenzy of team spirit she will bang him out of his
> mind and drop him right back where she found him when the
> manipulator has the last crumb of information he can use. . . .
> They [the manipulators] buzz around the country and the world
> in little groups, where everybody is always laughing, and at the
> resorts and airports and executive dining rooms, at the padded
> bars and the swinging casinos, in the groups there are always the
> Mary Smiths, pert, tidy, high-style, voracious and completely
> with it, eyes a-dance, freed by The Pill to happily pull down the
> game the manipulator fingers for her, the new Gal Friday who
> has become the Gal Friday Night. . . . She would be exquisite in
> all detail, from earlobes to cute little toes to the dimples at the
> base of the spine. She would be fragrant, immaculate, prehensile,
> and totally skilled, and she would ring all the changes, and pace
> herself beautifully, and draw me to her pace, and inflate my ego
> with her breathless astonishment at. . . .

This woman meets her fate in a brutally sexual stud called Hero, and in the later novels there is an increasing preoccupa-

tion with such men—McGees gone bad—who are often made
the villains. They are loathed, and often condemned to loath-
some deaths, sometimes of great brutality. And the sexual
women are sometimes sadistic too. In *The Long Lavender
Look* the villain is a girl of freakish physical strength. She is
so strong that she can lift a car, and she has an accomplice
waiting outside a window to kill the man who embraces her
when, in the moment of her orgasm, she will give the signal
and hold him in position. The whole complex clearly expresses a great fear of sex, combined with great enthusiasm
and fascination.

These are the features of MacDonald's interest in sex that
are the true equivalents of Sayers's snobberies. (He has also
similar failures of tone, sentimentalities like calling his car
Miss Agnes.) But much more than Sayers, he carries into the
world of popular entertainment the values and the techniques
established by the leading writers of his day. In his descriptions of action and of the boat, he emulates Hemingway, and
with considerable skill, while in his descriptions of sex he
follows Mailer, again at a respectable distance. Sayers did not
have such a relationship to her contemporary serious writers
—her similarity to Waugh is quite a different matter—but
rather to those more frivolous than herself like Wodehouse.
Her serious discipleship was to "the tradition," to Oxford
literary humanism, not to contemporary writers. It is notable
how often, and how unfavorably, D. H. Lawrence is referred to in her novels. *The Documents in the Case* (1930)
is a particularly striking example. (She herself said that this
was "a serious criticism of life, so far as it went.") The story
is told largely by Robert Munting, a poet, novelist, and
intellectual, who seems to derive some features from Aldous
Huxley. Munting writes a novel called *Deadlock*, which reminds him of *Point Counterpoint*, and is dark, thin, sardonic,
unpopular, nervous. His friend, Howard Lathom, is an amoral
artist, who seduces the wife of an elderly pedant in the name
of paganism: "She has the makings of a decent pagan soul
if one could teach her." He and she talk to each other about
"power," "beauty," and "emancipation." He has come to the
suburbs looking for "vitality." She, Margaret, is described as

being "not good-looking, but full of S.A. and all that." She is a prism, with no ideas of her own, needing an enthusiastic man to shine upon her and give her an idea of herself, whereupon she glows into life. Munting dislikes her, but admits that "this power of dramatization, coupled with a tremendous vitality and plenty of ill-regulated intelligence, has its fascination." He prefers her dry, scholarly husband, full of out-of-the-way knowledge, who is irritated by Margaret's enthusiasms and always snubs them, though he is very proud of her when she is not there. Munting (and Sayers) insists that Harrison *loves* his wife, and she *doesn't* love him.

Clearly this is a typical Lawrence story situation, interpreted the reverse way. But the interest is that the date of the novel invites us to wonder whether the Lady Chatterley scandal and the closure of the exhibition of Lawrence's paintings were making Dorothy Sayers write specifically about Lawrence and his own story. Margaret Harrison could be a hostile and ignorant portrait of Frieda, and her domestic situation was Frieda's in 1912. Lathom gives Margaret *Women in Love* to read, which she finds thrilling, like music, and a proof that the humdrum things in life don't really matter. "We shall build our temple of love." Soon after she persuades him to murder her husband. And the moral, presumably, is don't read D. H. Lawrence. This is one of Sayers's most ambitious attempts at a normative tract, combined with entertainment.

In *The Executioners* (1957) MacDonald made an interesting attempt at a wholly normative story in the form of a thriller. It does not include Travis McGee. *The Documents in the Case* did not include Wimsey, and both books are the poorer for lacking their heroes, but they make it clear how the two authors experimented and how they succeeded. MacDonald's hero, Sam Bowden, is a lawyer, a settled man with an absolutely typical and absolutely ideal American family. His ideal wife, Carol, is all woman, and reacts with primitive passion—"What kind of a man are you?"—while Sam believes in the law. His ideal daughter, Nancy, is just learning how to attract and hold boys. We are asked to note and admire her techniques, and his two sons are cute and funny. It is interesting to note how similar Sam is to McGee physically, and it helps one to see how much more successful McGee is. "The boys took after him," we are told. "Sandy-red hair, knobbly bone-structured, pale-blue eyes, freckles, over-sized teeth. It was evident that at maturity both boys would be like their father, incurably lean, shambling, stringy, tall men of physical indolence and ropy toughness. It would have been tragic if he had willed his only daughter such a fate." Girls have to be smooth and bright and sleek and curved, desirable objects, and boys have to be not that.

The family is threatened by Max Cady, a rapist of young girls, from the hill-people of West Virginia, with a feeble-minded mother and criminal brothers. We are told that dark hair grew low on his forehead and that he had small brown eyes set in deep and simian sockets. Sam tells his wife, "We all run in a pack—and he is a rogue beast." He is perfectly clear about the social substructure of legality and morality. "In our tidy little city of 125,000, Sam Bowden is reasonably well-known, and possibly respected. . . . I'm trying to say that I'm one of the boys. And the boys look after their own." But by the end of the book, Sam has been forced to give up trusting to the law and kill Cady himself. "I'm the king of this little tribe. I should be able to go put the fear of God in Cady. . . . My brood is threatened." The book is a ritual recapturing of the primitive sources of passion and aggression for the benefit of the average normal citizen, the average reader, rescuing passion and aggression, the life of the instincts, from the custody of the mad and the bad. This is in some sense what all the McGee novels are about, too, but less blatantly. While Sayers does not enact rituals of recapturing primitive passion, but the opposite rituals of re-signing the social contracts, regaining faith in the institutions and the intelligence and the taste of the past. (*Gaudy Night* was designed to show "intellectual integrity as the one great permanent value in an emotionally unstable world," Dorothy Sayers tells us.)

If we try to sum up all the differences between the two figures in one formula, we have to say that McGee is a much more *male* version of the detective hero than Wimsey. (The all-American rogue *male*, first cousin to Stephen Rojack, Steve

McQueen, and the guy next door.) Both are heroes of the
world of men, not of women; but McGee has the virtues of
the locker-room, Wimsey those of the drawing room. And
it is worth noting how many English writers of detective
stories—those with Wimsey-type heroes—have been women:
Margery Allingham, Agatha Christie, Ngaio Marsh, Josephine
Tey, and so forth. While the American writers of detective
stories have been men and have created *male* heroes. The
word *male* of course here conveys an enthusiasm, almost an
adoration. This is Promethean and Faustian man, the object
of America's worship over so long, the source of male
chauvinism.

The contemporary hero of this kind in England is James
Bond, and to return to Orwell for the last time, one might
say that England now has Raffles as written by James Hadley
Chase, and so has the worst of both worlds. Bond's adventures combine the sadism and immoralism of the one with the
social and class pretentiousness of the other. This is the
Americanized England that Orwell deplored at the end of his
essay, and it is undeniably significant that a leading English
novelist, Kingsley Amis, should have chosen to write a James
Bond adventure after Ian Fleming's death. It is all the more
significant that that novelist should have been one who began
his career as something of a follower of Orwell. Bond is
certainly a less attractive figure than any of the others we
have considered. There is no presence of ordinary England
or of normative concerns in these books. It is an England only
of clubs and espionage.

But though one cannot regard Bond as an encouraging
sign, one must regard him as a sign. It would be unhelpful
to treat him moralistically. One can say that treated mythically
he shows up the MacDonald myth as profoundly healthy by
comparison. Travis McGee is the hero of a strong, intelligent,
many-sided culture, though one obsessed with sexuality and
with male chauvinist sexuality, with its attendant nightmares
of emasculation and ambiguities of sado-masochism. Wimsey
was the hero of a self-doubtful culture, obsessed with class
and insistent that the dandy figure should take the place of the
figure of Anglo-Saxon virility which had been pre-empted

by America. And Bond is surely the hero of a corrupt culture, willing to "believe in" mere brutality of appetite, unrelated to any cultural idea. Above all, one can say that the Mac-Donald novels are much more interesting than Ian Fleming's, because they reveal the normative mind of their culture, working at a normal, alternately high and low, pitch of intensity. Like the Sayers novels, they give us a detailed scrutiny of its civilization by a highly moral and highly observant mind caught in that garrulous and unguarded mood in which we all tell most about ourselves. And that is what we go to detective novels for.

Chapter 10

ENGLAND AFTER 1918 I: OUR TURN TO CLICHÉ*

It seems that, after 1918, English culture gradually became riddled with cliché. The sense of *déjà vu* in matters of history and literature, of contemporary society and human types, of rhetoric and even of everyday vocabulary became so oppressive that people could hardly speak or write at all. On the topics their fathers had considered important or intimate, they had recourse to quotation marks and allusions and ellipses, to ironies and eccentricities of tone, to lispings and gigglings and affectations, because so many big words felt too philistine to use. and yet there was no way to renew them—no reason to believe one ever could renew the large meanings. This conviction spread sufficiently to amount to a profound imaginative and intellectual defeatism, and can be located at widely spaced and unconnected points of the culture. One can see a likeness between the habits of a certain kind of quoting, in matters of literature, a certain sense of period, in matters of history, a certain preoccupation with class and manners, but other new habits seem too disparate to connect by any "explanation" less vague than that there was "a turn to cliché."

Let me begin with two quotations from Waugh and Orwell. First of all, Waugh in *Labels*, 1930, discussing a "sense of

* This chapter appeared in the *Boston Arts Review* (December 1974), ed. Juan Alonso and Richard Burgin. Reprinted by permission.

period" and thus putting his finger on the meaning of "culture," as the English use the term.

> I do not really know how genuine or valuable this sense of period is. It is a product of the English public school and University education; it is, in fact, almost its only product which cannot be acquired far better and far more cheaply elsewhere. Cultured foreigners are lacking in it, and so are those admirably informed Englishmen whose education has been at secondary schools, technical colleges, and the modern Universities, or at the Royal Naval Colleges of Dartmouth and Greenwich. I am inclined to think that it is practically useless. It consists of a vague knowledge of History, Literature, and Art, an amateurish interest in architecture and costume, of social, religious, and political institutions, of drama, of the biographies of the chief characters of each century, of a few memorable anecdotes and jokes, scraps of diaries and correspondence and family history. All these snacks and tidbits of scholarship become fused together into a more or less homogenous and consistent whole, so that the cultured Englishman has a sense of the past, in a continuous series of clear and pretty *tableaux vivants*. This Sense of the Past lies at the back of most intelligent conversation and of the more respectable and worse-paid *genre* of weekly journalism.

Note how general is the function—"lies at the back of most intelligent conversation"—which Waugh ascribes to this Sense of the Past. It is the material core of all English culture. And note how trivial a thing he judges it to be, when measured by any larger criteria.

And now Orwell, during the war, showing us how that Sense of the Past was taught, and so how it could be counted on to be there at the back of every upper-class Englishman's mind, uniting them and distinguishing them from the men of "the secondary schools and the technical colleges." He is describing (in *Such, Such, Were the Joys*) how boys at his preparatory school were prepared to take the examination for the Harrow History Prize.

> They were the kind of stupid question that is answered by rapping out a name or a quotation. Who plundered the Begams? Who was beheaded in an open boat? Who caught the Whigs bathing and ran away with their clothes? . . . Disraeli brought peace with honour. Clive was astonished at his moderation. Pitt called in the New World to redress the balance of the Old. . . . I recall positive orgies of dates, with the keener boys leaping up

and down in their places in their eagerness to shout out the right answers, and at the same time not feeling the faintest interest in the meaning of the mysterious events they were naming. . . .

"1587?" "Massacre of St. Bartholomew!"
"1707?" "Death of Aurangzeeb!"
"1713?" "Treaty of Utrecht!"
"1773?" "Boston Tea Party!"
"1520?" "Oo, Mum, please, Mum—" "Please, Mum, please, Mum, Let me tell him, Mum!" "Well! 1520?" "Field of the Cloth of Gold!" And so on.

With Orwell at St. Cyprian's were Cecil Beaton (who had been at day-school with Waugh) and Cyril Connolly. Orwell won the Harrow History Prize for St. Cyprian's one year, Connolly the next. And Connolly went on at Eton to win the Rosebery History Scholarship to Balliol. In "A Georgian Boyhood" (1938) he says, "I had an excellent memory, I could learn by heart easily, gut a book in an hour and a half of arguments, allusions, and quotations . . . and remember them for just long enough to get them down in an examination paper. I was the perfect examinee." And in his novel, *The Rock Pool*, the hero is attacked in these words: "All you English boys are brought up on marks. You say you got marks for learning the collect, whatever that is, marks for taking out the best books from the library, marks for good conduct, for scholarships and examinations. Marks for every time you opened your mouth till you left Oxford, and now that they've stopped giving them, you don't know what to do."

The self-contempt there is important to us only insofar as it is connected with the self-knowledge—the sense of how his *mind* (and Waugh's and Orwell's) had been shaped by this education. And the central aspect of that education, from our point of view, is not its standardization of the students, but its standardization of the process of learning and of the history and literature learned.

After St. Cyprian's, Orwell like Connolly went on to Eton, where he was a contemporary also of Anthony Powell and Henry Green and Steven Runciman and Harold Acton. These people went on to Oxford, where they met Evelyn Waugh and Graham Greene and Peter Quennell and Kenneth Clark. Oxford was a confluence of people who had all been to such

schools, had had such an education, and out of it were building the culture they shared.

This was the intellectual material to which the imagination
of the dandy gave form, to which dandyism gave life. The
tableaux vivants of the past were just colorful clichés, but
modern middle-class life was all drab ones. So one turned back
to history, and art, and greatness, even knowing that all was
costume and pose. The Sitwells' books and life-performances
illustrate this scheme of values. Cyril Connolly may be said
to have made his life-work out of elaborating this sensibility
into a quasi-ideology. He has combined a strong sense of
period of the kind Waugh describes with the sensibility of a
dandy, to use his own phrase. "London is the capital of prose,
as Paris of art, or New York of modern living, and most of
this good prose is concerned with dandies or with slums or
with fog. . . . The London I like best is the one I can find
in books where it lies embalmed between 1760 and 1840, the
dandies still outnumbering the slums and the fog as yet barely
invented." But if this excerpt (from *Previous Convictions*,
1963) is typical, he more than other people has also turned
his attention on the modernist movement in the arts and on
the careers of the artists among his own generation. He has
brought the idea of the dandy into relation with all that. Thus,
in his critical essays we see again and again how attitudes
to literature and implicitly to politics belong together in the
essential cultural stance. For instance, he explains to us, again
in *Previous Connections*, why we *must* read French literature.
"The habit is unbreakable, for we need a literature whose
authors do not live on Green Line bus routes or lunch at their
clubs, whose civilization is observed through a sheet of glass.
. . . When we read too much English literature, we grow depressed by the unalterable bourgeois scene which has survived so many literary groups, even as it will outlast our own.
Oxford common rooms, London squares, Sussex cottages,
sausages, landladies, publishers' cocktail parties, Sunday af-
ternoons—one can fit almost every English writer into the
familiar scene. Tea is being served behind the house with
the blue plaque as expertly as when the great man lived
there. . . ." Thus dandyism did not die in the Twenties, nor

was its cultural material confined to history of the past. It was a sense of the present and future too. It was the English imagination. And in the fiction of the period, it is notable how many novels describe literal *tableaux vivants* or historical pageants to largely but not entirely comic effect. The most famous is of course Virginia Woolf's *Between the Acts*, which is all built round that event; but there were also Nancy Mitford's *Wigs on the Green*, and Anthony Powell's *From a View to a Death*, and others. Such events focused a lot of the dandies' sensibility, and attracted a lot of their energy in life as well as in art. There was much dressing up of that kind at weekends at Cecil Beaton's house, Ashcombe, and we often hear of Brian Howard appearing as Disraeli, Oliver Messel as Byron, or Harold Acton as Beckford, in various places.

This feeling for the historical pageant is closely connected to the feeling for history as concentrated in certain great houses. Behind Virginia Woolf's *Orlando* lies the history, the accumulated treasures and legends and records, of Knole, as becomes clear when one reads Victoria Sackville-West's *Knole and the Sackvilles*. That book came out in 1922, just after the war, and the same year saw Percy Lubbock's *Earlham*, about the great house in which he grew up. These books had many successors, including Elizabeth Bowen's *Bowen's Court* (1942), and John Betjeman's post-war television programs about old houses. These examples have been cited rather than others because of their special closeness to the fiction and poetry of their time; and besides Elizabeth Bowen's fiction, we must mention Joyce Cary's *To Be A Pilgrim* (1942) and Waugh's *Handful of Dust* (1934) and *Brideshead Revisited* (1945); and besides Betjeman's poetry, T. S. Eliot's *Four Quartets* (1943), also concentrated on particular great houses. The tendency of all such writing is to present history as a sequence of costumed episodes, to present it in terms of Waugh's Sense of the Past. (Raymond Williams's *The Country and the City* (1973) offers a convenient contrast, showing how differently history can be presented, even history seen in relation to the countryside. Williams is of course an anti-dandy.)

I myself have always had a strong sense of this. I remember deciding, when I prepared for my English Literature Tripos exams at Cambridge in 1948 that what one needed to get a First was a good sense of cliché. At least a feeling for it, if not a preference for it. Like most radical insights, this was no use. It could not be applied. At least I've always supposed that one reason I did so badly in those exams was that I overdid the commonplaces; that is to say, I showed a bad sense of cliché. But I still feel that it was an insight; that this was more true of these exams than of others I have taken since and more true of England than of other countries I have known.

By a cliché I mean primarily a standardized opinion, a judgment expressed in a phrase or sentence so standardized as to deprive it of all intellectual sincerity. But I also mean the taste or enthusiasm behind that judgment and also the object of that taste whether aesthetic or not. A poem or a building or an emotion or an institution like marriage can all become clichés, by becoming the object of a standard enthusiasm. When this happens a sensitive person must keep silent about them, or make them the butt of hostile irony, or—and this is what English culture after 1918 mostly did—*play* with them: ring the changes on them, invert them, exaggerate them, interweave and embroider them, stand them on their heads. And by extension cliché means the quotation, allusion, example by means of which—like so many handles—these ideas are grasped in order to be played with.

It happened that the habit of quotation and allusion was a particularly prominent one, and a particularly revealing index of this playfulness in England. Virginia Woolf's novels and her Common Reader essays are a high-level example of this, applied to literature. She makes constant allusion to and quotation from a narrow range of books, mostly English and French, and mostly eighteenth- and nineteenth-century "classics"—a word which in itself sums up the taste we are talking about. Rosamund Lehmann's *Dusty Answer* has a whole section of quotations from English poets to evoke her heroine's experience of Cambridge. And Dorothy Sayers's characters engage in the most extraordinary contests and cooperations of allusion, again to a similar range of books. In intention, these authors offer us the opposite of clichés—they are always wincing away from the standardized—but in effect it is a banquet of *different* clichés, saved from commonplaceness by being played with. The effect of all three authors is to make the reader feel that a certain range of literature (one notably lacking in challenge, adventure, or contemporaneity) is the whole universe of intellectual achievement, the whole humanist tradition, and that all that spontaneity can mean is playing within it. And the effect of the lectures at Cambridge I went to (with the exception of Leavis) was the same. Not that the standardization was flatfooted and monotone—quite the opposite. The pressure we felt was betrayed by our escapes *from* cliché—those escapes were what we were learning. But we were thus being highly sensitized *to* cliché, and we felt ourselves distinguished from other people by that sensitivity —by that shared sense of period, and power of quotation, and taste for epigrammatic summary, which Waugh and Orwell point to. And by a sensitivity to the "too obvious" wherever we found it.

Thus one thing that has distinguished the English from the Americans' sense of humor, sense of tact, sense of manners, has been the greater sensitivity of the former to clichés of behavior. There is a story of Matthew Arnold visiting Amherst which illustrates that. He had had various American breakfast specialities pressed on him by an effusive hostess, and when she then offered the blueberry pancakes (or blueberry muffins or whatever) to his wife, he endorsed them by saying something like, "Oh yes, try one, Lucy, they aren't half so nasty as they look." The point of the story is that the offense given was unwilling, even unwitting until the remark was out. And its motive was Arnold's need to avoid the clichés of enthusiasm and politeness that his hostess was inviting from him. That situation in which an American drives an Englishman to some anti-enthusiastic expression, which both then feel to be offensive, is the archetype of many social misunderstandings between the two peoples.

I don't know when to date the growth of that habit among the English to the status of a major national trait, but I should guess that it was post-Victorian, and coincided with the rise to power of the dandy. It is obviously closely connected to the growth of irony within the mode of humor, and a less good-humored irony than the American, a more defensive bristling of irritability. And that seems to have come to flowering after 1918. One can see why that might be so in the political history of those years. The patriotic propaganda of the war had been so contradicted by the experience of the men in the trenches that all loud patriotism was discredited. To some significant degree, so were all the social faiths in the major mode. There was much that worked indirectly to undermine naïveté and promote cynicism, in that slaughter of a generation and that decline of Britain from its world pre-eminence. One might say that the jokes of Beatrice Lillie, Noel Coward, Lytton Strachey, Aldous Huxley, Evelyn Waugh, all in different ways struck the same note. It was the humor of the dandy.

One example, which neatly ties the habit of quotation together with the confrontation with America, is the humor of Evelyn Waugh's *The Loved One* of 1946. The English poet, Denis Barlow, woos the American girl, Aimee Thanatogenos, by sending her poems. But she is so naïve, and he is so sophisticated, so intellectually dandified, that he copies out anthology war-horses, and changes the girls' names to Aimee, and claims them as spontaneous effusions of his own feelings for her. We are told that Aimee majored in Beauticraft, and took Art as a minor one year, though Psychology and Chinese were her real minors. Her mind is a mass of clichés, but naïve ones. She does not play with her clichés, and she knows nothing of the standardized culture he knows *so* well—so much *too* well. When Aimee discovers Denis's deception and reproaches him, he replies:

> I should be disillusioned that I have been squandering my affections on a girl ignorant of the commonest treasures of literature. But I realize that you have different educational standards from those I am used to. No doubt you know more than I about science and citizenship. But in the dying world I come from quotation is a national vice. No-one would think of making an after-dinner speech without the help of poetry. It used to be

the classics, now it's lyric verse. Liberal M.P.s constantly quote Shelley; Tories and Socialists don't get up and complain of being disillusioned when they learn that their ornaments are not original. They keep quiet and pretend they knew all the time.

This joke focuses shrewdly a general difference both nations have felt separating them—a very important feeling for England because it meant that America had usurped the functions of health and vigor and responsibility for Anglo-Saxon manhood, and that Englishmen must be dandies. So it is interesting that the joke and the difference could be expressed so naturally in terms of literary clichés.

In the 1920's, and for the men who became the leading writers of their generation in England, the dandy pose was struck outside as well as inside the limits of literature, above all by Brian Howard and Harold Acton, who became protégés of the Sitwells while still at Eton and who enacted the rebellion of the dandy for a whole Etonian and Oxonian generation. They symbolically overthrew domestic decency, flouted "father" and "mother," "work" and "home" in a way that captivated the imagination even of many who disapproved. (Waugh and Powell, for instance, disapproved of Brian Howard, and formed their own lives on very different models, but their sense of humor and their whole sensibilities were strongly influenced.) From the dandy's point of view, all of ordinary life was a series of clichés, and one "saw" only the fantastic, the eccentric, the resplendent or the preposterous. The most distinguished expression of this in verse was T. S. Eliot's early poetry.

From this time on, one may say that the characteristic names of British literature were of the order of Sebastian, Sacheverell, Basil, Osbert, Julian, Adrian, Lytton, Evelyn; instead of, as in the previous century, Charles, William, George, Emily, Charlotte, Jane, David, Thomas. (That "George Orwell" changed his name *to* George indicates how insistently he swam against the tide.) In literal fact, the fancy names were given before 1918 and by late Victorians. Sir Leslie Stephen named his daughters Virginia and Vanessa, and Leonard Huxley named his sons Aldous and Julian—names for princes or heroes of romance. But this is not a real anachronism. The protest against the values of the Victorian consensus, against plain living and high thinking, had begun in the 1890's. Indeed, names like Oscar and Aubrey and Dorian had been given before then. But it was left to the 1920's to carry the protest through and establish it in the national imagination. After the war had so badly damaged the confidence of the establishment, people were ready to respond to the fantastic (to *façade* and "Pierrot Lunaire") and to lump together all the old pieties of all clichés.

But it was only the boldest spirits who really committed themselves to dandyism. And they came to disaster. That is, the later careers of Howard and Acton after Oxford were not successes, and in England generally the aesthetes themselves achieved very little, so that even those dazzled by dandyism at Oxford turned back to being scholars and gentlemen. For the average English bookman, to discover that the old pieties were clichés did not mean to turn away from them, but rather to embrace them more consolingly and self-consolingly than before. For the more intellectually and morally rigorous, it meant to revive old orthodoxies that had lapsed during the pre-war liberalism—particularly religious orthodoxies, as the names of Waugh and Eliot will remind us. They renegotiated the old contracts, on stiffer terms. But they all remained imaginatively dazzled by the style of the dandies. Aestheticism and reaction made an alliance. And even the orthodoxy of the left was staffed by ex-dandies, who remained true to their original vocation—this was Orwell's complaint against them.

The major voice speaking against dandyism was that of D. H. Lawrence, speaking for Demeter against the ephebic Dionysus. Though one can find plenty of poems of his, among *Pansies* and *Nettles*, which belong to the rebellion against domesticity. There are even some fine stories, like "Two Blue Birds," which are almost entirely mocking and dandified. And there is that anecdote of his remark to Mabel Luhan, which makes him sound like a cousin of Brian Howard. But on the whole, Lawrence proclaimed the great alternative. And those people who have learned from him, Leavis and the school of *Scrutiny*, have spoken for marriage and the home and domestic pieties. That is the ultimate meaning of the quarrel between Leavis and the Sitwells.

This is a matter of literary form and techniques as well as of moral values. One sign of Lawrence's difference from all other modern British writers is his lack of clichés. In everyone else one finds that strong sense of things already categorized and standardized, which spread quite outside the range of "humour," and over people who were not dandies in any other sense. For instance, the characterization, the conversation, the description, nearly all the formal items in a Graham Greene novel, rely heavily on our accepting standardized categories of human personality and of social relationship. The novelist gives us a cue, a character's profession or his clothes or his accent, and we immediately feel we know all about him, and can fill in the rest of his dossier ourselves. The unsuccessful private detective, who is small and meager with watering eyes and frayed cuffs—the reader can go on from there, predicting in advance a whole series of traits, of character, belief, habit, and fate, which Greene will attribute to him. The same is true of opposite types, like the coarsely bouncing barmaid of *Brighton Rock* and the quiet American and the homosexual. The same techniques are employed in the serious Catholic novels. The point is insisted on, that these human beings *are* clichés.

Now of course all art relies on some system of conventional signs. If a character is given large eyes, we are set to find him/her sensitive or beautiful or some interesting variant on those. That Lawrence does not use clichés does not mean that he uses no system. It means that he "makes it new." Whereas Greene's work insists on the old, stale, conventional quality of his system. This is what gives the ideologically modern flavor to his work, and distinguishes it from that of Somerset Maugham. Maugham's clichés are not *obtruded* upon the reader; they are offered as a convenient shorthand for his range of experience. Greene insists that we notice the shorthand and give up our illusions that experience should be more than this. This accounts for his flavor of seediness even when he is describing something exotic or flamboyant. Implicitly, he is telling the reader that the number of human possibilities is so limited that all experience falls into patterns —patterns of disappointment, of course, but above all patterns. This implicit message of his form thus confirms and is confirmed by the more explicit ideology of his work.

The same is true of Evelyn Waugh's work both as a satirist and as a Catholic novelist. The more explicit ideology cooperates with the formal shorthand that tells one everything about a character in a single line of dialogue. We accept it from Evelyn Waugh that anyone who would say the few words that Lady Granchester says about Lady Metroland must be rich, titled, dowdy, stuffy, and so forth. In this case, there is a thrill of conscious wickedness for the reader, in agreeing to accept this, to himself make such snap judgments and so despise dull people, which makes Waugh's use of cliché more attractive than Greene's. But culturally the significance of the two novelists' strategies must be the same. It is a slighting of human possibility.

This is, I take it, a received opinion about the Catholic writers of the time. It will also be easily granted perhaps that the British detective novels and science fiction and romance and entertainments in this period relied heavily on the reader's sense of cliché, of standardization, in depicting people and places. I mean that in the work of C. S. Lewis, Dorothy Sayers, Somerset Maugham, where one might expect to find something apparently fresh, one does not. I am not saying that they were not creative novelists, but that as romancers their materials were obviously and complacently standardized. They used clichés with an emotional resonance which varied from case to case, but which had always some ring of "let's be comfortable." (That stress on comfort is what made them not ideologically modern, like Greene, who offered discomfort.) "The people who try to escape the traditional, to create and explore," they say, "always turn out to be either pushy or shady, don't they?" They say this not only in terms of events and values but also in terms of form and technique. This comfortableness is what makes these books so soothing, as much as their descriptions of desirable manners and meals and charming people. In other words, this is a very conservative formal convention.

But in all the authors of the post-war period, the most large-scale and significant mode of cliché thought and feeling was class thought and feeling. Characters, by means of not only their clothes, speech, and ideas but also localities, houses, landscapes, whole towns, are insistently placed on the class-scale, and everything else about them is related to that placing, if not *explained* by that. Authors act as though they confidently thought that class was the only thing that mattered, though really they are expressing a doubt about, an incapacity to believe in, the life-enhancing alternatives. Thus a lot of the snobbery of British light fiction in this period—and of British behavior outside fiction—is to be counted as intellectual conservatism as much as social. These perspectives are what make Dorothy Sayers, Nicholas Blake, Michael Innes, and some others so interesting.

And what is so striking about English culture after 1918 is the way this reliance on class cliché spread across the whole range of literature, and up into the heights of talent—often, of course, accompanied by other manifestations of dandy temperament. For instance, Charles Tansley in *To The Lighthouse* and Doris Kilman in *Mrs. Dalloway* are good examples of this class-shorthand; and they are also said to be very "uncharming," an adjective that expresses a central stress of dandy sensibility. We need not mention Virginia Woolf's comic charladies or her "mothers of Pimlico" who "give suck to their young." The disastrous thing artistically is not that the author has so much passionate interest in class, but that she has so little—that she uses class clichés. One need only think of Proust to realize that a passionate interest in class ("morally" no better than hers) could be a motive force of great fiction. Nor is it lack of talent or simple failure in writing. One need only think of E. M. Forster—he also failed with the Basts in *Howard's End*, but one need only think of them to realize that Forster was trying and Virginia Woolf wasn't—she was using class—characterological clichés.

And from her novels descended a long line of similar works, down to *Mrs. Miniver*. One quite insipid example that won serious consideration in its day was Rosamund Lehmann's *Dusty Answer*, which came out in 1927, and had had eight impressions by 1928. Its middle-class heroine, Judith Earle, wants to be accepted by the beautiful, brilliant, upper-class Fyfes. She goes to Cambridge, which is very romantically evoked, and adores the beautiful, brilliant, decadent Jennifer Baird, and is adored by the ugly, common, hard-working Mabel Fuller. In the portrait of Mabel the class prejudice is morally crudest, but the romantic clichés about the upper-class types are even more distressing intellectually.

This novel derives its major interest from these Cambridge episodes, just because the university novel became in this period one of the classic forms for dealing with class themes. Both *Gaudy Night* and *Brideshead Revisited* are strikingly like *Dusty Answer*. (It is no accident that, as I pointed out, the Sayers and the Lehmann novels are both festivals of cliché quotations. Oxbridge was the major float in that carnival of paper flowers.) In all three the central consciousness represents the middle or professional class, but meets at Oxbridge some brilliant and dashing example of the upper classes, and casts off his/her dull, cocoa-drinking antecedents. Judith Earle's Jennifer in *Dusty Answer* is a silly equivalent of Charles Ryder's Sebastian in *Brideshead Revisited*, and Mabel Fuller is a vulgar equivalent of Charles's cousin Jasper. And in *Gaudy Night* Harriet Vane, who is after all a more interesting version of Judith Earle, meets in Oxford Lord Peter Wimsey (much the same thing as Lord Sebastian Flyte, as the names indicate) and therewith she too shakes off the dull and earnest companions of her youth. Symbolically, this is an example from standardized middle-class reality into fantasy. Oxbridge in fiction and in life was the Checkpoint Charlie of the British class-system, and there was plenty of publicity for any individual who made it across to the land of titles, the land of fantasy. But even this adventure was standardized, and needed to be played with. Evelyn Waugh tells us in his autobiography that he had read all the Oxford novels from *Sinister Street* on before he went up, and knew exactly what he should find there. Harold Acton tells us that publishers asked him to write an Oxford novel when he came down, but he knew it had already been written—*Žuleika Dobson*. Waugh of course found what he expected, what he wanted, and followed it up out of his middle-class origins, up into the land of faerie. It is no accident that along with his enthusiasm—for "Brideshead"—went an appalling boredom, along with his appetite for the fantastic, a distaste for more and more of reality.

Nor is this feeling that ordinary things in England are standardized a thing of the past. Perhaps the most generally respected novelist now writing in England makes as much use of class-and-character cliché as any of those we have mentioned, and with the same effect of imaginative conservatism. Anthony Powell was at Eton and Oxford with Harold Acton and Brian Howard. He belonged to the generation whose imagination they imprinted. In his novel series, *The Music of Time*, all the interest derives from the recurrence of the same faces at different places in the gridwork of time, place, and status. The people are interesting because of their movements across that gridwork, not for their intrinsic life. Their faces do change, but the changes are observed from outside, and occasion curiosity rather than concern. Any passionate interest the reader might have, though the phrase is inappropriate, would go to the social gridwork. That is why Powell's war novels are his best. During the war years that social gridwork bulked so large, bore down on individual lives so heavily, that it *was* a large part of our experience. In the peace-time novels, when his characters are building their own lives, their own fates, one is oppressed by how little the author feels about them, how little importance he can ascribe to them. He relies essentially on standardized categories to convey to us their psychology, their character, their interests, and so forth. Though he goes on to point out in what contradictory directions of interpretation such conventional clues lead one, the effect is not to make one want to know these people in some more substantial and immediate way, but only to make one conclude that nobody can be known.

This conviction amounts to imaginative defeatism, and it is to be found in various forms in many British writers of the period. In *The Acceptance World*, Powell has his hero, Nicholas Jenkins, say, "I began to brood on the complexity of writing a novel about English life, a subject difficult enough to handle with authenticity even of a crudely naturalistic sort, even more to convey the inner truth of the things observed. Those South Americans sitting opposite, coming from a continent I had never visited, regarding which I possessed only the most superficial scraps of information, seemed in some respects easier to conceive in terms of a novel than most of the English people sitting round the room. Intricacies of social life make English habits unyielding to simplification, while understatement and irony—in which all classes of this island converse—upset the normal emphasis of reported speech."

The things that differentiate one English person from another and so specify each one's personality are too subtle for a writer to record. V. S. Naipaul quoted this passage, in an essay in the *Times Literary Supplement*, and said that Powell "gets to the heart of the matter." He suggested that these difficulties were the cause of the fact that so many English writers were depending more and more on "gimmicks." He remarked on how often he had heard people in England deplore the disappearance of "characters," and agreed that English life presents quite peculiar problems to the imaginative writer. This is what I have called imaginative defeatism.

It was paralleled by an intellectual defeatism of which the most important example is no doubt the obvious one, the absence of Marx and Freud from the British literary scene. (There have been moments, like that created by John Strachey's popularizations of Marx in the 1930's, which prevent one from saying that they have never been present on the *intellectual* scene, though their disappearances from it each time have been very complete.) This absence is particularly striking because of the contrast provided by the American scene in the same years. In Britain, moreover, centrally placed individuals certainly were acquainted with both Freud and Marx—Auden and his circle provide one good example, and Virginia Woolf's nephew and niece were psychiatrists. But these interests remained curiously private, entering public discussion with a note of quaintness, and imaginatively ineffective. Virginia Woolf herself could not be persuaded to consult a psychiatrist in her illness, and Auden's evocations of his "healers"—in country houses at the ends of drives—made them seem eccentricities. A representative British figure is Aldous Huxley, who "kept up with" everything, but discussed the new ideas in old-fashioned rhetoric. At the end of his life he still used the same quotations from Blake and Wordsworth as he did at the beginning. He still had the same standardized "humanist" taste, after all those experiments with drugs and religion. The same thing was true of George Orwell, who insisted on defining his political radicalism in the most old-fashioned of terms, and who created his novels out of well-worn materials.

The only new ideas that were translated into a passionate and unself-consciously contemporary style were the ideas of D. H. Lawrence, translated by F. R. Leavis. These were offered as saving truths that needed no ironical quotation marks round them, needed no playing with. But there was a limitation to Leavis's contemporaneity, because he insisted on relating Lawrence to George Eliot and the British past. Moreover, a striking feature of Leavis's intellectual career has been its negativeness—the new ideas he has refused to deal with, for one reason or another. He has refused, for instance, any tincture of the Freudian or Marxist categories or those of philosophical aesthetics. This British provincialism has had many admirable aspects, but they cannot disguise the central fact that this was a provincialism, expressing a distrust of new possibilities of intellectual life. And in most cases of university intellectuals, there was nothing admirable about it. But this conjunction of Leavis with the others was, I think, the source of my feeling about the Tripos that in order to succeed I should *cultivate* a sense of cliché. He never implied I should do that, but he did imply that to try for *new* ideas was to invite intellectual and moral as well as practical failure.

At the other end of the scale of importance from exam techniques, this sense of cliché expressed a failure of faith in all human possibility. The adventure of life-renewal begun by Lawrence was not followed—the worship of Demeter was neglected for that of the ephebic Dionysus—for the dandy style and aestheticism. There was imaginative potential in *that*, of course. But one of the most striking events of the period in England was the *failure* of the aesthetic movement there. The ideas of that movement—ideas represented by the names of Diaghilev, Cocteau, Stravinsky, Picasso—were brought to Eton and Oxford and London in the 1920's by eager publicists. But in a sense, that was all. The strongest characters of that generation, Eliot, Leavis, Orwell, and Waugh, all turned decisively away from aestheticism, as we shall see. It had mostly a negative influence, devaluing the ordinary, and the positive influences were repetitions of old pieties. No new gods were worshipped. The sense of cliché was turned in upon itself, and it was precisely the old formulas that were to be endorsed again, the old rules that were to be enforced. In the imaginative work of Orwell and Waugh this policy has both dignity and pathos, but even as they expressed it, it could not lead others out to imaginative life. England after 1918 gradually lost imaginative life.

Chapter 11

ENGLAND AFTER 1918 II:
WAUGH AND ORWELL
AS CULTURE CRITICS

There is a rather striking parallelism and contrast between the life and work of Evelyn Waugh and those of George Orwell. They were born in the same year, 1903, and into roughly the same class situation, though Orwell's father worked in the Indian Civil Service, while Waugh's was a publisher's editor and literary journalist. They both went to prep schools and then public schools, and, being very clever boys, seemed destined to rise by scholarships to join their country's ruling class. And both, Orwell at Eton and Waugh at Oxford, came in contact with dandy-aestheticism in the persons of Harold Acton and Brian Howard. But though both rejected the dandy's irresponsibility, they themselves balked at the university section of their own upward progress and at everything planned for them by their families and their class. Waugh took only a third-class degree at Oxford, having refused the university's discipline, while Orwell refused to go to a university at all, and joined the Burma Police instead. In 1928 he came back to England, determined to drop down socially out of his class and to immerse himself in the experience of being one of society's rejects. This led to his first book, *Down and Out in Paris and London*. Nineteen twenty-eight was also the year when Evelyn Waugh also may be said to have left his class, but he rose up out of it, by becoming engaged to Lord Burghclere's daughter. He had cultivated titled friends at Oxford, as he had neglected the middle-class disciplines of work. Now he found a way to turn that experience to literary and monetary profit by writing *Decline and Fall*, which is about the aristocracy, and by marrying into the same class on the proceeds.

These were opposite books, in nearly every way, but both turned away from the new aestheticism. Orwell committed himself to an opposite reality, vowed, as it were, never to even refer to dandyism. Waugh devoted himself to it as a subject, but made a conservative-ironic judgment on it. (In his life of Rossetti, published the same year, his tone is as moralistic and conservative as Orwell's, or Leavis's.) More obviously, and just as importantly, both turned away from middle-class, middle-of-the-road England.

In the 1930's both men committed themselves to large-scale social and ideological movements, and their books reflect that. Waugh joined the Roman Catholic Church, and wrote a Catholic biography of Blessed Edmund Campion. Orwell joined the Socialist movement, and wrote *The Road to Wigan Pier* for the New Left Book Club. Both traveled abroad and became involved in foreign wars, though their sympathies lay with opposite sides. Orwell fought against Franco in the Spanish Civil War. Waugh sympathized with Franco, and reported on the Abyssianian war on Mussolini's side, which Orwell hated.

During the war against Hitler, however, both were enthusiastically on the same side, enthusiastic at least while Russia as well as Germany seemed the enemy. This was presumably because Waugh, like his character Guy Crouchback, felt that he was fighting against the whole modern world, while Orwell had decided that, however bad the British Empire had been, it had been replaced by something much worse in the totalitarian empires of the twentieth century.

Both were in this sense deeply conservative and patriotically British, and both were soldierly types.

After the war, both produced striking satires, *Animal Farm* and *The Loved One*, satirical attacks, one on Russia, the other on America. And both wrote successful novels, *Brideshead Revisited* and *1984*—very different in style, form, and subject, but both written in warning against the future and in celebration of the past. When *Brideshead* provoked serious attacks from everyone else on the Left in England, Orwell defended it, and planned a five thousand word essay on Waugh for the *Partisan Review* though he was too ill to complete it. And in 1950, as Orwell lay dying, Waugh was one of the last men to go to visit him. Opposite as they were in ideological position, one can well imagine that they respected each other, not only for their literary talents but also for their personal integrities. They were of similar temperaments.

Moreover, they were both brilliant cultural historians. Both men's books are marked by lists of the points that characterize contemporary types of men, houses, towns, newspapers, lectures, parties, and so forth. *Coming Up For Air* and *Put Out More Flags* map different parts of modern England, and from different points of view, but both are much concerned to map it. England's reaction to war approaching in one case, to war present in the other, is crystallized for us in *typical* conversations, moments of panic, plans of action, and so forth. The infinitely various national scene is clarified for us by a typology whose intellectual vigor is one of each book's major achievements.

Both authors build for us representative modern men with representative modern experiences, of course painful ones, Tony Last in *A Handful of Dust* and Gordon Comstock in *Keep The Aspidistra Flying*. It is quite explicitly a portrait of the modern experience, as it feels to most Englishmen, that each novelist is working at here, and it stands or falls largely by the authenticity of its design and its detail.

Finally, both authors extend their cultural history into autobiography. Orwell does this explicitly, in Part 2 of *The*

Road to Wigan Pier and in "Such Such Were the Joys," and implicitly in *Keep The Aspidistra Flying*. This autobiographical cultural criticism is brilliantly done and has been widely recognized—it is one of the two or three major categories of Orwell's achievements, so there is no need to describe it again here. For our purposes, we want to mention it only in order to claim an analogy between it and Waugh's unrecognized work of the same kind. Waugh extends cultural history into autobiography in *Brideshead Revisited* and *Unconditional Surrender*. *Gilbert Pinfold* of course also reports autobiographical experience, but it is personal rather than cultural in its interest. The other two books' autobiographical revelations are of cultural-history interest, though its focus is primarily literary. It is Waugh's autobiography as a writer that he obliquely discusses with us. In *Unconditional Surrender* he implicitly condemns *Brideshead Revisited* as "trash" (and mentions Dorothy Sayers to show what he means by trash), as a novelette though one of enormous length, as "inspired" by a death wish the author completely yielded to, and as a riot of sensual and sentimental vulgarity. And he places it (shrewdly) among the other books of that cultural moment in England which "would turn from the drab alleys of the thirties into the odorous gardens of a recent past transformed and illuminated by disordered memory and imagination." Waugh says there were half a dozen English authors then "averting themselves sickly from privations of war and apprehensions of the social consequences of the peace," and preparing to compose such books. Presumably he was thinking of Nancy Mitford, Angela Thirkell, Anthony Powell, and so forth among whose works *Brideshead Revisited* (though more interesting) must be placed.

He even suggests that the war trilogy itself is not much better—at least that its "heroine," Virginia Troy, "sounds like the heroine of Major Ludovic's dreadful *Death Wish*." He clearly, though obliquely, says that Virginia was a version of the same idea as Myra Viveash in *Antic Hay*, and Iris Storm in *The Green Hat*, and Brett in *The Sun Also Rises*, the last of "the exquisite, the doomed, and the damned, with expiring voices."

Waugh thus places himself and his work on the map of the imaginative history of his times. But he does so, in *Unconditional Surrender*, by very crude artistic means, by in effect abandoning his form, by dropping his attempt at a novel and speaking through it and about it to his readers and himself. In *Brideshead Revisited* (this is why it is so interesting) he talks about his development and the development of his whole group *within* the novel. There is a fable at the heart of it that is an implicit cultural theory of England after 1918, which we can compare with Orwell's better-known theories.

It is usually agreed that the central character of *Brideshead*, Charles Ryder, represents Waugh. He has been given exactly Waugh's age, his years at Oxford, and his career there. He has the same relation to his family, has the same unfortunate first marriage, and has a career as artist that is strikingly parallel to Waugh's. Charles makes a great success painting English country houses with charm; Waugh made his success writing about English country houses with humor. (In *Work Suspended* Waugh makes the man who represents him a writer of detective stories—the three activities have the same cultural character.) Both men escape from their unsuccessful first marriage to find happiness with another woman. Both find ultimate peace in the Roman Catholic Church.

The novel begins in Oxford, and the first thing we see Charles do is fall in love with Lord Sebastian Flyte. Sebastian takes Charles on a picnic in somebody else's car, with strawberries and white wine, after which they lie on the grass. "Sebastian's eyes on the leaves above him, mine on his profile." The magic door into the walled garden of romance has opened for Charles, we are told. After an austere school life, and alienated family, he finds love and wit and beauty and style all in one. And this love is anarchy, "The hot spring of anarchy rose from deep furnaces where was no solid earth, and burst into the sunlight—a rainbow in its cooling vapors—with a power the rocks could not repress."

A contrast is drawn between all that Sebastian represents to Charles and all that his cousin Jasper represents, which is the prudent, middle-class, career-oriented attitude to Oxford. Even more interesting is the effect on Charles's taste which is ascribed to Sebastian. He arrived at Oxford with Bloomsbury taste.

> On my first afternoon I proudly hung a reproduction of Van Gogh's "Sunflowers" over the fire and set up a screen, painted by Roger Fry with a Provencal landscape, which I had bought inexpensively when the Omega workshops were sold up. I displayed also a poster by McKnight Kauffer and Rhyme Sheets from the Poetry Bookshop, and, most painful to recall, a porcelain figure of Polly Peachum which stood between black tapers on the chimney-piece. My books were meagre and commonplace —Roger Fry's *Vision and Design*; the Medici Press edition of *A Shropshire Lad*; *Eminent Victorians*; some volumes of *Georgian Poetry*; *Sinister Street*; and *South Wind*—and my earliest friends fitted well into this background. . . .

But immediately after his first lunch with Sebastian, "when at length I returned to my rooms and found them exactly as I had left them that morning, I detected a jejune air that had not irked me before. What was wrong? Nothing except the golden daffodils seemed to be real. Was it the screen? I turned it to face the wall. That was better." Exit Roger Fry—the influence of Bloomsbury is ended—and it is the work of Sebastian. Collins, one of Charles's intellectual friends, had exposed to Charles the fallacy of Bloomsbury aesthetics. "But it was not until Sebastian, idly turning the page of Clive Bell's *Art*, read, 'Does anyone feel the same kind of emotion for a butterfly or a flower that he feels for a cathedral or a picture? Yes. I do,' that my eyes were opened."

Sebastian represents that Etonian version of modern aestheticism that Brian Howard and Harold Acton brought to Oxford, and Ryder/Waugh turn away from Bloomsbury to follow it. First, he comes to know Sebastian's Oxford and then Brideshead, the house to which Sebastian drives him on that first expedition, the great baroque mansion with the fountain imported from Italy; and beyond Brideshead stands Venice, which is the imaginative domain of Lord Marchmain, Sebastian's father, a Byronic voluptuary and magnifico. These are the perspectives of beauty, art, sensuality, magnificence, the Renaissance. But Lord Marchmain has been defeated by his wife, and Sebastian can represent those perspectives only in child-like, playful, nursery form. His addiction to his teddy bear is serious as well as playful, a real refusal to grow up. Sebastian stands for the pleasure principle, that which *must* be superseded by the reality principle. The latter is represented by Lady Marchmain and her eldest son, Bridey, both devout Catholics, who accept the Church and all its juggernaut truth. We are told that Bridey's face looks like an Aztec sculptor's version of Sebastian's and that Lady Marchmain's brothers, also Catholics and war-heroes, have the same primitiveness in their faces.

They (and Cordelia Flyte, simple and good) stand in polar opposition to the brilliantly overdeveloped and decadent mind of Anthony Blanche, who was drawn from Howard and Acton and who stands for modern aestheticism. Between those two poles Sebastian is fatally divided. He cannot bear adult reality of either kind. He takes to drink and achieves only spiritual redemption as a church acolyte.

Between those poles Charles also will be divided. But at the moment of choosing between Sebastian and Jasper, all the Bridesheads and Blanche seem to be in the same party. Charles then sees boldness and brilliance in Sebastian, and meets Anthony Blanche in his company as a natural extension of Sebastian. Anthony also flouts middle-class seriousness and conscientiousness; he also lives for beauty and wit; he also inhabits exotic terrains of the imagination. But his challenge to his enemies is much more vigorous and risk-taking. While Sebastian is the object of homosexual love, Anthony declares himself its agent. While Sebastian discovers quaint and charming corners of past taste, Anthony explores modern and foreign art. While Sebastian's rebellion against the world of authority and responsibility is implicit and playful, Anthony's is explicit and aggressive. The former refuses to grow up, but remains a wholly delightful child, the latter riots in elaborate and fantastic but malevolent blasphemy against every British tradition of respectability and type of success. While Sebastian inhabits Brideshead and Marchmain House, the English past, Anthony inhabits contemporary Paris and Berlin.

Anthony recognizes Charles's artistic gifts and tries to claim him for modernism. He invites Charles to dinner, offers him friendship, tries to turn him against Sebastian, warns him against the fatal effect on his art of his love for Sebastian. He says that Charles will be, as an artist, "strangled with charm." Charles refuses Anthony's friendship and sees only malice in his warnings. This is the crucial moment in the story, though its full significance is not made clear until later. Charles is afraid of Anthony. He is afraid of his flaunted homosexuality, of the size and scope of his rebellion against the normal, the traditional, the decent, of the modernist art towards which Anthony tries to direct him. He chooses Sebastian.

He chooses the quaint and the charming, and turns away from the dangerous and the bizarre. Sebastian is not interested in Charles as an artist or in modern art. His rebellion in aesthetics as in other things is purely playful. Anthony is associated with Cocteau, Diaghilev, Picasso, with modern art at its boldest. Charles prefers the art of painting British country houses. He prefers charm. But when his first exhibition is held, Anthony attends it, and he alone understands what Charles is doing and what has gone wrong with his artistic development. He tells Charles that he has succumbed to English charm in just the way he had warned him against in their conversation about Sebastian. And Charles admits that Anthony is right. Anthony is established as He Who Knows. He has been right all along and about the author himself. Charles is bored by his wife, by his art, by his friends, by everything. (In *Gilbert Pinfold* Waugh portrays a terrifying boredom in a character who is obviously autobiographical.)

The reader therefore feels that he must go back to that first conversation, take Anthony more seriously, ask what his analysis means, when translated from remarks about Charles Ryder into remarks about Evelyn Waugh. Waugh, we are to understand, passed up some opportunity represented by Anthony Blanche, and therewith wasted his artistic vocation. One can see easily enough how Waugh's novels could seem inadequate to him, when measured against his sense of his own talents. But what contemporary artistic alternative could Anthony stand for? In what direction was Waugh pointing when he hinted at that artistic possibility which he himself had betrayed? Howard and Acton were not themselves great novelists, and I think it is clear that the Sitwells did not seem to Waugh to represent great art. It seems likely that if he was thinking of anyone in particular it was Proust; there are reminiscences of *A La Recherche du Temps Perdu* in *Brideshead*—orchestrated themes of memory and romances of manners—and Anthony's homosexual persona and fate also suggest Proust. And it *is* likely that Proust's example was a great lost opportunity to English literature, because so many of the Bloomsbury and dandy writers tried to imitate features of his work without similar acts of courage and self-commitment. But whatever Waugh was at that moment thinking of, a modern reader might get a better sense of the possibility Charles Ryder missed by thinking of Vladimir Nabokov. The art of *Lolita* particularly is one that can be legitimately aligned with that of Diaghilev, Cocteau, Picasso, Proust, and it conveys a vivid sense of an artist's career, lived out in defiance of social morality and ideology, during the same years as Waugh wrote.

While he was writing *Brideshead Revisited*, Waugh wrote in his diary how much he regretted being unable to describe his hero's sexual experiences in the same detail as he was devoting to his eating and drinking, and defined himself more than once as an artist, whose moral obligations and concerns led him in directions opposite to those of men of action—both very Nabokovian themes. Moreover, more than once in his later work, Waugh can be seen attempting Nabokovian subjects—the fathering of *Brideshead* on to Ludovic in *Unconditional Surrender* (the construction of an alter-ego corrupt aesthete, like Nabokov's Clare Quilty in *Lolita*) and the whole fantasy experience of *Gilbert Pinfold*. Waugh's artistic destiny brought him to Nabokov's subjects in those books, and his failure with them is owing to his lack of Nabokov's artistic techniques. Anthony Blanche, we can safely assume, would have loved *Lolita*. Waugh, willfully, did not, just as, like Charles Ryder, he willfully rejected "modern art." The moral scheme he offers is of course that Charles Ryder and he had a greater vocation than that of artist, that of Christian. But to read (in Frances Donaldson's book) that Waugh suspected Nabokov's novel of being a plot to corrupt public morals by decorating pornography with literary jewels, is to feel that here is another example of how right Anthony was and how high a price Charles paid for rejecting him.

Charles chose Sebastian, which was in the long run to choose Cordelia and Catholicism, because Sebastian represented only an antithesis within the Catholic dialectic, the pleasure principle that must succumb to reality. Charles gives up Sebastian when he sees his weakness, and passes by way of Julia (like her father, a figure of *grown-up* beauty and sensuality) to Cordelia, the devout Catholic. His chance of painting a really great picture, a really brilliant piece of modern art, disappears almost without another word. *Brideshead* was of course a Catholic novel, and Waugh proclaimed other values than the aesthetic. He wanted to show the proper subordination of aesthetic values to religious ones. That is why he could regret being denied the freedom of obscenity and still disapprove of Nabokov's using it. He was quite ready to think that he had had to give up "art" for "religion." But for us the fate of "art" is the most important in the book, because it is the fate of the English imagination. More than Waugh's work as a writer was at stake in Charles Ryder's choice. All the writers of Waugh's group chose with him the engagement of a generation hung in the balance. To choose Sebastian was to choose dandyism in a fatally half-hearted form, to choose aestheticism and modernism while hanging on to tradition and beginning reaction. Sebastian represents that fatal compromise, that combination of the riskily elegant and the dowdily safe, which England as a whole did choose.

It is this fable, in some sense concealed within the book, which redeems it from a blatant vulgarity (obvious not only in the descriptions of food and wine but also in the names and the architecture—*everything* is overdone) and a very unpalatable and unconvincing "Catholicism." Nor can the rest of the book engage our attention at a very high level. The eroticism of the affair with Julia is too Parnassian to be interesting. The alternation of sex and romance in her appeal for Charles (the alternation of the pornographic succubus and the hollow-cheeked *quattrocento* sadness) reminds one too schematically of the alternation of herself and Sebastian before. This is a fatally theoretical and stiff-jointed eroticism, like something out of Mario Praz. To compare it with *Lolita* is to see Waugh as a non-starter. But the concealed fable is very richly rewarding, because what it says about Waugh is corroborated by the successes and failures of his other work, and also by the successes and failures of other writers of the time.

Here we can perhaps call on the testimony of W. H. Auden, talking about Max Beerbohm—but talking also about himself in relation to Max Beerbohm.

> Greatly as I admire both the man and his work, I consider Max Beerbohm a dangerous influence—just how dangerous one must perhaps have been brought up in England to know. His attitude both to life and to art, charming enough in him, when taken up by others as a general cultural ideal becomes something deadly, especially for the English, an intelligent but very lazy people, far too easily bored. . . . "Good sense about trivialities," he once wrote, "is better than nonsense about things that matter." True enough, but how easily this can lead to the conclusion that anyone who attempts to deal with things that matter must be a bore, that rather than run the risk of talking nonsense one should play it safe and stick to charming trifles. . . . he slyly suggests that minor artists may look down their noses at major ones and that 'important' work may be left to persons of an inferior kennel, like the Russians, the Germans, the American, who, poor dears, know no better. The great cultural danger for the English is, to my mind, their tendency to judge the arts by the values appropriate to the conduct of family life. Among brothers and sisters it is becoming to entertain each other with witty remarks, hoaxes, family games and jokes, unbecoming to be solemn, to monopolize the conversation, to talk shop, to create emotional scenes. But no art, major or minor, can be governed by the rules of social amenity. The English have a greater talent than any other people for creating an agreeable family life; that is why it is such a threat to their artistic and intellectual life. If the atmosphere were not so charming, it would be less of a temptation.

I would suggest that one can take Beerbohm to represent, in terms of writing, what Sebastian represented in terms of personality, and that Auden is speaking from the position of Anthony Blanche. Waugh, like Auden, delighted in Beerbohm, and one can take Auden's later artistic strategy, his distrust of England as a whole, as deriving from a fear of such Sebastian-figures, endowed with all that charm on which both writers so insist.

Perhaps Wodehouse even more than Beerbohm should be taken as Sebastian's literary equivalent, because he has been the private vice of so many of the dandy writers. In 1973 a volume called *Homage to P. G. Wodehouse* included enthusiastic essays by Lord David Cecil, Claud Cockburn, John Betjeman, Malcolm Muggeridge, Compton Mackenzie, and Auberon Waugh; and if Evelyn Waugh had been alive he presumably would have contributed also, for he had written often and well about Wodehouse—in the naughty style appropriate to the subject, semi-seriously hyperbolic. Among those who did contribute, Auberon Waugh wrote the most interesting essay, and one of the things he said may be usefully added to Auden's remarks about family life, and may link them back to *Brideshead* in particular. He tells us that his ten-year-old daughter has just begun to appreciate the Wodehouse books, that his own youth was "entirely rescued" by them, that his father and grandfather both loved them. When one thinks of the sharp conflicts between Evelyn Waugh and his father, the sharp oppositions between their tastes, one can see how useful to *that* family life, and many others, must have been a taste like this which could be shared just because it was so innocuous. Wodehouse was and is the kind of author who can be read aloud on evenings of family tension because everyone will enjoy him, just as at Brideshead Lady Marchmain would read aloud Father Brown stories or *The Diary of a Nobody* on such evenings. Implicit in such scenes is the conflict between the needs of family life and those of the intellectual and artistic life. Waugh was certainly as aware of that conflict as Auden, but he *liked* Wodehouse and Beerbohm and the rest—*liked* them willfully and naughtily—liked them as self-destructively as Charles Ryder had liked Sebastian.

And it was the whole of English dandyism, in some sense, which chose Sebastian over Anthony, which fell for charm, played safe, and lost. We already have pointed out how like to Waugh's world is that of Anthony Powell's and Nancy

Mitford's fiction; how like to Waugh's sensibility is that of both Dorothy Sayers and P. G. Wodehouse; how strikingly his passion for architecture parallels that of John Betjeman and the Sitwells; and how like his literary taste is that of Cyril Connolly and Peter Quennell. There are even significant likenesses between Waugh's art and that of Virginia Woolf and Aldous Huxley. Waugh does things that both of them attempt, and he carries those things through to artistically successful completion. In *Mrs. Dalloway*, for instance, the preference for the aristocracy as fictional subjects, the interest in handsome mansions, and particularly country houses, the small scene technique, the sampling of different social levels, the primary social stress on clubs and ballrooms: all these things. In *Point Counterpoint* we think of Waugh even more significantly, because there Huxley is trying to speak for D. H. Lawrence, but his voice is not even apprenticed to Lawrence's—it is apprenticed to Waugh's, or rather sounds as if it were.

Lawrence's presence was of course felt in this period, and he was calling people away from either accepting or refusing Anthony Blanche's invitations. And Leavis's voice, also calling to people to merely turn away, has continued to stand for a different cultural option. So has Orwell's. Orwell's criticism of left-wing intellectuals was not unlike Waugh's. Both rooted themselves back in traditional Englishness and repudiated the dandyism that lay beneath modish Marxism as well as beneath aestheticism. Waugh, as early as *Rossetti*, tried to align British aestheticism with Rossetti and Ford Madox Brown instead of with Burne-Jones, and so to connect it with intellectual and moral masculinity. But of course his imagination was imprinted with dandyism at Oxford, and when he wrote comedy it was dandy comedy. Even when he wrote as a Catholic and spoke for the Reality Principle, most of what he had to say, and his most characteristic voice, was the opposite of Lawrence, Leavis, and Orwell.

For of course Waugh and Orwell represent opposite imaginative options, if one concentrates on their work and on the most striking and authentic tones of each voice. Orwell chose to fix his affections and admiration on the average man;

Waugh loved the brilliant, the fantastic, the exceptional. Dobbin or George Bowling are the opposite of Margot Metroland or Basil Seal or Sebastian Flyte. (In Waugh's war trilogy Guy Crouchback *is* a Dobbin, and Ivo Claire, the brilliant and beautiful dandy, is a traitor, and so the most important strains of feeling are quite Orwellian. But just for that reason, it seems to me, the trilogy is not Waugh at his best. Certainly, it is not what I here mean by striking and authentic Waugh.) Orwell stood for decency, Waugh for outrageousness.

And to some extent we can see subsequent British writing in terms of these two options. We can see Doris Lessing as Orwellian, Anthony Powell as Waughian. Above all, we can see Kingsley Amis, perhaps the liveliest fictional talent to emerge since their deaths, as following Orwell to begin with and then switching to Waugh. In *Lucky Jim* and *That Uncertain Feeling* and *I Like It Here*, the imagination is controlled by an Orwellian conscience, by sympathy with the underdog and hatred of the pretentious and phony. But Amis was always on guard against Orwell, as his Fabian pamphlet shows, and with *Take a Girl Like You* he declared himself a Cavalier and not a Roundhead after all. Since then he has appeared consistently as anti-Left, politically and imaginatively, and his gestures remind one more and more of Evelyn Waugh's. *The Anti-Death League* even shows a very Waugh-like attitude to the army.

In making this switch, Amis probably showed the right instinct as a novelist, despite or because of the opprobrium it brought him. The left-wing virtue and decency of which Orwell was the greatest example became a righteousness in the England of the 1950's, and for other people besides Amis —though particularly for him—represented a constraint on imaginative truth, a restraint of imaginative life. Indeed, that is probably still true today, as I shall argue in another essay. But the point to which we must return is the antithesis between these two imaginative options—between Waugh and Orwell (and Lawrence and Leavis). Because it is disciples of the latter option who have made the major criticisms of modern British culture, and directed the modern cultural conscience, No one has read Waugh while asking the questions one asks while reading Orwell. So it is time to realize that he has something important to add to what Orwell (and Lawrence and Leavis) say. He can tell from the inside the story of twentieth-century dandyism in England, what went wrong with it, and what it meant to the writers who were fascinated by it. He has authority by virtue of his (dialectical) involvement in the movement himself.

Since the heritage of Lawrence and Orwell has passed from Leavis to Raymond Williams, the need to confront and assimilate the testimony of Waugh and Nabokov has grown greater. We have innumerable essays on Lawrence and Orwell and the great tradition, from the party of righteousness, but nothing on Waugh. Left-wing radicalism has been petrified into a rigidity that falsifies its imaginative truth. Perhaps it can be brought to life again by having it embrace the complementary truths that Waugh represents. Both heritages bear vitally on the tragi-comic plight of the British imagination today, and both are necessary to redeem it. Donald Davie has been calling for a "new aestheticism" in British poetry, and the same is true for the novel and for criticism.

Chapter 12

ENGLAND AFTER 1918 III:
LITERARY VALUES
AND LEFT POLITICS

I am in an uncomfortable position here,* offering to criticize the faith and the purposes of the other members of the conference, standing outside and—to that extent—against what brings them together. And it is doubly uncomfortable when one's own standpoint is liberal and yours is radical, because there is inevitably something feeble about a liberal. From your point of view, and even from my own, I have gone half way and stuck, refusing to let go of what stands behind me, even though I want what stands ahead. Once one admits the existence of a radical position on any question, the liberal position is bound to feel half way.

This is a humiliating feeling. I find myself involuntarily

---

* This essay was a talk given at a *Slant* conference in Birmingham, England, in 1967. *Slant* was a Catholic-Marxist magazine, linked to Sheed and Ward, Ltd. In those days, both the magazine and the publishing house specialized in aggressively radical papers and books. The talks given at this conference, for instance, were brought out as a book with the title, *From Culture to Revolution* (London: Sheed and Ward).

identifying with Ambrose Silk in Evelyn Waugh's *Put Out More Flags*. Ambrose, you may remember, is much troubled by this half-way feeling in his ideological disagreements with Parsnip and Pimpernell, the politically radical poets who presumably represent Auden and Isherwood, at the beginning of the war. I quote. "I can't come all the way with you," he said once to Parsnip and Pimpernell when they explained that only by becoming proletarian could he hope to become a valuable writer. "I can't come all the way with you, dear Parsnip and Pimpernell. But at least you know I have never sold myself to the upper class." And he has a vision of himself walking through some aristocratic neighborhood, sternly refusing the solicitations of dukes and their butlers.

We are told that Ambrose always speaks nodding and fluttering his eyelids and as though with a repressed giggle. "I belong," he says, "hopelessly, to the age of the ivory tower." He has of course lost his manhood, a fact which goes naturally with his ideological position in the novel. "I belong, hopelessly, to the age of the ivory tower." What I shall say is bound to end up, after all my circumlocutions, sounding not essentially different from that. So you must expect a touch of malice in my criticism. A liberal in radical company feels his manhood always under imputation.

At the same time, Ambrose Silk is, in the comic mode, a serious figure, a serious representative of Waugh himself, and of one major trend in modern literature, the elegant and mandarin and aesthetic trend. He is, for Waugh, a major artist, and for me too his experience and his testimony have some validity. He has some right to speak and to be heard, on these questions of literature and ideology, as one representative of the literary mind. The part of literature he represents, and the position on these matters he dramatises, is not of course radical. Neither is it liberal. It is conservative. But it has its validity. It does represent a considerable bloc of experience and achievement in our time.

The criticism I am going to make of the idea of a common culture is from the point of view of the literary mind. I shall confine my attention to what you have to say about literature, what you imply about it, and the use you make of it. I would not feel confident enough of my own thinking to make any criticism from a political or philosophical position. So my relevance is in one sense quite partial. But literature is, like politics and like philosophy, something you make use of in your synthesis, so you must listen—in a tough-minded way, of course—to the reactions of those who try to speak in the name of each speciality. And it is a part of my argument that the use you make of literature has been quite crucial to your whole enterprise. So, if you accept my argument, my criticism is in fact quite important.

My argument is going to be made up out of two propositions. That you derive significant moral and intellectual authority from your references to literature, and that that authority is in certain significant ways illegitimate. As you can forsee, I shall spend most of my time arguing the second point, but I must devote a little attention to the first, or you will always be able to say, whenever you feel in danger of assenting, "That is probably true in general, in the abstract, but it does not apply to us." However, I don't want to demonstrate this first point in detail, with references to particular books and authors, because most of them are present at the conference. This fact both makes the task of reference a case for elaborate literary-polemical manners, and also makes it largely unnecessary.

(After I'd finished talking, some people reproached me with not naming names, and said my discreetness made my whole point vague to them. Other people said they knew exactly what I meant. But as an essay in print I must expect this to catch the eye of a much less specialized audience, for some of whom the relevant passages *will* jump much less immediately to mind as parts of their recent experience. So let me say—as I said then, in discussion—that I would apply the analysis in my paper to the work of Raymond Williams. I would apply it to other people's work, too, and in some cases with more confidence in it as a complete diagnostic criticism, but he has such a special place in the intellectual hierarchy of the New Left—he was quoted so reverently by so many members of the conference—that he must be the one the pebbles are slung at, like the first Goliath. So let me say that I think

Williams's achievement as a whole depends quite a bit on his achievement as a critic—that is, on the quality of his purely literary work—and that that quality suffers from the radical consistency of his beliefs, the systematization of his mind. His taste, as contrasted with Leavis's, expresses a temperament which has externalized its conflicts, and this makes for authoritarian processes of thought and platitudinous formulations. I hope I needn't say there is a great deal to admire in his work—I have learned a great deal from it myself—but when he is made so much a model of imitation and a source of authority, it becomes necessary to protest. As a purely literary figure—and he is that, whatever else he is—he is an eccentric, and so as a champion he is as vulnerable as he is formidable, a Goliath.)

I presume we can all agree that there is a remarkably large number of pages devoted to the discussion of literature in books and essays about the common culture—in *Slant* books in general. That many of these are closer to being literary criticism than to any other conventional category. That much of the discussion of ideas and of experience has a marked flavor of literary criticism. That other things, for instance, the other arts, are notably less often referred to; music, painting, film have no comparable place. And that these references are not merely illustrative. They are the sources of some major sanctions, both by means of their own splendor of expression, and by means of the professionalism with which you handle them. That you present yourselves as —among other things—priests of the muse of literature. Literature, you make the reader feel, has spoken on your side.

Obviously, since I am not naming names or citing passages, I cannot work out my case fully; I must leave it a little loose and general. There are some of you to whom what I am saying applies less than to others, some to whom it applies very little. My claim is that it applies to the group as a whole, in the work it has published, the part of itself it has made public.

To specify a bit more, though still non-personally, there seem to be two main ways in which you invoke the authority of literature. The first is as a philosophical model. The way literature works illustrates for us the way other kinds of reality work. The two premises of this are that the various kinds of reality have been explained to us up to now in other models, which this will improve on; and that we are all agreed about how literature works, which means for instance how the relations between a work of art and the common culture explain the quality of the work of art.

This use of literature as a model has many branches. For instance, it includes a theory of symbolism, in literature and in religion. It includes an epistemology which stresses the activity of the subject's imagination in the act of knowledge —an epistemology which therefore, like Coleridge's, assigns a very important role to the aesthetic kind of knowledge. It includes a theory of the sacred. Here I must quote and name, because I don't understand well enough to adapt without falsifying:

> The answer to the problem is to see the sacred not as a separated category but as an illuminating one, to see it not as arrogating meaning to itself but as bestowing it on the whole. This involves the further sense that the sacred is not a *possession*, to be jealously guarded and hoarded, but as a means of understanding, participation, and service. It is, in a word, representative; and I would suggest that it is so in a way analogous to that in which works of literature are representative.

That is Vincent Buckley's idea about Brian Wicker's very similar idea of the sacred in *Culture and Theology*. I quote it, as I cited those other ideas, just to remind you how often a sentence like that last one turns up in *Slant* and *New Blackfriars*.

I don't myself get much out of either of the two lines of thought I called premises to the model of reality argument. At least if I restricted myself to their bearing on literature itself, I think I could show that they aren't very profitable. The negative applications, of course, I can agree with. I quite see the disadvantages of understanding experience as split between hard categories of subjective and objective; and I quite see that the romantic theory of lonely genius will not explain what we admire in, say, Shakespeare. But the positive applications are not so clear to me. The common culture theory of literature seems to me just as tangential to an author like Dostoevski as the romantic genius theory does to Shakespeare. But, as I said, I don't fully understand those lines of thought, especially in their non-literary bearings, so it would be presumptuous of me to object at length. I had better pass on to the other main way in which literature is invoked.

This is by means of citing names of authors, titles of books, quoting poems and passages of prose, using dicta and insights, which derive from a certain literary taste, a tradition of criticism and of the authors that criticism prefers. That tradition in criticism is best identified by the name of Leavis, and in terms of creative work by that of Lawrence. There are of course ways in which *Slant* authors move outside and against that tradition and that taste, but they seem to me to do so without ceasing to belong to it. What they like and the way they like it, and even more perhaps what they dislike, ignore, instinctively pass over, bears all the marks of the same intellectual and moral temperament as Leavis's own. This becomes clear as soon as one thinks of other important critics, their taste and their temperament. The family likeness is obviously to Leavis.

This invocation of literature is less explicit, less rational, less philosophical than the other, but I assume that it is no less powerful. For instance, one of those two premises I mentioned was an agreement about the way literature works; an agreement which in fact you find only within this tradition of literary study; and without which—here I am guessing—the model of reality argument would lose much of its power, wouldn't it? But there is something even more important. I assume that, to put it crudely, the figures of Leavis and Lawrence, their total careers, their achievements, work for you as guarantees that a concern for literature can be combined with a concern for culture in a way that invigorates both the concerns combined. The concern for literary critical values in Leavis becomes more exact and exacting, more lively and more spontaneous, in purely literary terms, because of his concern for other things. And his concern for culture, for social values and life values, becomes more complex and more scrupulous, more discriminatory and more passionate, because of its testing and its dramatization in literary terms.

Now I think that that is true. But I think it is also true that Leavis combined his two concerns in a way that you are not imitating, that you would not want to imitate, that is really a liberal-individualist's way. He insisted on the primacy of his literary interests over his potential, social, etc., interests; he insisted on the autarchy of his own temperament and taste, in ways that made the two together express a passionate individualness. The primacy of the literary interest is evident mostly in his practical criticism; but whenever any question of primacy came up, he insisted on it in principle as well as in practice.

In "Under Which King, Bezonian?" he says,* "But to identify *Scrutiny* with a social, economic or political creed or platform would be to compromise and impede its special function . . . one does not necessarily take one's social and political responsibilities the less seriously because one is not quick to see salvation in a formula or in any simple creed." That is unexceptionable in its manifest content, but I think we are justified in pointing out the latent content of a phrase like "not quick to see." Leavis said that in 1932. It is now 1967. He has not indeed been quick, and I think we have the right to say he never intended to be quick, in any relevant sense of the word "intend." The duty to choose any creed, any policy, is one he has found indefinitely deferable, as long as it was in competition—as it was always in competition—with that other duty to maintain critical standards, to discharge the special function of *Scrutiny*. He declined to line up behind either the Marxists or the Anglo-Catholics or anybody else. And he has continued to refuse. His ideological battles have been frequent enough, but they have been over other issues and on his own ground, where he was not behind anybody else. The primacy of the literary interest has been closely related to the primacy of his private judgment, of his individual self.

* *Scrutiny*, 1, 3 (December 1932), 205–14.

Now of course the idea of culture has been very important to Leavis. In the same essay he says:

> A culture expressing itself in a tradition of literature and art—such a tradition as represents the finer consciousness of the race and provides the currency of finer living—can be in a healthy state only if this tradition is in a living relation with a real culture, shared by the people at large. The point might be enforced by saying (there is no need to elaborate) that Shakespeare did not invent the language he used.

This is the kind of sentence *Slant* writers most often quote from Leavis, and the kind of idea in which they feel most at one with him. But surely they can feel that only because the phrasing is so loose that the sentence can mean different things to different people. The living relation with a real culture that invigorates literature can only mean to Leavis —on the evidence of his critical judgments—any lively, vivid, interesting relation, including the relation of negation, of rejection, of self-dissociation. If Shakespeare did not invent the language he used, Henry James did; in the sense that its relation to that shared by people at large was so ironically condescending as to be transformative and appropriative. The taste that can respond so much to James as well as to Shakespeare is a highly flexible one, and if you stretch the formula I quoted to accord with all its judgments, you will make it so elastic as to be shapeless—meaningless. And if you find you have to choose between keeping Leavis's cultural formulas and keeping his practical criticism, there can be no doubt which is the more valuable. The formula must be abandoned, at least as something given meaning by Leavis. If it *is* true, you must make it true. Leavis's use of it gives it no weight, no precision, as a tool of abstract thought.

Again, he has entitled one of his best books *The Common Pursuit*, and he has made much of the idea that all literary study is cooperative, is a matter of saying, "This is so, isn't it?" "I find this here, what do you find?" But his practice has surely been essentially different from his theory; and his essential achievement is surely that of an unrestrained individualist. One could guess that the ideal of cooperation and cultural solidity derives some of its value for him just from being an unachieved intention; and from being a defence against the inner necessity of unadapted egotism. His support, his value as an emblem, goes properly to other liberal-individualists, not to common culturists.

It is significant that that very book takes as its epigraph a quotation from James which repudiates cooperation (November 11, 1912):

> For me, frankly, my dear John, there is simply no question of these things; I am a mere stony, ugly monster of Dissociation and Detachment. I have never in all my life gone in for these things, but have dodged and shirked and successfully evaded them—to the best of my power at least, and so far as they have in fact assaulted me: all my instincts and the very essence of any poor thing that I might, or even still may, trump up for the occasion as my 'genius' have been against them, and are even more against them at this day than ever. . . . I can't go into it all much—but the rough sense of it is that I believe only in absolutely independent, individual, and lonely virtue, and in the serenely unsociable (or if need be at a pinch sulky and sullen) practice of the same; the observation of a lifetime having convinced me that no fruit ripens but under that temporarily graceless rigour, and that the associational process for bringing it on is but a bright and hollow artifice, all vain and delusive.

It seems to me there is a good deal of conviction behind James's writing of that, and behind Leavis's choosing of it. Of course literary study is a common pursuit for him in some sense, but that must seem a very abstract sense when we remind ourselves of the gusto with which he has acted out the role James describes there. Not to mention the savagery of his attacks on both rivals and apostates, and the unrestrained fullness of flow of both his pride and his vanity. It was surely himself he was thinking of when he added, as another epigraph to *The Common Pursuit*, that quotation from the Knut Hamsun obituary notice: "The Norwegian Society of Authors gave him a loving cup, but he asked them to scratch off the inscription, and give it to somebody else." Isn't *that* Leavis's true note? Isn't *that* the clue that leads us to the source of his power? Individualism is after all a source of power. I take it we haven't got to the point of denying that.

Surely it is clear that this individualist dissociation and detachment in Leavis, as in James, this absolutely independent, individual, and lonely virtue, is not merely a matter of personal temperament, while the idea of a common pursuit and a common culture is his message? To me at least it seems clear that that passionate individualism is a matter of intellectual temperament, and has much to do with everything he achieved intellectually. After all, who could be more different from each other, in merely personal temperament, than Leavis and James? It is a matter of intellectual salvation which drove them both to this extreme privacy of individualism. Without it they would not have been, it seems clear, great writers of the kind they were. The kind of common pursuit they could engage in, the kind of common culture they could be part of, must be of a very abstract kind, and of very little relevance, I would have thought, to concrete political and social enterprises or even thinking.

As for Lawrence, we all think at once how he complained that the societal instinct in him had been ruined, and declared that the societal instinct was the deepest thing in man, deeper than the sex instinct itself. That seems to me not only a very poignant thing for Lawrence to say about himself, but a very true thing for anyone to say about Lawrence. But Lawrence said many true things about himself, some of which are quite opposite in tendency. I should have thought it quite improper to pick on any one of those things as the sum of Lawrence's wisdom, or any one of those tendencies as the source of Lawrence's vitality. Improper, that is, to do so on the evidence of Lawrence's own experience, and Lawrence's own analysis of that experience. Of course, if you know beforehand, on other grounds, what must be the source of his strength and what the source of his weakness, then you need not hesitate to say so. But you do need, in that case, to admit the purely illustrative role Lawrence is playing in your argument. He is not proving your point for you. He proves an opposite point equally well; and neither point conclusively. What his total evidence comes down on the side of is the value of a passionate inner dialectic between two principles.

Lawrence was of course marvelously aware of just how belonging to the right community benefited the individual, and of just how belonging to the wrong community harmed him—whether the family community or the city or the state or the whole civilization—and of the agonies and deformations of the individual who has cut himself off from all community. But he remained aware also of the opposite, more nineteenth-century values of self-reliance, of individualism, of the personal integrity and intensity of truth that derive from a man's renouncing every kind of social sanction and communal reassurance. It is in *Kangaroo* that he argues out and acts out the conflict between the two tendencies in himself. And he decides in favor of individualism, though with a bitter sense of defeat in having to choose one and reject the other.

The major form given to the societal tendency in *Kangaroo* is political, in the sense of a national political party and political policy. What Lawrence has to say about politics that is political seems to me of very little value, but what he has to say about the conflict within Richard Lovat Somers between politics and privacy, between the societal instinct and the individualist, seems to me very interesting and very impressive. Lawrence's gift for representing sympathetically and forcefully the point of view he is fighting against, for imposing his own rationalization of the issues on a highly resistant representation of them, that gift is at work in *Kangaroo* as brilliantly as anywhere else. Lawrence is telling the truth there, and we should pay attention to what he says.

For instance. "So he discovered the great secret: to stand alone as his own judge of himself absolutely. He took his stand absolutely on his own judgement of himself. Then, the mongrel-mouthed world would say and do what it liked. This is the greatest secret of behaviour: to stand alone and judge oneself from the deeps of one's own soul." And the political and cultural consequences of this are made clear in a passage like this. "The individuality which each of us has got and which makes him a wayward, wilful, dangerous, untrustworthy quantity to every other individual, because every individuality is bound to react at some time against every other individuality, without exception—or else lose its own integrity; because of the inevitable necessity of each individual to react away from any other individual, at certain times, human love is truly a relative thing."

The love he is referring to there is the love of a man for his mate, the modern political passion. But the analysis is of course relevant to the love of man and woman, and the struggle between Somers and his wife. All the themes of the book are in fact shaped and controlled by the central idea of a conflict between the individual's relation to himself, and his relations to other people and things. What Lawrence rejects love in the name of is God, the God who is the source of all passion; once go down before the God-passion, and human passions take their right rhythm. And this God-passion is essentially private and individualist.

The chapter everyone remembers from *Kangaroo* is "Nightmare" and the whole point of its powerful and disturbing rhetoric is Somers's inability to accept any invasion or mitigation of his privacy. This principle is so large for him that it subsumes the whole phenomenon of the Great War and the whole issue of conscripted military service; both become mere examples of the invasion of privacy; and it is so passionately important a principle that he declares he would die if it were denied in him. "If ever," he said, looking up from his own knees in their old gray flannel trousers, as he sat by the fire, "if ever I see my legs in khaki, I shall die. But they shall never put my legs into khaki."

Lawrence admits fully the irrationality of what he is saying, and makes that admission the guarantee of his seriousness in saying it. It must be said, however foolish or wrong it makes him sound. It must be said because it is the truth of what he feels, of what he is.

Of course it was all necessary, the conscription, the medical examinations. Of course, of course. We all know it. . . .

It was *necessary* to put Richard Lovat and the ugly collier through that business at Derby. Many men were put through things a thousand times worse. Agreed! Oh, entirely agreed! The war couldn't be lost, at that hour. Quite, quite, quite! Even Richard, even now, agreed fully to all these contentions. *But—*!

> And there you are. *But—*! He was full of a lava-fire of rage and hate, at the bottom of his soul. And he knew it was the same with most men. He felt desecrated. And he knew it was the same with most men. He felt sold. And he knew most men felt the same.

Here we surely have Lawrence making one of his fundamental affirmations. He was a creature of privacy and individuality essentially. Deprive him of those conditions and you deprived him of his self. This is after all the point of another major theme in *Kangaroo*, the democratic atmosphere of Australia. Lawrence felt himself, in contact with that atmosphere, essentially an aristocrat, because the democratic feeling denied the value he placed on privacy and individuality. And so at the end of the novel he sails away from Australia, humiliated, sore, self-contemptuous for his self-preserving retreat, but convinced he has no other self to change into, no way to be different. And if we think of *The Plumed Serpent*, that subsequent attempt to overcome his limiting privacy, to join in the societal enterprise at least imaginatively, we shall have to agree that he was right. He had indeed no other self, at least of remotely equal quality. This is what Leavis means by calling *The Plumed Serpent* artistically insincere.

One last quotation.

> The man by himself.
> That was one of the names for Erasmus of Rotterdam.
> The man by himself. . . .
> This is the innermost symbol of man: alone in the darkness of the cavern of himself, listening to the soundlessness of inflowing fate. Inflowing fate, inflowing doom, what does it matter? The man by himself—that is the absolute—listening—that is the relativity—for the influx of his fate, or doom.
> The man by himself. The listener.

There is a special poignancy for me in Lawrence citing Erasmus, because Erasmus also is an important figure for me as a liberal, and one who belongs in a very different perspective from Lawrence. Erasmus belongs with von Hügel for me. But apart from the personal poignancy there is surely a nonpersonal significance in this unique alignment of the two figures. They come together here for once because here for once Lawrence acknowledges his roots in liberal individualism, acknowledges an identity he at other times tends to deny, or neglect. That truth about himself, the nineteenth-century Emersonian truth, was what he started from; he need not affirm that; he had other, opposite truths to explore; but once deny that truth, once attack that privacy, and, as *Kangaroo* makes clear, his whole nature rocked and tilted and crashed together in panic until that base of being was reestablished.

Now of course you know this side of Lawrence, and the equivalent in Leavis. You know that they have been individualists, and of a particularly strenuous kind, of no ordinary pitch and tempo of individualism. You are trying, I take it, to design a society in which a man of their sensitiveness will not need to separate himself from his fellows, into their kind of privacy. In that sense, I take it, your whole enterprise acknowledges this fact about Lawrence and Leavis, is in response to their cry of pain. But that cry is ultimately ambiguous. What I am asking you to acknowledge is that their individualism is so central to their achievement, to their selfhood, that they belong, as sources of authority, as much on the other side. They denounce individualism, as the source of what they suffer from, but the energy and pride with which they do so derive from the same source. And therefore you cannot say that this extreme individualism was merely what they suffered from; because it was also what they achieved, aimed at, built on.

(After my talk I was asked whether I had not confused an individualism special to Lawrence and Leavis with the individualism natural to all artists. In a sense I had; what I was pointing out in them is also to be seen in most other artists, and is theirs just insofar as they *are* artists; but that is a truism I had to come the long way round to. Those interested in a common culture are concerned to point out (rightly) the obverse side of the romantic cliché of the solitary artist. All I am doing is returning to that cliché, reminding them of the obverse side of *their* half-truth. But if they accept that return, that truism, that strong element of individualization and privatization in the artist, then there are important consequences for them. The artist then becomes a very poor ally for them in their battle, one of the least appropriate figureheads to march behind, and the paradox of their constant invocation of the artist in literature, the paradox of *The Long Revolution* and *Culture and Society*, becomes more puzzling, more debilitating for them.)

Let me assume that you acknowledge their individualism of temperament, without seeing it as theoretically significant. Let me anticipate your objections to my argument that it is. Do you say that the community you want will be one to which they would want to belong? I don't think that is convincing to anyone who knows the people they *are*—what they might have been, under other cultural conditions, is of course hypothetical. Do you say that the community you want could be belonged to in one of the ways we can imagine in them? Either the mode of wistful yearning after the ideal city, or the mode of bitter carping at the real one? I don't think such a community, that could be belonged to in such a way, would be a community. Do you say Lawrence and Leavis are not totally exemplary figures from your point of view, and you are not responsible for them? Then you are agreeing with me. You are not responsible for them, nor they for you. You do not, fundamentally, stand for the same values. They know what's wrong with being a bourgeois individualist, but they aren't ready, in fact, to stop being one. You, I presume, are.

Now, to diversify the attack, I should like to take a few different literary examples; writers who have been discussed from a common culture point of view, who have been interpreted and to that extent appropriated under the aspect they bear for you. My point is of course to argue that that aspect is too sharp-angled, that profile too partial and eccentric. First of all, Wordsworth.

> Bliss was it in that dawn to be alive,
> But to be young was very Heaven! O times,
> In which the meagre, stale, forbidding ways
> Of custom, law, and statute, took at once
> The attraction of a country in romance! . . .
> Not favoured spots alone, but the whole Earth,
> The beauty wore of promise. . . .
> Now was it that *both* found, the meek and lofty
> Did both find helpers to their hearts' desire,

And stuff at hand, plastic as they could wish,—
Were called upon to exercise their skill,
Not in Utopia,—subterranean fields,—
Or some secreted island, Heaven knows where!
But in the very world, which is the world
Of all of us,—the place where, in the end,
We find our happiness or not at all.
                    (*The Prelude*, Book xi; 1850).

It is because Wordsworth had thought that, and still thought it at the time of writing enough to be able to write those lines, that he was a great poet. The energy of mind and generosity of heart manifested there, the capacity to be a radical and a revolutionary, shown in the changed sensibility towards social classes and work as well as towards landscape, this is what we recognize and respond to in his poetic tactics and strategies. His engagement in the common cause in this sense made him a great poet.

That I take to be the New Left point about Wordsworth, and I entirely agree with it. But Wordsworth himself felt that something else was even more the point. That he was betrayed by those political hopes; by those speculative schemes that promised "to abstract the hopes of Man/Out of his feelings, to be fixed thenceforth/For ever in a purer element— . . . Tempting region *that*/For Zeal to enter and refresh herself,/Where passions had the privilege to work/And never hear the sound of their own names."

And that he was saved from the ruin into which radical politics betrayed him by his sister Dorothy, the representative of nature.

She, in the midst of all, preserved me still
A Poet, made me seek beneath that name,
And that alone, my office upon earth.
                    (*The Prelude*, Book xi).

In other words, it was his turning away from primarily political hopes that made him Wordsworth the poet we know. I don't think anyone can rejoice whole-heartedly over that turning away, which does have, for me too, the character of a resignation, a compromise, a defeat. But on the other hand, can anyone deny that this is how Wordsworth came to be Wordsworth? For instance, the monumental effort that produced the *Prelude* was the effort of a man concentrating his strength on one narrow field of activity because of the defeats he had suffered elsewhere. Obviously the bulk of work a poet produces is likely to be greater if he seeks, beneath that name and that alone, his office upon earth. Obviously, too, the bulk of a poet's work is not the only or the major criterion by which we judge him. But surely several other of those criteria equally derive from singleness of passion, total dedication, undivided attention.

Or let us take George Eliot. I have no quarrel with what Raymond Williams says about her in *Culture and Society*. It is true that in Felix Holt's *Address to Working Men* George Eliot's thinking is very far from her best. It is a fact that when she touches, as she chooses to touch, the lives and the problems of working people, her personal observation and conclusion surrender, virtually without a fight, to the general structure of feeling about these matters which was the common property of her generation, and which she was at once too hesitant to transcend, and too intelligent to raise into any lively embodiment. That seems to me vigorous and useful literary criticism. And I assent too when he goes on to say, "It is indeed the mark of a deadlock in society when so fine an intelligence and so quick a sympathy can conceive no more than this. For patience and caution, without detailed intention, are very easily converted into acquiescence, and there is no right to acquiesce if society is known to be vicious."

Perhaps I don't really assent to that last phrase, but to argue against it would take me away from the literary argument. Here my point is only one that Raymond Williams himself makes from another point of view. "It is clear that, inadequate as her attempts at a position may be, it proceeds, though not fruitfully, from that sense of society as a complicated inheritance which is at the root of her finest work." I would only expand that a bit and say that George Eliot's weaknesses as a whole proceed from the same sources as her strengths. That she compromised with that general structure of feeling which was the common property of her generation about much more than working-class problems. Not that I deny that there was a failure there by her own standards. But her successes were also achieved through compromising with that general feeling. It seems to me that George Eliot's wisdom and her art were both essentially matters of inclusiveness, of forgiveness, of acceptance of things as they are. She forgives better than anybody else. Though in a sense the quantity of unforgiving sharpness and rigor she includes is the real measure of her achievement, still that quantity was dictated by the opposite, primary, tendency. It was as much as could be contained by, and within, her dominant drive, to accept and forgive. The quality of her forgiveness is constituted by the amount of unforgivingness it assimilates. I think the very structure of George Eliot's sentences, their expansiveness, their blend of balance and drive with straying leisureliness, their rolling hills quality, expresses that. As does the richly playful, indulgent, chiaroscuro character of her imagery. In other words, George Eliot *is* an acceptance novelist, *is* the creature of her retreat from political activism, not just in her weaknesses but in her strengths, too.

Last let me take Pasternak. In this case I do not agree with most of the criticism I have read, but we can take it for granted that *Dr. Zhivago* is in some sense an apologia for the author's life. And presumably we can agree that the novel as well as its main character affirms life values and denies those we might call "historical." Thus he says:

> . . . those who inspired the revolution aren't at home in anything except change and turmoil, they aren't happy with anything that's on less than a world scale. For them transitional periods, worlds in the making, are an end in themselves. They aren't trained for anything else, they don't know anything except that. And do you know why these never-ending preparations are so futile? It's because these men haven't any real capacities, they are incompetent. Man is born to live, not to prepare for life. Life itself, the phenomenon of life, the gift of life, is so breathtakingly serious! So why substitute this childish harlequinade of immature fantasies, these schoolboy escapades?

Real capacities, real competence, is for life (as understood here, private life) and for art. Public life is seen as unreal, as a preparation for, or a scaffolding around, private life.

Public events are treated in the novel by the traditional symbolist technique as natural phenomena, sweeping down upon individuals, and altering their lives, their real lives, from outside. The most frequent image is of a storm; rain and wind, ice and snow, avalanche and glacier. When public events demand to be taken on their own terms, as the action of people-in-society, the novel runs into difficulty. Zhivago's voice, and Pasternak's, becomes shrill and cracked. Yurii makes an attempt to describe public events in "his own language," when he comments on the Bolsheviks' seizing of power. He says, "It has something of Pushkin's uncompromising clarity and of Tolstoy's unwavering faithfulness to the facts." There is obviously something very strained in this, something incipiently foolish, and in fact Yurii lives to repent bitterly this one attempt to confront public events directly.

> Only once in his life had this uncompromising language and single-mindedness filled him with enthusiasm. Was it possible that he must pay for that rash enthusiasm all his life by never hearing, year after year, anything but these unchanging shrill, crazy exclamations and demands, which became progressively more impractical, meaningless, and unfulfillable as time went by? Was it possible that because of one moment of overgenerous response he had been enslaved for ever?

The first passage occurs a third of the way through the novel, the second two-thirds of the way through. The second, recalling the first, announces that this is a major theme, and invites us to scrutinize its treatment. But when we do so, we must surely be disappointed. Yurii deserves our sympathy, but his way of handling the experience surely cannot impress, and the novel gives us no hint of how to criticize him while remaining loyal to Pasternak. The shrill petulance of the second quotation is the natural complement of the shrill eagerness of before, and the exaggerated egotism of the final exclamation is ultimately the hero's, and the author's responsibility. Yurii cannot, in fact, deal with public events as human behavior. He and Pasternak can only deal with them as phenomena of "nature."

But my point here is just that Zhivago repudiates the revolution, however valid we judge his repudiation to be, and retreats to find fulfillment in personal relations, and in the writing of poetry. He becomes a poet in much the same sense as Wordsworth. And, like Wordsworth, Pasternak tells us that he could only write because he repudiated, because he disengaged himself.

Well, of course, all this is painfully obvious. And so is the conclusion I wish these analyses to lead us to. That you have no right to use the writers' testimony as to where their power comes from in the one case when you don't in the other; the first case being their cultural and political engagement, the second their disengagement. Surely nobody could deny that Wordsworth, George Eliot, Pasternak, gave us what they did because of their disengagement from social/political action as well as because of their engagement in it? Surely, even, their political defeatism, their cultural separation, their unhealth, is at the source of their literary validity? In other words, literature is a very partial and treacherous ally of your enterprise, really going a dozen ways, living according to a different rhythm.

Of course these are liberal truths, many-faceted, facing everywhere, leading nowhere. But are they not also literary truths? Isn't this the way the truth about an author or a book organizes itself? Where you are giving a faithful account of a novel in its relations to culture or politics, faithful primarily to the book, that is, do you not find that the different things you have to say organize themselves like that most of the time? I have chosen authors who are remarkable for the energy or the fullness of what they have to say about the history of their time and place, writers whose work shows the benefit of engagement. There are many others I could have chosen whose work abounds in richness and brilliance in defiant independence of any such engagement. Yet even in the case of these three, it seems to me clear that their engagement has been temporary, oblique, irregular, inert; from the point of view of their activist contemporaries has looked like disengagement. Of course, there are exceptions like Sartre. But then there are also exceptions like Proust. And I think there are a larger number of larger figures like Proust.

You may object that this is liberal logic and not binding

on a radical. I am taking the words of the writers themselves, only checking it against a very common sense and unadventurous appraisal of what they wrote and how they lived. I am not trusting to cultural or political insights that would tell me more decisively which of their remarks about themselves are to be listened to and which to be re-interpreted. My arguments aim at the assent of the average man, whose process of judgment, from your point of view, has been corrupted by the influence of liberal philosophy. And consequently the conclusions I come to are liberal conclusions, inert and depressing, essentially on the side of the status quo.

I think that is fair. My argument is liberal, though not conservative. A conservative position on these matters I would call one which would stress the incompatibility of the political passion with the literary, the need to choose between ideology and art. A Nabokovian position, let us say. I don't believe you have to choose one or the other. I believe you can have both, and indeed the literature I care about most is that in which both have had play. But I believe in their relationship being dialectical, and the value for the writer deriving in the first case (indeed the only sure case) from the struggle beween them and not from any particular issue to that struggle. That I would call liberalism. Conservatism means for me some impulse to triumph in the defeat of the liberal endeavor to make sense of life, to identify oneself with the disharmonies, the paradoxes, the ugly or cynical truths. Conservatism, insofar as it admitted political duties, would stress the suitability for a writer of attitudes that picturesquely defined his personality, gestures and postures that expressed primarily his dissent from the pieties, liberal and radical, of his contemporaries. There was a good deal of this in Evelyn Waugh's ideology, and in Kingsley Amis's today. And clearly both men are serious, and clearly this is one of the ways in which literature and politics, literature and culture, do interact in men of talent. The radical point of view presumably sees the literary and the political passions fitting together perfectly when properly understood, competing against each other only for the individual's time. Such internecine conflicts as Doris Lessing reports, in *The Golden Notebook*, presumably appear as merely personal, merely sick, seen from that point of view. The difficulty is that such a point of view is so lofty as to be little use—to the man interested in the books discussed for instance—so far above the phenomena it offers to put together as to be out of touch with them.

Perhaps this is inevitable, once you offer to apply radical insights to literature. The literature we have to talk about is the product of a society divided in fatal ways. It is liberal literature and therefore liberal logic applies to it much more easily than radical logic. All I need say to you here is to recite truisms, while you have to prove paradoxes. Obviously this is inequitable, but my conclusion is that therefore you should not be talking about literature. One can only write significant literary criticism about the books that are already written. It is a retrospective trade, and the preserve of the inert-minded liberal—inert as seen from your point of view.

I should have thought that the real lesson of Leavis's career was just that. That he triumphed in the end over his early ideological foes just because only a great critic can speak for literature in his time, can say what needs to be done now, what books need to be read now, and which of the possible relations between literature and culture will not prove fruitful. And that he was a great critic in part because he put literature first, established a hegemony for it over his other interests. By putting literature first, I mean for instance defining one's values in phrases like "quality of life" and "living relationship with a real culture" which have a more than literary scope, and yet can only be fruitfully applied in literary ways. I know what Leavis means by those terms; I find them useful on occasion myself; but that's because the structure of my interests is very like his. They are very slippery terms indeed, and quite unusable, I should think, for anyone with a different structure of interests. Nevertheless, I believe Leavis was right in those early definings of his position or refusings to define it. And not right only because he has since produced better criticism than Trotsky or Wellek. He was right in his description of how a vigorous mind with many interests should in his time relate them to literature, to the act of reading. He was right because only a liberal critic could be right about our literature and in our conditions. (Of course, I admit that Leavis was radical in certain ways and that his relevance as a critic derives from his partial radicalism too; what I am arguing is that the liberalism in him is absolutely fundamental.) Anyway he did speak in the name of literature.

But you, it seems to me, cannot speak in the name of literature, because your structure of interests is quite different. You are using literature to supply you with examples and insights, and relying largely on a taste you have inherited, not one you are creating, as he was. You are not trying to become great critics, at least as I have defined the term and the activity. You have no right—from the literary point of view—to ignore and simplify and dramatize as he did. So insofar as you are, unconsciously or consciously, deriving reassurance from his example, beware. Literary history will not support you as it has supported him. The cry of rape will not fade away as it did in his case, but grow louder.

Let me put the same thing a different way. Literature is speaking on your side only in small part, with a small voice. For instance, much of the most brilliant and interesting writing today accords with your analysis neither consciously nor unconsciously. More important, the part that is on your side is something we are all familiar with. We know the cultural insights of D. H. Lawrence and George Eliot, and the strength they give to the novels in which they are at work. And we know the equivalents in writers since them. We are trained to recognize them. Effectively, therefore, the testimony that literature bears to your argument is dull. This is the price you pay for so convenient a legacy. When you began to write, we all saw immediately what you meant about literature and its relation to culture. That was your advantage. But it is now your disadvantage.

Only those who have something creative to say about literature in their time can speak in its name, can count on its support. And that creativity in liberal-capitalist times comes from an ideological submission to literature, the subduing after struggle of other interests and passions to that one, the embarking on an essentially individualist autarchic adventure of the mind. Of course, there are exceptions to that rule, but I think it's a rule; and I'm sure the figures you have leaned on are not exceptions to it.

I don't know what, if any, ideology will be able to ally itself fruitfully with literature in our time, fertilize literary study itself as well as being fertilized by it. But for you I think the moment has come to cut yourselves off from that library of examples, that fund of insights, that source of prophetic power. The Hesperidean apples are going to turn to ashes in your grasp, otherwise.

Chapter 13

AMERICA AFTER 1945 I:
FAUSTIANISM IN AMERICA

One can group intellectuals according to their temperaments as well as according to their ideologies, and one can describe a temperament in terms of a psychic bargain, or an exchange of one set of personal potentialities for another. To use another metaphor, it is an investment transfer of one's psychic resources, capital and work-force, from one enterprise to another. And this is important not so much because capital or work force is limited in quantity, as because the act of transference arouses and energizes the whole psyche. This is often just as firm and clear a classification of minds as ideology provides, or the political positions of conservative, liberal, and radical. In the case of certain modern American intellectuals, like Norman Mailer and Leslie Fiedler, it seems a more meaningful classification.

Their constant theme, which they write out of as well as about, is what is traditionally called the Faustian or diabolic or daimonic contract, in which a man sells his soul to the devil in exchange for forbidden knowledge and forbidden powers, giant faculties and forces. This idea of excess is connected to the idea of the incorporation of meaning, their appropriation to the body in the Faustian type. This connec-

tion between the expressive body and the excessive ego is a
constant theme in Tolstoy, for instance. These are not necessarily or exclusively the forces or faculties of genius. Mabel
Dodge possessed them, as well as D. H. Lawrence. But they
are the forces and faculties that both of *them* possessed and
that T. S. Eliot and E. M. Forster did not possess.

Goethe took the title of his play, *Faust*, from a sixteenth
century magician. But in his own lifetime, it was science and
rationalism, rather than Christianity as in the sixteenth century, which had to be denied or evaded in order to acquire
giant powers, as we see in both his and Blake's attacks on
Newton and Locke. They attacked Newtonian science and
rationalist philosophy as the blighting reign of Urizen. They
were determined to make a world within which there would
be free play for their own giant powers of intellect and
imagination. In the twentieth century, the Faustian bargain
for writers has been typically, as we see in Mailer's books, the
sacrifice of decency in exchange for indecent sexual and sensual
knowledge; the sense of disgust and recoil, and the sexuality
of degradation and perversity. It is in all ages the selling of the
soul for the body, and today it is for the possession of one's
physical apparatus in fullest imaginative detail.

This temperament will express itself in a conservative political position if the power acquired for the individual personality is "paid for" by the imaginative endorsement, intensification, of social rules and limitations for other people. This
frequently happens in men of notably powerful persona; it is
an element in Mailer's left conservatism, and can be felt in
Armies of the Night. These rules and traditions are external
to their endorser, and leave a zone of freedom around his
personality, but they guarantee the order of society in general against too much freedom. But if the forbidden power is
not "paid for," compensated for, in this way, if it is rejoiced
in as a universal and absolute good, then the Faustian temperament takes up a radical position—as Mailer seems to do in
"The White Negro."

The American writers I picked on to admire in *Reapprais-
als*, Emerson and Salinger, are not in the least Faustian. Salinger's gradual dematerialization, his fading from the national

retina, is a striking demonstration of the hegemony gradually established by the Faustian temperament over the American imagination since 1945. He and Emerson are exemplars of a different temperament, the results of a different bargain, one in which a writer sells his body in exchange for freedom of the spirit. This is the angelic pact, as opposed to the diabolic, and I associate it with Erasmus as opposed to Faust. Writers like Forster and Trilling are also good examples of this temperament, and to some degree everyone who is at home in recent British literature as opposed to American, belongs to it.

Within American literature itself, its locus is, predictably enough, criticism. I use this term for that extension of literary criticism which, while continuing to regard literature as its main concern, looks through it and beyond it to history, politics, science, whatever it may be, to bring that too into some relation to the same sensibility and judgment. Trilling again is a major example of this kind of writing, as are Frye and Wilson, though it is only the first two I discuss in the essay that follows. All of these writers are essentially men of judgment, and their intellectual temperament must be based on the Erasmian pact.

This pact is an intensified version of the one every man enters into by the process of maturing, by the very process of becoming human, as described by Freud in *Civilization and Its Discontents*. It is the exchange of sensual pleasure for mental, of immediate gratification of appetite for indirect and subtle gratification, of nature for culture. It is repression, suppression, and sublimation. It causes the uniformity and rationalization of civilized man, and that two-dimensionality which so many intellectuals rebel against in themselves. Intellectuals, writers among them, enter into this contract more largely than other people, are especially its beneficiaries and its victims. They are its sponsors in society, and feel especially responsible for it. They get more from it and lose more by it. They especially yearn for the three-dimensional world of free, rich, full, vivid, unmediated experience. They often contract, or try to contract, the Faustian bargain as well, and are therefore often *its* sponsors, or would-be sponsors, as against the Erasmian.

The Calvinist bargain is the other way of escaping from Erasmian limitations, the opposite way to the Faustian. While the latter intensifies the powers of the individual as an individual, personal power, personal intuition, and personal imagination, the former makes one participate in the intensified powers of a group, of the elect, the redeemed, the saints. By this social contract, the saints' bargain, one sacrifices individual freedom and gains party infallibility. But we need not dwell on the Calvinist imagination here, since it plays an unimportant part in the American imagination of this period. What concerns us is above all the Faustian.

It is most typically Jewish writers who have made the signing of the Faustian contract the subject of their imaginative work and the core of their psychic drama as personalities. The part played by the Jews in recent world history and their special position in America, give a greater resonance to their acquisition of power than it has in other writers. The American Jewish writers have felt that they were giving up the roles associated with suffering for those associated with aggression, giving up the modest irony and humorous wise scholarship of their race, and reaching out to acquire the big brutal energies they had attributed only to *goyim* before. Mailer has spoken of a Jewish modesty in himself and a Jewish softness—as of someone too much loved by his mother—which are what he has always hated in himself. Leslie Fiedler has pointed to the scenes in Mailer's and Bellow's fiction in which the author of his representative can be seen dreaming of the truculent *goy* toughness he is going to acquire. And Susan Sontag in *Trip to Hanoi* has described her bewilderment at meeting a different contract established in North Vietnamese culture, and the reflections she then made on her own culture, her America, which is predominantly Jewish and New York.

The city of New York is itself a Faustian temperament; in its buildings, in its street scenes, in its racial and political tensions, in its social harshness, it contains a series of violent reachings toward power, which a visitor, even if he arrives from another of the world's metropoles, can feel on his nerves as a dangerous stimulant and challenge. It is no wonder that now, at the climax of the city's world-historical career, a group of writers are to be found who express it, take its temperament as their subject, re-enact that in their style and sensibility. And it is no wonder, though it could not have been predicted, that the genius among them should be the one who expresses his city, relates to it, represents it, in the most various ways—including straight political representation, as we saw in 1969, when Norman Mailer ran as candidate for Democratic nomination as mayor of New York.

Mailer's is the imaginative style that has become dominant in American culture since 1945, and it could hardly be more unlike the style dominant in England. Though there are elements of the Faustian temperament in both Lawrence and Leavis, their work is largely in the service of "maturity" and "manliness," "decency," and "marriage," which are virtues of the Erasmian temperament. And the work of the dandy-gentlemen, so different from theirs in every other way, is like it in service of "tradition" and "realism" and "taste." The most striking new work in the imaginative-cultural field in England is that of Raymond Williams and his allies and followers, which can be called Calvinist. Of course, the antithesis between the two countries is by no means complete, and the two cultures legitimately can be analyzed in other ways that would not issue in any antithesis at all. But in my experience of the two there is a marked difference between them, which I can articulate in this way. And one of its symptoms is the way in which Whitman remains an American and not a British poet.

Chapter 14

AMERICA AFTER 1945 II: WHITMAN AS A TWENTIETH-CENTURY POET*

By twentieth century I mean just one segment of our contemporary literary sensibility and theory, but it is a large segment, it includes several varieties, it is powerful and still growing in power. The label I will give it is post-Freudian (though post-Nietzschean would be in some ways better). My thesis is that Whitman prefigures this, and that they throw light on each other, he on it, and it on him.

Post-Freudian "Modernism"

By post-Freudian I mean something different from Freudian, as that word was used in the 1930's—to indicate an interest in sex or in the process of psychoanalysis. I mean the Freud of *Civilization and its Discontents*, speculative Freud, not the Freud of *The Interpretation of Dreams*; and by using the pre-

* This chapter appeared in *The Month* (August/September 1969).

fix post I mean to imply that the people I am interested in have done some impressive speculating in their own right, using Freud as a starting point. The most extreme theorists of this movement are Norman Brown in *Life Against Death* and *Love's Body*, and Herbert Marcuse in *Eros and Civilization*.[1] They assume a profound opposition within the human personality between the interests of the body, including all of pre-mental life, the instincts as well as the senses, and the interests of the mind, that is civilization representing itself within the personality as morality, systematic thought, patriotism, religious duty, and so on. The body's spokesman in literature is Blake; "Energy is the only life, and is from the body," and "Energy is Eternal Delight;" the mind is obviously spoken for by a thousand great names, but typically by Plato and Descartes, with their insistence on the abstract, the ideal, the disembodied, the sublimated.

As we are most concerned with the theory of art within this general theory of culture, here are some representative quotations from Brown.

> The function of art is to help us find our way back to the sources of pleasure that have been rendered inaccessible by the capitulation to the reality principle which we call education or maturity . . . In contrast with the repressive structure of the authoritarian group, the aim of the partenership between the artist and the audience is instinctual liberation . . . Art, if its object is to undo repressions, and if civilisation is essentially repressive, is in this sense subversive of civilisation.

Obviously, in saying that, Brown is thinking of the cultures of the past only.

That theoretical position may seem remote from not only Whitman, but any widespread modern habit of thought, any practical thinking. But I think it is vitally related to a quite widespread contemporary set of attitudes to cultural problems, and a quite practical contemporary literary sensibility; which one finds expressed in, to take some striking examples, Susan Sontag in *Against Interpretation*, Philip Rieff in *The*

---

[1] Marcuse's total position is of course very unlike Brown's but in *Eros and Civilization* he seems to me to be saying something similar.

Triumph of the Therapeutic, Norman Mailer in *Advertisements for Myself*, and Marshall McLuhan. These people differ from each other considerably, in their interests as well as in their values, but what they all have to say about, and to, modern culture, is essentially similar, and essentially post-Freudian.

Like McLuhan, Miss Sontag and Mr. Rieff believe that we are at the end of the literary phase of our culture; that literature will decline in importance; and that along with it will decline (as primary cultural values) literacy, privacy, individualism, liberalism, the conscience, self-sacrifice, self-improvement, "standards," culture itself in the Matthew Arnold sense. They think that the art of the future will and should return to its (they believe) essential function of releasing man's sensuality—in the widest sense of that phrase. The classic dilemma of our culture, Miss Sontag says, is the hypertrophy of the intellect at the expense of energy and sensual capability. They see the values I just listed as profoundly ascetic, the enemies of sensual capability, the servants of the old (nineteenth century) civilization, and essentially hostile to art and the new (twenty-first century) civilization.

Sontag is less ready than Rieff to anticipate the post-literary future with eagerness. But she rejoices equally in the extinction of the Matthew Arnold idea of culture, in which literature was so central; she rejoices in the decline of the hegemony of conscience, and the rise of aesthetic and formal autonomy in the arts. She and Norman Mailer, the more purely literary minds of those I mentioned, are perhaps attuned rather to the extinction of our race along with its culture, while Mr. Rieff and Marshall McLuhan are tuning themselves in to the new culture which will replace ours.

Rieff and McLuhan's view of the future is quite strikingly apolitical and in any traditional sense amoral. They question the usefulness today of (in Rieff's phrase) all the traditional modes of self-salvation through self-identification with a communal cause. Susan Sontag and Norman Mailer say rather that those modes of salvation have been put out of our reach; that a moral and responsible life, in America in the twentieth century, has been made too difficult. The years in which one could complacently accept oneself as part of an elite by being a radical are forever gone, Mailer says. The only courage that we have been witness to has been the isolated courage of isolated people, sexual adventurers. They refer us to the murder of the Jews during the war, to the threat of the hydrogen bomb, to the hypocrisy and immorality of American politics at home and abroad. And they report to us, with participatory excitement, the phenomena of decadence. Whereas Rieff and McLuhan, on the other hand, are more concerned to describe how peaceful everything will be once we have stopped being moral and responsible and how well we shall probably like the new state of affairs once we've got used to it. They report the speed with which our culture is changing, new technologies are being developed, and the ratios between our senses are being transformed. But they all look forward equally to a greater variety of and prestige for sensuality, and to the withering away of most forms of corporate ethical action.

That is all I want to say to show how these four people are related to the theoretical position I described before. To put it briefly, they all see our present situation in post-Freudian terms, as the end of civilization as we have known it, repressive civilization, characterized in morality by ascetic values and in art by literature, especially the novel, and they see our future, if we have one, as a non-repressive civilization, characterized by a relaxed morality, sensuality, and very different forms of art.

However, I want to add a few more remarks that will be useful later, to show how they are related to Whitman. This general attitude is implicitly hostile to what might be called the orthodox British configuration of taste with its nineteenth-century traditions of moral responsibility. Arnold and Ruskin are representative figures it reacts against. "What we decidedly do not need now is further to assimilate Art into Thought, or (worse yet) into Culture," says Sontag. The modern representatives of that tradition, like Leavis, are not mentioned, and presumably could seem only provincial, priggish, and reactionary to Miss Sontag, who refers rather to Sartre, Genêt and Lévi-Strauss. Even D. H. Lawrence, who is of course mentioned, is not dwelt on or unreservedly praised. He is not accepted in the way that say Yeats is.

Marx's name is often invoked, but not Marxism, which is clearly a nineteenth-century mode of thought, belonging to a repressive civilization. As Rieff says,

> our revolution is more Freudian than Marxist, more analytic than polemic, more cultural than socialist . . . The Communist movement belongs to the classical tradition of moral demand systems . . . It is a terrible error to see the West as conservative and the East as revolutionary.
>
> We are the true revolutionaries . . . Our cultural revolution does not aim, like its predecessors, at victory for some rival commitment, but rather at a way of using all commitments, which amounts to loyalty towards none. By psychologising about themselves interminably, Western men are learning to use their internality against the primacy of any particular organisation of personality.

And Norman Mailer predicts that the revolutionary vision of the twentieth century will differ from Marx's nineteenth-century vision by not being concerned with political economy but with the mass media. This takes us back again to McLuhan, and Susan Sontag remarks explicitly on how odd it is that

> such strongly apolitical critics as Marshall McLuhan have got so much better grasp on the texture of contemporary reality . . . than the Marxist critics . . . Despite their commitment to the notion of historical progress the neo-Marxist critics have shown themselves to be singularly insensitive to most of the interesting and creative features of contemporary culture in non-socialist countries.

That is, of course, the features *she* finds interesting and creative.

And this brings me to my final point. The specifically literary taste we find in the post-Freudians is a kind of modernism. Susan Sontag distinguishes between the pantheon of high culture, George Eliot, Homer, Tolstoy, Bach and Beethoven, Rembrandt and Chartres, and a sensibility whose trademark, she says is "anguish, cruelty, derangement. Think of Bosch, Sade, Rimbaud, Jarry, Kafka, Artaud, think of most of the important works of art of the twentieth century, that is, art whose goal is not that of creating harmonies but of overstraining the medium and introducing more and more violent and unresolvable, subject-matter." That is what I call modernism, and it is clearly that kind of art to which her own taste turns most eagerly, and it is that idea of art which influences Norman Mailer's own fiction.

Whitman and "New Sensory Mixes"

But what has all this, this manifestation of twentieth-century life, to do with Whitman, in many ways so essentially of the nineteenth century? Clearly it hasn't much to do with the Whitman of *Democratic Vistas*, or with the poet of the great elegies. But there are other Whitmans, and I think I can claim that the one I shall refer to, the Whitman of *Song of Myself*, and *Children of Adam*, and the *Calamus* poems, is the most important from most points of view. And this Whitman seems to me vitally related to the cultural attitude and literary taste I have been describing.

To take the most obvious aspect first, Whitman was a great prophet of sensuality:

Sex contains all,
Bodies, Souls, meanings, proofs, purities, delicacies, results,
    promulgations,
Songs, commands, health, pride, the maternal mystery, the seminal
    milk,
All hopes, benefactions, bestowals,
All the passions, loves, beauties, delights of the earth,
These are contained in sex, as part of itself, and justification of itself.
                                            ("A Woman Waits For Me").

This, however obvious, is very important. Of all nineteenth-century writers, Whitman was surely the boldest and most insistent in his claims for sensuality; and the redemption of the senses is quite primary in the twentieth-century, post-Freudian creed. From that first tenet follow a dozen others, a dozen major values. Mailer says, "The trouble is that it's enormously difficult to return to the senses now . . . Our danger is that civilisation is so strong, so divorced from the senses, that we have come to the point where we can liquidate millions of people in concentration camps by orderly process." Proper sensuality woud make that impossible. And Susan Sontag says, "If civilisation may be defined as that stage of human life at which objectively, the body becomes a problem, then our moment of civilisation may be described as that stage at which men are subjectively aware of, and feel trapped by, this problem." That problem of the body is probably the major theme of all Whitman's poetry.

For the word sensuality can mean many different things, and what it means in Whitman is much closer to what it means in the modern writers than is the sensuality of the other great sensualist writers of the nineteenth century. It is when one puts him up against, for instance, Baudelaire, or for that matter D. H. Lawrence, that one sees how much closer Whitman is to the modern thinkers—though he is the further from their thoughts and the one they are least apt to quote. Baudelaire was in one meaning of the word a great sensualist, but in him the senses are the means of damnation. In Whitman they are rather the means—though also the end—of salvation. In Lawrence there is salvation through the senses, but it is something that involves more action, more purposefulness, more moral integrity; in Whitman it means relaxation, purposelessness, moral multiplicity, acceptance of everything, identification with everything. Moreover, in neither Baudelaire nor Lawrence are we aware, as we are in Whitman, of the senses as independent agents, being encouraged to reach out centrifugally into the world and absorb it and mix it up inextricably with the self behind the senses, encouraged to be infinitely inventive in their variations and uninhibited in their pan-sexuality. It is in fact the word body, in its modern post-Freudian meaning, which suits Whitman's sensuality; and does not suit Baudelaire or Lawrence.

O my Body! I dare not desert the likes of you in other men and women, not the like of the parts of you.

("The Body Electric").

And this, in which an ecstasy of libidinal awareness transcends the limits of heterosexuality and even of genitality in a very modern way:

The expression of the face balks account;
But the expression of a well-made man appears not only in his face
It is in his limbs and joints also, it is curiously in the joints of his hips and wrists;
It is in his walk, the carriage of his neck, the flex of his waist and knees—dress does not hide him
The strong sweet supple quality he has strikes through the cotton and flannel;
To see him pass conveys as much as the best poem, perhaps more;
You linger to see his back, and the back of his neck and shoulder-side.

(ibid.).

But most striking of all is the narcissistic quality, carried far beyond normal reaches of thought and feeling. The inside of Whitman's body becomes an object of love for him, and the whole world becomes an extension of his body. In one sense of Brown's phrase, the whole world is eroticized:

The smoke of my own breath;
Echoes, ripples, buzz'd whispers, love-root, silk-thread, crotch and vine;
My respiration and inspiration, the beating of my heart, the passing of blood and air through my lungs;
The sniff of green leaves and dry leaves, and of the shore and dark-coloured sea-rocks, and of hay in the barn.
The sound of the belch'd words of my voice, words loos'd to the eddies of the wind;
A few light kisses, a few embraces, a reaching around of arms;
The play of shine and shade on the trees as the supple boughs wag.

("Song of Myself," 2).

This is narcissism of the kind Marcuse embodies in Narcissus; but it is also the world eroticized, and with that inexhaustibly inventive sensuality which Susan Sontag tells us she finds in underground movies. And that key phrase of Norman Brown's, polymorphous perversity, that stage of sexual development which civilized people are not allowed to live through in their infancy, which is repressed and thus never outgrown, surely it is Whitman who has found for that an adult and literary equivalent.

For Whitman the whole world kept turning into his sensorium. Moreover, his work is a recipe for the reader, telling him how to make that happen in himself. Whitman shows us how to escape that genital organization of strictly heterosexual sensuality on which Norman Brown blames our neuroses, our civilization's plight, and which held the other great sensualists captive. It is just for that sexual puritanism, for instance, that Susan Sontag blames D. H. Lawrence:

Through me forbidden voices;
Voices of sexes and lusts—voices veil'd and I remove the veil;
Voices indecent, by me clarified and transfigured.
If I worship one thing more than another, it shall be the spread of
   my own body, or any part of it. . . .

(ibid., 24).

O span of youth! Ever-pushed elasticity!
O manhood, balanced, florid, and full.
My lovers suffocate me!
Crowding my lips, thick in the pores of my skin,
Jostling me through streets and public halls—coming naked to
   me at night,
Crying by day Ahoy! from the rocks of the river—swinging
   and chirping over my head,
Calling my name from flower beds, vines, tangled underbush,
Lighting on every moment of my life,
Bussing my body with soft balsamic busses,
Noiselessly passing handfuls out of their hearts, and giving
   them to be mine.
Ages and ages, returning at intervals,
Undestroy'd wandering immortal,
Lusty, phallic, with the potent original loins, perfectly sweet,
I chanter to Adamic songs,
Through the new garden, the West, the great cities calling,
Deliriate, thus prelude what is generated, offering them,
   offering myself,
Bathing myself, bathing my songs in sex,
Offspring of my loins.

(ibid., 45).

I am he that aches with amorous love;
Does the earth gravitate? Does not all matter, aching, attract
   all matter?

So the Body of me, to all I meet or know.
I too had been struck from the float forever held in solution;
I too had receiv'd identity by my Body;
That I was, I knew was of my Body—and what I should be,
  I knew I should be of my Body.
               ("I Am He That Aches with Love").

A key phrase for the post-Freudians is "new sensory mixes"; new deployments of the senses. McLuhan says civilization depends on the artist because he can "correct the sense ratios before the blow of the new technology has numbed conscious procedures." And Susan Sontag says the new sensibility understands art as the extension of life, not the criticism of life, and such art is experimental just as science is, experimenting in new sensory mixes. It seems to me that enigmatic phrase is more comprehensible in relation to Whitman than in any other literary context, and that Whitman is more comprehensible when you use that phrase; with its suggestion of the external control and combination of the senses, their exploitation in experiments in sensuality yet disinfected of all cynical immoralism.

The Poet as Prophet

So much for the most obvious, but the most important factor, Whitman's sensuality. Next, as we saw in the quotations from McLuhan and Marcuse, the modern culture critics assign a role of great importance to the poet, the artist, in bringing about the transition from our present stage of civilization to the next. Philip Rieff says there is a religious power inherent in the work of modern artists. The artist represents what we are trying to become, the shape we are trying to take in our effort to escape. He does so in the most obvious sense because he has broken with the middle-class moral demand system. But more essentially it is because, as an artist, he externalizes his inner life in forms valid first to his own psychological economy, and invalid to the outside world, indifferent to its rationalizing and moralizing disciplines.

Whitman, despite his sensual anarchy and moral diffuseness, saw himself as a prophet teaching the world. Indeed it
was just for his sensuality and his diffuseness that he saw himself as that—they were his message.

> I hear you have been asking for something to represent the new
>   race, our self-poised Democracy,
> Therefore I send you my poems, that you behold in them what
>   you wanted.
>
> ("To Foreign Lands").

But the message of those poems, Whitman's new way of taking the world, had its religious and philosophic implications, as
well as the sensual and psychological. He was inventing "Laws
for Creations."

> What do you suppose Creation is?
> What do you suppose will satisfy the soul, except to walk free
>   and own no superior?
> What do you suppose I would intimate to you in a hundred
>   ways but that man or woman is as good as God?
> And that there is no God any more divine than yourself?
> And that that is what the oldest and newest myths finally mean?
> And that you or any one must approach Creation through
>   such laws?
>
> ("Laws for Creations").

Philip Rieff says that Christian culture is over now, and the
great modern question is whether our culture can be so recon-
structed that no faith—that is, no symbol of some self-integrat-
ing communal purpose—need any longer superintend the organization of personality. Whitman answered that question, in
his own case, a hundred years ago; he showed us a personality
organizing itself out of relation to all faiths. We must make a
partial exception for his faith in Democracy; but it is partial,
democracy for him was not a purposive activity. Effectively it
was rather a relaxer of those bonds and obligations on the
soul which other political creeds brought. Whitman valued
faith; but he defined it as "the antiseptic of the soul"—it is
faith in that very modern meaning of the belief in oneself that
saves one from inhibiting guilt or shame.

We should notice too that reference to myths in the last
quotation. McLuhan takes our interest in the myths of other

times and cultures to be peculiarly characteristic of our age, and Rieff explains this by saying that our cultural revolution aims at a way of using all commitments which amounts to loyalty toward none. That is, by appreciating with equal sympathy the customs of monogamy, polygamy, polyandry, and so on, we are able to keep our moral self-respect through every change of behavior. And to understand and see the point of every religion, is to save oneself from the moral and psychological cramp which believing one alone might cause. It is also to save oneself from the moral and psychological dryness which having no religion might cause—for this attitude to religion is the reverse, in one sense, of atheism. This is what Whitman says here:

> I do not despise you, priests;
> My faith is the greatest of faiths, and the least of faiths,
> Enclosing worship ancient and modern, and all between
> ancient and modern.
>
> ("Song of Myself").

And here, for example, he imagines himself,

> Walking the old hills of Judea, with the beautiful gentle
> God by my side;
> Speeding through space—speeding through heaven and the stars,
> Speeding amid the seven satellites, and the broad ring,
> and the diameter of 80,000 miles;
> Speeding with tail'd meteors—throwing fireballs like the rest;
> Carrying the crescent child that carries its own full mother in
> its belly;
>
> (ibid.).

And so on. All of human experience, and more than human, seemed to Whitman to be brought within his grasp by his way of taking the world, and that he could participate as much as he wanted to in every mode of being. He took in Christianity, he took in science. He responded fully to both, he had no quarrel with either, and he was not committed to either in any restrictive way:

> To see nothing anywhere but what you may reach it and pass it,
> To conceive no time, however distant, but what you may reach
> it and pass it.
>
> ("Song of the Open Road").

We can perhaps take Longfellow as representing the orthodox nineteenth-century way of taking an interest in the cultures of other times and other countries. He too knew a great deal about other cultures and other literatures, and he too referred to them a lot in writing his own poetry. But he always knew they were foreign, not his own beliefs, and their function was always exotic. By contrast, Whitman's was the twentieth-century way of taking them, appropriating them, making them resolve tensions of one's own life.

Next, this new experimental art the modern critics tell us of, with its new sensory mixes, will also be notably unpolitical. And this combination is strikingly true of Whitman, despite his invocation of Democracy:

I hear it was charged against me that I sought to destroy
    institutions,
But really I am neither for nor against institutions;
(What indeed have I in common with them?—or what with the
    destruction of them?)
Only I will establish in the Mannahatta, and in every city of
    These States, inland and seaboard,
And in the fields and woods, and above every keel, little or large,
    that dents the water,
Without edifices, or rules, or trustees, or any argument,
The institution of the dear love of comrades.
               ("I Hear It Was Charged Against Me").

Whitman refused to concern himself with institutional or organizational facts, he was interested only in individuals, he said:

Underneath all, individuals!
I swear nothing is good to me now that ignores individuals,
The American compact is altogether with individuals,
The only government is that which makes minute of individuals,
The whole theory of the universe is directed to one single
    individual—namely, to You.
               ("By Blue Ontario's Shore").

But in fact Whitman is not so much concerned with individuals as with the elements that make up one individual. He has not much to tell us about the relations between people, however private and personal you make those relations, but he has a lot to say about the relation between the parts that go to make up a personality. As he says:

> I will effuse egotism, and show it underlying all—and I will be
> the bard of personality.
> ("Starting From Panmanok").

He tells us how to relate those parts so as to produce the totally free, unconstrained, unconcentrated, self-sufficing, self-delighting, totally playful, personality which our modern prophets foretell for our future.

They not only foretell it, they prescribe it. Freud's most important ideas for us, according to Philip Rieff, have to do not with sexual impulse but with ambivalence. These are so important because it is only if man can understand his ambivalence, the instability and ambiguity of his emotions, their tendency to reverse themselves and to mean the opposite of what they seem to, that he has a chance of survival as a race. "What hope there is," I quote Philip Rieff in *The Triumph of the Therapeutic*:

> Derives from Freud's assumption that human nature is not so much a hierarchy of high/low, and good/bad, as his predecessors believed, but rather a jostling democracy of contending predispositions, deposited in every nature in roughly equal intensities. Where there is love, there is the lurking eventuality of hatred. Where there is ambition there is the ironic desire for failure . . .

And so on. When man realizes that, he will no longer believe in his own passions or moral judgments enough to risk his happiness or his existence for them. No one was more profoundly ambivalent than Whitman, and more important, no one so fully used his awareness of his ambivalence to evade moral and emotional simplicities and militancies. Certainly Whitman's is a peace-preserving doctrine, and probably that is because his psychology broke down the hierarchies of high and low, good and bad, because his nature was a jostling democracy of differing predispositions, each one always being displaced by the next.

The central problem in reading Whitman, according to Richard Chase, has to do with his varying personality. Chase, who wrote very well about Whitman, points out how many different meanings are to be attached to the pronoun "I" in the poems. Sometimes it is very intimate, and even ironic about itself, sometimes very self-conscious and coy, and just as often brazenly self-proclaiming in a way hard to reconcile with the other meanings. It is this last which is so hard to take. For instance:

His shape arises,
Arrogant, masculine, naive, rowdyish,
Laugher, weeper, worker, idler, citizen, countryman,
Saunterer of wood, stander upon hills, summer swimmer in rivers or by the sea,
Of pure American breed, of reckless health, his body perfect, free from taint from top to toe, free forever from headache and dyspepsia, clean-breathed,
Ample-limbed, a good feeder, weight 180 lbs, full-blooded, 6' high, 40" round the breast and back,
Countenance sun-burnt, bearded, calm, unrefined,
Reminder of animals, meeter of savage and gentleman on equal terms,
Attitudes lithe and erect, costume free, neck gray and open, of slow movement on foot,
Passer of his right arm around the shoulders of his friends, companion of the street,
Persuader always of people to give him their sweetest touches and never their meanest . . .
Teacher of the unquenchable creed, namely, egotism,
Inviter of others continually henceforth to try their strength against him.

("Song of the Broad Axe").

In that passage we have Whitman, as so often, mythifying himself. The detail could not be more specific to one person—his weight, his height, his walk, etc., but at the same time we are told that this is one of the two shapes of Democracy. The other shape, the female, is very generalized and this description begins I think with fairly general intentions:

Laugher, weeper, worker, idler, citizen, countryman, but then it slides into building this statue of and to Walt Whitman himself. And at other times. Whitman identifies himself with the American continent, with all animal life, with all material, and his identification is not an admission of a kinship with these things outside himself, but a presentation of that kinship to us, these things interfused with his personality, their and his claims on our attention inextricable.

Chase's case for Whitman is that the interplay between these senses of Walt Whitman is witty and comic, and that *Song of Myself* is a witty and comic poem. Of many passages this is clearly true, but in other cases the shift from one meaning to the other is a slide rather than an interplay, and the effect is not witty but rather the reverse, if by witty one means a sharp sense of likenesses and unlikenesses, congruities and incongruities, and a game played between these. In the passage I quoted the effect depends on our not using that sense—indeed on our positively putting it to sleep. And since that sense is one which a literary man normally cultivates, the literary appreciation of Whitman is a problem, a difficult matter. This way of handling his identity probably lies at the root of a hundred things in Whitman's poetry which makes so many readers recoil from it.

Certainly it was these things that gave me my early problems with Whitman, when I wrote about him in *Re-appraisals*, and again the modern critics help to explain why. I spoke there of

his remarkable indeterminate slidings from one into another self. The self-responsible personality disappears. The crucial distinction, between what the poet felt, and what he might have felt if he had been somebody else, is fatally blurred; and this blurring extends to his tone as well as his vision. He is not speaking *to* any more than *as* a person. The social situation he sets up with his readers is always tending to become that of a speaker before a huge shapeless crowd, highly excitable and responsive and uncritical, each of whom he has to merge with himself, and with each other . . .

Whitman is not only non-literary. He offers to discuss personal experience, and then forces on us everything but that—catalogues of objects, political exhortations, ideas of sexuality, day-dreams, grotesque posturings. Even his catalogues are of things he had read about, not seen and heard himself. In a word, he does not tell us the truth. Quite often he tells lies—he says he has felt and seen things which he has not. Again and again, he makes a fool of himself . . . And all the time he asks his readers to cease to be persons—people who respect their own emotions—and to become partisans, members of a crowd, merging with each other in a stock response. In reading Whitman, therefore, despite moments of pleasure, a reader has to force himself to go against his nature as a reader.

I made there a rather risky connection between the reader, as a human role and the self-responsible, self-defining, personality, and asserted a disconnection, a discontinuity, between those and Whitman. It is interesting to find Philip Rieff and Marshall McLuhan making the same connection from a different point of view with almost opposite sympathies and with no reference to Whitman. Philip Rieff says, "We are probably witnessing the end of a cultural history dominated by book religions and word-makers." And then, he says, "Then the brief historic fling of the individual, celebrating himself as a being in himself, divine and therefore essentially unknowable, would be truly ended." And the new cultural history that will succeed that he says will be characterized by our "getting to know one another."

> Reticence, secrecy, concealment of self have been transformed into social problems; once they were aspects of civility, when the great Western formulary summed up in the credal phrase 'Know thyself' encouraged obedience to communal purposes rather than suspicion of them.
>
> (The Triumph of the Therapeutic, 1966).

Clearly Whitman was a forerunner of this new cultural history. He was reticent in his own way, but only as a cover over an enormous indiscretion. And for him "know thyself" meant learn how to outmaneuver the claims of communal purposes on your inner life; not learn how to enforce those claims against your own selfish impulses to avoid them. And therefore it is natural that in him the classical sense of identity, and of the tones possible in talking about oneself, and of the gestures and postures of the self permissible in presenting oneself, should be so defective, judged from the classical point of view. He had a quite different sense of identity, and the different sense of tone and gesture that followed from that. (It is interesting, incidentally, that Mr. Rieff, though he presents us with psychological man as a creation of the future, only just beginning to emerge in the present, admits that in *American* culture—though in no other—he may be in some degree native. He may have a nineteenth-century history. Rieff quotes de Tocqueville on American individualism, but he never mentions Whitman.)

That phrase about the end of book culture today reminds us of McLuhan, and McLuhan makes the same connection between bookreading and values like integrity of personality and privacy of judgment. He says, "The highly literate and individualist liberal mind is tormented by the pressure to become collectively oriented." This pressure towards collective orientation and total human interdependence McLuhan thinks is being exerted by the new electric technology:

> The literate liberal is convinced that all real values are private, personal, individual. Such is the message of mere literacy. . . .
> The partial and specialized character of the viewpoint, however noble, will not serve at all in the electric age.
> (The Gutenberg Galaxy, 1962).

But long before the electric age, Whitman had transcended this viewpoint as too partial and specialized, had become collectively oriented. This is just what Lawrence objected to in Whitman—his insistence on identifying himself with everybody else, his sacrifice of his own point of view, of his own limited integrity. (And incidentally I think Lawrence's insistence, in his own life, on integrity of feeling and limited identity at all times is related to what Miss Sontag objects to in him, his limitedly masculine and genital sexuality. She belongs on the same side of the dispute as Whitman.)

Whitman and McLuhan

McLuhan has many things to say that seem to me relevant to Whitman, and the final point I would like to take is his idea that field method characterizes modern habits of thought and consciousness in general. What he means by the phrase is perhaps best made clear by a few examples of how he uses it. Thus he calls the stream of consciousness, both as a literary technique and as a psychoanalytic technique, a field method, as contrasted with the assembly line of rational logic. And he calls the technique of suspended judgment, that is the use of not single but multiple models for experimental exploration, another example, and the great discovery of the twentieth century in art as well as in physics. And the time sense of typographic man, cinematic and sequential and pictorial, will be replaced in the next age by a field perception of time.

In field perception, then, a number of things are held in mind at the same time, with the relations between them and between each one and the perceiving subject not arranged in any fixed order of priority, and therefore, from any ordinary point of view, left ambiguous if not vague. Sometimes McLuhan uses the term mosaic for this, and connects it with communal participation and communal response as opposed to private, judgmental response. "The mosaic is the mode of the corporate or collective image and commands deep participation. This participation is communal rather than private, inclusive rather than exclusive."

This clearly fits the diagnosis of Whitman I formed in *Re-appraisals*, both in the effect of the poetry, its inclusivity and centrifugality of feeling, and in its means, the mosaic pattern of the catalogues and the inset stories and the multiple roles Whitman acts out for us. It is equally clear why McLuhan associates this mosaic form with the newspaper, and sets it in antithesis to the book form.

> As forms, as media, the book and the newspaper would seem to be as incompatible as any two media could be . . . The book form is not a communal mosaic or corporate image but a private voice. As the book page yields the inside story of the author's mental adventures, so the press page yields the inside story of the community in action and interaction.
>
> (*The Gutenberg Galaxy*).

McLuhan does not mention Whitman—he speaks rather of "the poets after Baudelaire" using the press format—but if we apply it to Whitman, we see that it amounts to another way of saying what I said in *Re-appraisals*, that there is something anti-literary in what Whitman is doing.

A hundred examples from *Song of Myself* will remind us how exactly that idea of McLuhan's answers—all unintendedly —to Whitman's method:

This is the city, and I am one of the citizens;
Whatever interests the rest interests me—politics, wars, markets,
newspapers, schools,
Benevolent societies, improvements, banks, tariffs, steamships,
factories, stocks, stores, real estate, and personal estate.

"Human interest" McLuhan describes as just a technical term

> meaning what happens when multiple book pages or multiple
> information items are arranged in a mosaic on one sheet. The
> book is a private confessional form that provides a point of
> view. The press is a group confessional form that provides com-
> munal participation just by means of its exposure of multiple
> items in juxtaposition.
>
> (*The Gutenberg Galaxy*).

Here is one example of Whitman following this policy:

I understand the large hearts of heroes,
The courage of present times and all times;
How the skipper saw the crowded and rudderless wreck of the
steamship and Death chasing it up and down the storm;
How he knuckled tight, and gave not back one inch, and was
faithful of days and faithful of nights.
And chalked in large letters, on a board, *Be of good cheer, we will
not desert you*;
How he followed with them and tacked with them—and would
not give it up;
How he saved the drifting company at last;
How the lank loose-gowned women looked when boated from the
side of their prepared graves;
How the silent old-faced infants, and the lifted sick, and the sharp-
lipped unshaven man;
All this I swallow—it tastes good—I like it well—it becomes mine;
I am the man—I suffered—I was there.
The disdain and calmness of olden martyrs;
The mother condemned for a witch, burnt with dry wood, her
children gazing on;
The hounded slave that flags in the race, leans by the fence, blowing
covered with sweat;
The twinges that sting like needles his legs and neck—the murderous
buckshot and the bullets;
All these I feel, or am.

("Song of Myself").

Now of course everyone knows that Whitman was a newspaper man by training and occupation, and that he remained
acutely attuned to, for instance, the chances of personal pub-

licity, all his life. And most people have always agreed that his poetry as well as his personality shows the influence of newspaper work. There is nothing new in that. What seems to me interesting is the connection of this fact with the others I have been discussing; the confusion of identity, the ambivalent personality, the giving up of privacy and decency, the evasion of political commitment, the multiple awareness of other cultures, religions, philosophies, the awareness of any belief as a thing to be participated in but not yielded to, and the development of a new sensuality, very powerful and yet oddly indeterminate, multiform, pervasive. What interests me above all is that all these things, each so separate from the others, and all so important to a group of thinkers I have called post-Freudian, should go together in Whitman. And the fact that none of these people mention Whitman, that they take their literary examples from other writers, who fit their purposes much worse—McLuhan citing Mallarmé and Eliot as examples of press format influencing poetry—this seems to me a guarantee of this connection. These people have not forced their arguments to fit this case. They have not been aware of this case. It is then history itself which corroborates them.

But I claimed at the beginning that bringing these people together with Whitman would enable each to throw light on the other. The light Whitman throws on them must be broken and discontinuous, because there are such big differences between members of the group; indeed the word group is not really appropriate. But I will *suggest* two points.

If Whitman's case is one which shows McLuhan to be on the right track in his distinction between the book and the newspaper as forms, it equally casts doubt on the importance he assigns to print as such. If anyone qualifies for the title Typographic Man, Whitman does; and yet his sensibility is a prime example of post-typographic man. Surely we must conclude that typography by itself is far from so important a determinant of sensibility and consciousness as McLuhan insists. It is in cooperation with other things—in this case, in cooperation with total literary format—that typography is important.

The second point is this: the sensibility which Susan Sontag and Norman Mailer express in their work—the sensibility I called modernist—is in some ways less in accord with their post-Freudian principles than Whitman's. They are much more angry and anguished, less cool and poised, more personally involved in the old style of the liberal point of view. Whitman is much freer, more amoral, self-sufficing, and self-emancipating. They are inconsistent. I needn't say I don't make this observation in any spirit of triumph over them. Consistency in matters of this kind is not to be called a virtue. It is more likely to be a vice. But as an observation this has its use in understanding these writers, I think.

The light thrown on Whitman I see as revealing the connection in him between the features we have discussed, the unified character of his work, its morality, its psychology, its aesthetic; a character quite unlike most other things in the nineteenth century and—I would agree with Rieff and McLuhan—closer to features of the culture of the present and possible future. And I think this helps us to understand better some of our difficulties in reading Whitman. That is all I would claim for the moment, as it were.

But of course I am not indifferent to the possibility that Whitman may prove to be a portent of part of our future, a sign of some things to come to us. That is the more disturbing idea to which I wish to point, but without taking full responsibility for advancing it.

Chapter 15

AMERICA AFTER 1945 III: CRITICISM AND THE SOCIAL CONTRACT NOW

We seem to be now in the trough of a wave of crisis in high-culture, that crisis when students repudiated study, and universities, those ships of intellectual state, pitched and tossed and wallowed and nearly wrecked. It may seem to be a teacher's parochiality to take *that* series of events as a general crisis in high-culture, but I suspect that most people—certainly more than would admit it—invest faith in the universities. They take the universities at their best to be the major manifestations of mind in our society, our major institutional investment in the life of the imagination, and so to be crucial investments in value. I myself take universities that way, as I discover with some surprise when I imagine abolishing them and transferring that function to some other body. And certainly the books I want to discuss here "believe in" universities.

These are three books written by literary critics out of the stress and strain the late 1960's imposed on them. The writers try to formulate a view of literature and criticism (and society and culture) which will justify their careers. The books have a good deal in common in their sense of contemporary conditions and of the modern period which led up to the crisis; in their autobiographical or at least existential character; in their more or less liberal position; and even in their method—they all slice the cultural organism at a psycho-historical angle, and set before us types of personality or modes of feeling (rather than books or authors or literary genres) as major exhibits and even arguments in their case.

The three books I have in mind are Lionel Trilling's *Sincerity and Authenticity*, the Norton Lectures for 1971; Northrop Frye's *Critical Path: An Essay on the Social Contex of Literary Criticism*, 1971; and my own *Cities of Light and Sons of the Morning*.* I don't really intend to discuss *Cities of Light*, but I want to point out certain resemblances between it and the other two books, in order to give them (and thus my present thesis) a greater substantiality, a representativeness. Even the contradictions of one book by another can be seen as variations on the themes they share. Examining those themes can, I think, show us how the general crisis made itself felt, and how that crisis bears on the practice of criticism.

Trilling's and Frye's books share a chronological scheme which revolves around certain changes which altered Western consciousness during the Renaissance. In Frye's scheme, the great change was the transfer of creativity from God to man, in Trilling's the birth of sincerity. Another great moment of change seems to be understood much the same way by both; that moment when books (for instance, Dostoevski's novels) began to embody revolutionary moral and even religious meanings; which Trilling describes as the triumph of Spirit in literature, or of spirituality, and Frye describes as the poets' resuming of that function of social lawgiver which had been theirs in the old oral cultures but had been lost for centuries. (But it is worth noting, though Frye does not make much of this, that in oral culture the poet's spirituality sanctions the society's normal practices, while, in modern culture, it usually denounces those practices.) Trilling dates this

* I shall give page references to these books (and others by Trilling and Frye) in their paperback editions. Details are given in the bibliography at the end of the essay.

change as occurring in the late nineteenth century, while Frye seems to set it earlier, but he does date the decay of humanism in the late nineteenth century, and perhaps he conceives of humanism as the force which till then held that poetic ambition in check. *Cities of Light* is ahistorical, in the sense that its idea of history is cyclical rather than linear, but its Faustian, Erasmian, and Calvinist types are defined psycho-historically, and its Faustianism—in that book's scheme—corresponds to the spirituality of the other two. Trilling's sincere personality or honest soul corresponds to my Erasmian temperament, and Frye's educational contract is an institutionalized version of my Erasmian contract. But of course each book has its own scheme of ideas, and must be taken primarily on its own terms.

Trilling's book draws a contrast between two forms of honesty, or the two kinds of personal honor that base themselves thereon. The first form, sincerity, he defines by referring to Polonius's injunction, "To thine own self be true," with its further bearing and rationalization, "It must follow, as the night the day, Thou canst not then be false to any man." The further bearing of this kind of honor is then peculiarly social. Trilling thinks it rose to prominence in the sixteenth century, in reaction to the new social mobility of those times, which tempted people to disguise their class origins and to invent new identities as they rose socially. He associates the ideal of sincerity with the opposite contemporary image of the villain, who was essentially a dissembler, a conscious hypocrite, like Iago. (Trilling says that to us, just because we are no longer "sincere" as the Elizabethan audience was, Iago's villainy seems exaggerated—demands explanation or subtilization—as does also Othello's heroic sincerity.)

Authenticity Trilling defines by referring to Diderot's dialogue, "Le Neveu de Rameau." In this dialogue between the nephew and Diderot himself, the former is angrily honest about his dishonesty in society, but his anger does not issue in any loyalty, however theoretical, to sincerity. It issues rather in the conviction that sincerity is impossible in practice—is only an ideal, a noble lie, or a self-deceiving nobility of style.

(Trilling associates this "noble style" with the belief in pleasure—in honor, wealth, beauty, the "fair courts of life"—the belief that the rewards which nature and society can give us have moral and aesthetic dignity. Authenticity denies that belief and so mocks that style.) The new man's style is ignoble, is consciously base. His honor lies all in defiantly acting out his anger at society's dishonesty, and in outraging social decorum, and in exceeding socially agreed limits of personality. Thus one of the things the nephew does within the dialogue is to perform a whole opera to his interlocutor, taking every part and mimicking every effect; which leaves Diderot, the honest soul, thoroughly uneasy and deeply embarrassed; but for himself as well as for the nephew. For the latter has shown himself to be more authentic than the former; that is how Trilling defines authenticity—a pursuit of self-expression beyond the limits of decency and decorum; and he thinks that our sensibility, in this century, has been increasingly dominated by an authentic kind of honesty and honor, which have gradually deprived the sincere kinds of imaginative validity.

A related phenomenon, at the end of the last century and the beginning of this one, was the magical value attached to masks (by Nietzsche, Wilde, Yeats, the 1890's aesthetes, and so forth.) This cult of masks indirectly implied that the pursuit of sincerity could lead only to dishonesty—to inauthenticity. But Trilling is more concerned with the active (indeed violent) pursuit of authenticity itself. He sees that cult as underlying today's repudiation of reason and culture and objectivity and even sanity—all the liberal values for which he himself stands.

Thus his interest in these concepts is shaped by contemporary concerns. But he stresses the indirect or negative effects of authenticity rather than its self-affirming manifestations. For instance, he leaves it to his readers to add that the rebellion of the students (his students at Columbia among others) often bore the stamp of authenticity in a primitivism of emotion and of action.

Sincerity and Authenticity is a difficult book to read just because Trilling left it to the reader to make many such explanatory additions. His ideas bear on (in some sense derive from) his immediate and personal concerns, but he defines them instead by reference to the past and to the books of the past. The closest he comes to naming what has troubled him personally is to cite R. D. Laing's and Douglas Cooper's and Norman O. Brown's theories of madness. But the reader who is familiar with Trilling's work and career can make some illuminating connections.

Let us take the incidents involving Allen Ginsberg and Trilling's story, "Of This Time, Of That Place," (*Best American Short Stories of 1944*) and Ginsberg's poem, "A Lion in the Room." Ginsberg was Trilling's student at Columbia (c.1943–1948) and apparently laid his personal problems in Trilling's hands, made them his emotional responsibility. The story, being about an imaginative and unstable student who invokes his teacher's protection for abnormalities which develop into outright madness, was taken by Ginsberg to refer to himself. Diana Trilling tells us, in "The Other Night at Columbia," (*Claremont Essays*, 1964) that Ginsberg would phone her husband, very late at night, to get him to say that the mad student was less mad than the sane society that condemned him. We gather that Trilling was deeply distressed, not least by the appeal to declare himself against society, and to return to Ginsberg, the enemy of society, as much feeling as he was getting from him. And in the same essay Mrs. Trilling describes attending a reading by the Beat poets, ten years later, at which Ginsberg read his poem, which she took to be a repentant declaration of grateful love for her husband.

The relevance of these incidents to this book is that Ginsberg's behavior, as a student, and as a Beat poet, and later, has been "authentic." Mrs. Trilling tells us of "flagrancies" of behavior, imagined and committed, which he insisted on recounting to her husband against the latter's will. Ginsberg was using them aggressively against the philistines of his society, but also against its most "sincere," most nobly sensitive, members, like Trilling. The latter was put into the position of Diderot, the honest soul, in their dialogues. So was Mrs. Trilling, though she, by her own account, simply disapproved of Ginsberg when he was a student, and when he emerged as a national celebrity, forgave him very condescendingly. In her essay she still takes the tone of a brisk mother-figure, sure that these bearded would-be poets are only being so shocking in order to attract her attention. She and her husband, in their different ways and degrees, have both cultivated sincerity, the form of honor which serves social purposes. But the liveliest writing of the last twenty years has come from men like Ginsberg, who cultivated authenticity instead. (Trilling comments sadly on Bellow's ineffectual attempt to resist that tendency, in *Herzog*.) Behind the text of *Sincerity and Authenticity* one hears a more private rumination. "You mean then that I have been inauthentic? Perhaps. It is my penalty for trying so hard to be sincere."

Since Trilling did not make this connection for us, the connection between *Sincerity and Authenticity* and his own life, it may be that he did not want us to make it either. But his ideas gain so much, in precision and power as well as pathos, when we do make that connection, that we cannot feel guilty toward him. We then see Trilling as a central figure in the cultural drama of the last ten years, and as criticism's protagonist. He has never assumed a heroic style, being very unlike Leavis in his discretion, his quietness, his elusiveness; and then the narrowness of his social range, his self-referral almost exclusively to New York Jewish liberalism, have made him seem less "representative" of America than other critics. But so much of the best writing of the last twenty years has come from these liberals or their rebellious sons or their close allies, and Trilling's relation to them has been peculiarly close and his example has worked on them with peculiar power both in attraction and in repulsion.

For instance, Trilling's preoccupation with Freud has surely been of major importance in both Freud's acceptance by the "orthodox" intelligentsia of New York, and his rejection by "heretics" like Mailer. Trilling attributed to Freud the tragic view of life, the Shakespearian vision of good and evil, the weighting and stiffening of life with that stern dignity which religion had used to give it. He made Freud the renewer of traditional values. The heretics perhaps saw in this a refurbishing of old inhibitions and prudences—at any rate they rebelled against Freud and traditional culture and everything liberal.

But even then they were following Trilling's suggestion and encouragement, his implicit advice. As early as 1943, in his book on E. M. Forster, Trilling was defining the weaknesses of the liberal imagination in very much the same way as Mailer was to do in *Armies of the Night*, in 1968. Trilling says that Forster, and by implication he himself, is at war with the liberal imagination, and that liberalism's one desperate weakness is the inadequacy of its imagination. Moreover, whatever liberals *say*, in practice they require absolutes and ideals in conduct; "it [liberalism] prefers to make its alliances only where it thinks it catches the scent of Utopia in parties and governments, the odor of sanctity in men" (p. 14). Twenty-five years later, Mailer says, "Like the scent of the void which comes off the pages of a Xerox copy, so was he always depressed in such homes [those of liberal intellectuals] by their hint of over-security. If the republic was now managing to convert the citizenry to a plastic mass . . . the author was ready to cast much of the blame for such success into the under-nourished lap, the over-psychologized loins, of the liberal academic intelligentsia . . . they were the natural managers of that future air-conditioned vault where the last of human life would still exist" (p. 26).

Trilling says that the moral and pious aspect of the intellectual's tradition is very important. "Intellectuals as a class do not live by ideas alone, but also by ideals . . . [They feel themselves responsible for] the freedom and privilege of groups less advantageously placed than their own. . . . Consequently, liberal intellectuals have always moved in an aura of self-congratulation. . . . To these people ["the people"] he vaguely supposes himself to be in a benevolent superior relation, paternal, pedagogic, even priestlike. He believes it necessary to suppose that they are entirely good. . . ." (*E. M. Forster*, pp. 123–125). Mailer also accuses liberals of having no passions of their own. "The private loves of the ideologues were attached to no gold-standard of the psyche." Love and power, guilt, greed, compassion, trust, are all only concepts to them. "The Freud-ridden embers of Marxism, good old American anxiety strata—the urban middle class, with their proliferated monumental adenoidal resentments, their secret slavish love for the oncoming hegemony of the computer and the suburb." (*Armies of the Night.*)

The two rhetorics are much the same, though the tone of the one is ironic, while that of the other is angry. But of course that makes as large a difference as tone can ever encompass. Trilling ruefully remarks the limitations of the liberal mind he himself shares, and recommends a compensatory regime of relaxed playfulness and profound irony. Mailer angrily repudiates that mind, changes himself away from being a liberal, by a regime of commitment, passion, action, authenticity.

To take another example, Trilling read Isaac Babel's *Red Cavalry* in 1929 with profound disturbance, he tells us. He found in it the fate of being a Jew dichotomized into a tragic dilemma—a Jew has to choose between being violent and being over-gentle. Babel tells how at the age of nine he had seen his Jewish father kneel in humiliation before a Cossack captain "who gazed ahead like one who rides through a mountain pass." The nine year old boy was already an intellectual, a student of the Torah, "with spectacles on my nose and autumn in my heart." But he rebelled against his fate. After the Revolution he joined a Cossack troop, adored its leader, a giant called Savitsky, and forced himself to kill, as a test of his manhood. This was the myth of the Jewish fate which Trilling found in *Red Cavalry*, and it disturbed him very deeply. It was later to be the myth that haunted Mailer and Bellow and later Jewish writers. As Leslie Fiedler points out in *Waiting for the End*, both Mailer and Bellow invented (for themselves or for Jewish representatives in their fiction) fantasy personas who were *goy* figures of power and violence, like Sergius O'Shaughnessy and Henderson the Rain King.

There is plenty of evidence that the problems of being Jewish, understood along these lines, have been a major preoccupation of Trilling's. His early pieces, especially those written during 1925 and 1926, his year of exile from New York in Wisconsin, seem to echo a crisis of identity of which the two poles were his Jewishness and his genius. He was very consciously a Jew, doubly alienated from the dominant philistines of his society, and called to the traditional Jewish accommodation of the intellectual life. On the other hand, he felt himself more gifted than others, Jewish or *goyim*, a proud athlete of the mind, in some way akin to the boldest Byrons and Rimbauds. (Keats consciously wanted to be a *hero*, and in a young man this is always most winning, Trilling tells us in his 1951 essay on Keats; and he shows the same special fondness for Dickens, another genius of boldness and fecundity.) He finally chose an ironic version of the first option, he chose Arnold and Forster, ironic sincerity and criticism; but he carried with him the traces of more heroic destinies he had declined, and what he wrote carried the seeds of those destinies to both his disciples and his antagonists, and to that large class who were both in part.

The most striking example of that class for me is Mailer, who may well have had no personal contact with Trilling at all, but whose work seems often to *answer* Trilling's quite directly. Or sometimes Trilling's work answers Mailer's. Thus Trilling's categories of sincerity and authenticity leap to life the moment they are used to interpret *Armies of the Night*. And Mailer's long digressions there about Lowell (and Macdonald and Goodman) justify themselves once one sees that he is defining his own politics as authentic and Lowell's as sincere. (He even uses the terms "base" for himself and "noble" for Lowell.) Mailer is claiming that *his* is the kind of politics we must trust, *his* is the account of the Pentagon we must believe, because it is authentic. His drunken stage performance before the March, recounted to us at such length, is a demonstration of his authenticity, very like the nephew's rendition of the opera in Diderot's dialogue, and we, as readers, are left (as were Lowell, Macdonald, Goodman, on the right) in the embarrassed position of honest souls, acknowledging a witness to the truth who has passed beyond all decorum, beyond all limits, beyond *us*, in his quest for total honesty, total commitment, total self-revelation.

Trilling's categories this time enable us to understand what Mailer was doing, and Mailer's performance explains why Trilling had to work out these categories afterward. More often, Trilling's categories came first, and Mailer's performance took them up to contradict them, to contradict the spirit behind them. In both cases, Trilling emerges as the man who has, more than any other, defined the situations and set up the options for his younger contemporaries. And if they used what he taught them to repudiate his own choices and his whole teaching that only adds to the interest and dignity of his position. He has been "the critic" for them. By what he has done, and not done, he has embodied criticism for them. Turning away from him, they turned away from all criticism. And he has pursued them with his mind, and understood them, and so re-established criticism's reign over them.

Northrop Frye does not practice criticism, in my sense of the term, and he is criticism's professed enemy. Or those things *were* true. In *The Critical Path* and *The Stubborn Structure*, writings of the 1970's, he has turned his attention to literature-and-society, and so become a critic. Of course he had talked about literature and society before, but in a way that denied the possibility of those intimate interactions between the two concerns which we symbolize by the compound noun. He had said that the study of literature as a whole, the formalist study of literature, ultimately had a social function, because it developed men's imaginations, and so taught them to formulate their ideals for society; but that our study of society, our political values, and so forth, had no literary function, or a deleterious one; so that in our experience of reading a book we should not try to bring that other experience into play, but should focus on purely literary matters. So he was not a critic. Now he is, in the sense that he admits *some* legitimate interaction between the two concerns and directs *some* attention to it, but he still is not a critic in my sense, because he still refuses to make the connections that seem life-giving to me. So his book will be described polemically.

Frye's equivalents, in importance of concept, for Trilling's sincerity and authenticity, are the myth of concern and the myth of freedom. A society's myth of concern is its ideology of values, political, legal, social, and so forth, seen under the aspect of myths, which are sometimes religious, sometimes patriotic, and so forth, in their coloring. The myth of freedom embodies a somewhat contrary set of values, which acknowledge an ultimate loyalty to the concerns of that society, but belong to a distinct subset and partially threaten the values of concern, inasmuch as they center in objectivity, rationality, critical skepticism, free play of mind. The values of freedom are close to what Trilling means by mind, and Trilling would no doubt accept Frye's terms, and agree that the crisis of our times is that the myth of freedom has been discredited among its natural adherents in the universities. The study of literature is of course quite crucially related to both myths. But what Frye means by saying that is not what criticism means.

Frye began his career by taking up a radical position (Tory-radical) about the relations of literature to society. He declared most criticism to be either vulgar response (to the author's life or his opinions) or stock response (to things in art taken as if they were out of art). These inadequate and irrelevant responses expressed the reader's "values," and Frye set himself to eradicate value-judgments root and branch. (Even in "Reflections in a Mirror", as late as 1966, he says, "My approach to criticism makes no *functional* use of value-judgments; but then no criticism does, that gives us any knowledge of art.") His position was a further development of the anti-humanism implicit in T. S. Eliot's criticism, which was fairly openly "Tory." Frye, however, declared the English tradition in poetry to be Protestant, romantic, and revolutionary, a neat reversal of Eliot's cultural slogans of Catholic, classical, and royalist. He derived his poetics not from Dante but from Blake. This contradiction at least confused the issue and baffled those who sought to classify Frye as aesthetically Tory. Moreover, he appeared to be politically radical. Despite the prim and professional character of his wit—he was from the start a very witty and entertaining writer—he also spoke seriously for social change and in alliance with social radicals. He took as examples of his High Demotic style both the Sermon on the Mount and a contemporary statement by a participant in the struggle for desegregation. So that Frye seemed to propagandize radical social dogma at the same time as he insisted on aesthetic dogma that divorced art from social values entirely. Thus for twenty years after *Fearful Symmetry*, 1947, Frye seemed to represent a significant, though enigmatic, new option in literary criticism.

The events of the 1960's of course imposed a severe strain on Frye, as on other literary critics. But Frye's literary persona does not express strain as simply as, say, Trilling's; Trilling's is quite subtle enough, but he is full of pathos, giving readers the sense that just off the page he is conducting a self-interrogation and even judgment with full panoply of axe and organ and red velvet. Frye expresses strain by firing off a new sheaf of epigrams and paradoxes and *obiter dicta*, each more sparkling than the last. His strain is to be measured only by the incompatibility of these pronouncements with the preceding set and with each other. For when you subject these chapters to close scrutiny, it becomes clear that Frye is not at his best at pronouncing on "the social context of literary criticism." His attempts to rationalize literary-and-social experience are full of twists and tricks and cheats—perhaps unconscious and certainly masked by the style of a grand master, but cheats nevertheless. Each sentence is beautifully clear and sharpens to an unmistakable point or hook; and each sentence links on to the last and the next with the click of precision tooling. But if you align sentence one with sentence ten you are likely to find them pointing in very different directions.

One reason for this is the radical concessions he makes, in this book, to the position he so long attacked, to criticism. A passage, though not entirely unambiguous, seems to announce this. "Criticism will always have two aspects, one turned toward the structure of literature and one turned toward the other cultural phenomena that form the social environment of literature. Together, they balance each other; when one is worked on to the exclusion of the other, the critical perspective goes out of focus." [Surely Frye would have to admit that what he used to do, and teach others to do, was precisely to work on the first aspect to the exclusion of the other? Unfortunately he doesn't *say* that.] "If criticism is in proper balance, the tendency of critics to move from criticism to larger social issues becomes more intelligible." [More intelligible then when? Than when criticism is not in proper balance, presumably. Does that mean Leavis's criticism—Frye names Leavis as the representative of value-judgment criticism—and that Frye originally reacted against the "movement to larger social issues" because he first met it in such unbalanced critics? Again, it seems a pity he does not *tell* us.] "Such a movement need not, and should not, be due to a dissatisfaction with the narrowness of criticism as a discipline, but should be simply the result of a sense of social context, a sense present in all critics from whom one is in the least likely to learn anything" (p. 25). This last sentence seems to resolve the passage into a large and generous concession. One's only disappointment then is that it does not lead to larger consequences in Frye's critical procedures—that he keeps saying much the same things as before about the study of literature—remains in practice hostile to criticism, and inconsistent with his own new theory. Except that the connection he now admits between the study of literature and the criticism of society we must call mystical. By *possessing* works of literature in our imaginations, by incorporating their powers into ourselves, we shall be enabled to apply the criteria of imagination to social reality (p. 126). But we come to possess them by not looking at them critically—to scrutinize them as objects, as agents of meaning and value, would be aestheticism. (This curious use of "aestheticism" seems largely designed to put Frye into the position of being able to call Leavis an aesthete, which he then does. Several curious items in Frye's intellectual weaponry have to be explained the same way, as anti-personnel items, designed to cause maximum distress to highly specified members of the enemy forces.) Instead we must look *through* the criteria. As Blake says we must look *through* our senses to see imaginative reality. This use of Blake's idea is characteristic of Frye, not so much in the fact that he uses Blake, as in the way he appropriates a poetic idea for a professorial purpose. Another example is his theory that literature is a mythological language, or code, of concern. It makes no statements of value itself—being art—but it enables such statements to be made by, for instance, religion, and to be understood by the general reader (p. 128). This seems to me strikingly analogous to Wordsworth's theory of Nature, as teaching us the *language* of religious feeling.

Both of Frye's applications of these ideas are ingenious; but that is all, surely. Of course, we want to possess great poems imaginatively and to see *through* them, but the obvious way to achieve that is first to look at them as works of meaning, to criticize them, to embrace them searchingly and evaluatively. And of course literature is a language of concern, but it is so because each great poem makes statements of concern, which have to be encountered at some point in much the same way that such statements are encountered outside art—certainly if that particular poem is ever to become an imaginative possession of ours. One cannot take either idea quite seriously. One cannot feel that Frye takes literature-and-society quite seriously. He is not really at ease with it.

Frye sees himself as a modern equivalent of those Renaissance humanists he often discusses. At least he often hints that we should make that connection; he defines those humanists as scholars and not poets, and as insiders not outsiders of the culture of their day, and as the men who defined the social function of the poets, and in effect ruled them. Such a theory of the two types' relationship, and of his own performance as humanist is surely what is always implied by Frye's voice and persona. But he also says that humanism was the intellectual expression of an aristocratic social structure, and so became impossible under democracy, so that he calls Matthew Arnold the *last* of the great humanists. Presumably Frye used to see himself as—he certainly presented himself as—an avatar of Blake rather than Arnold; he was the critic-as-Blake, revolutionary and romantic as well as professor, minister, and college president. But in these books of the 1970's he only half-heartedly hints at that role for himself, and yet he insists on the non-viability of humanism. So when he discusses the theory of a completely democratic culture with no fine arts and no high culture (Morris's theory in *News from Nowhere*) the reader wonders if Frye is not fascinated by that ideal as the culmination of his own tendencies. Has he not worked himself into a false position, a position of decreeing his own extinction?

One often senses that Frye has talked himself into a proposition that rings false to his deeper feelings, his settled convictions, lured there by his love of surprising the reader. For instance, in "Speculation and Concern," an essay in *The Stubborn Structure*, we find him suggesting that perhaps the arts are *all* inferior to the sciences (p. 39). And from the beginning his critical theory was marked by the boldness with which he stole the poet's thunder for the critic. (The word "stole" is suggested by the neat paradoxical impudence with which he reapplied to the critic formulas that traditionally described the poet; and by his air of having got away with something which he would of course restore to the rightful owner if we could catch him.) The encyclopedic scope of his poetics, including every myth and every work of literature in every language, is the largest example of that boldness. Another is his cool condescension to poets and novelists as being simple-minded folk, who often mistake their own poetic devices for reality, and who are, at their best, scholarly technicians of myth, cool-headed, hard-working transmitters of tradition like scholars (*The Educated Imagination*, pp. 25, 28, and passim). Another is his deriving his poetics so directly from Blake. This also had the effect of silencing the spokesmen for poetic freedom and imagination, who are the usual enemies of scholarly law-givers. Frye seems to speak in the *name* of freedom, in the very voice of imagination; he spoke *through* Blake, because he possessed Blake.

But now that the pressure of events has forced Frye to discuss current crises and their bearing on literature-and-society in his own voice, it becomes clear that that was all a maneuver, all only the boldest of his many bold feats of ingenuity. Frye's relation to the larger social issues, and even imaginative issues, is very unlike Blake's. Frye is a spokesman for his own class, and that is a very different class from Blake's. He had been hijacking Blake for the managerial establishment, hijacking poetry for scholarship, hijacking revolution for the university and the church and the government commission. (As C. S. Lewis "occupied" heaven and hell for the Establishment in England. Frye often reminds us of Lewis, another Establishment egghead adept at disguise—painting a cowboy's kerchief over his clerical collar and impersonating the outdoors man to popular applause.) Frye, we now see, had been using Blake's corpse as a shield and deepening his voice in imitation of Blake's, as he strode boldly into the gambling hell of squabbling poets and revolutionaries; and in effect he struck them all dumb for twenty years. The trick was so neat it would be a shame to unmask him, if one didn't have to in order to talk seriously about these matters.

One could point to many fraudulent items in Frye's vocabulary by which that trick is worked. Those interested might look at "aestheticism," "culture," and "literature"—the last being a force spoken for sometimes by the poet and sometimes by the critic, even when the latter two are supposed to be at loggerheads. But perhaps one case is enough, his use of the word "revolutionary." The most vivid examples of this come in *The Stubborn Structure*, where we find, "The Platonic conception of the relation of education to society is a revolutionary one: the shape of a just society, as education conceives it, is so different from that of society as we know it that the two cannot coexist: one is bound to regard the other as its enemy" (p. 8). "Realism in a healthy condition is another form of socially revolutionary art: it explores society, shows compassion with misery . . ." (p. 59). "Democracy is a genuinely revolutionary society, neither about to be revolutionized nor trying to retain its present structure, but mature enough to provide for both change and stability" (p. 60). It is surely undeniable that Frye uses "revolutionary" to mean what the English language means by "idealistic" (or "liberal" or "critical") and that he does so in order to capture the afflatus of the former word for his argument, and to avoid the tarnished defeatism of the latter word. This is so light-hearted an intellectual tactic as to be quite winning, but of course it means the end of serious argument. If we intended to go on giving Frye serious attention, we should have to call this light-minded rather than light-hearted.

Northrop Frye is, on cultural topics, a performer of professorial vaudeville, who skips around the ring giving an expert mimicry of real boxing, but not landing or taking any real blows. He is a dandy paradoxist, and his sponsor should be Nabokov rather than Blake. Indeed, his critical method would apply very well to *Pale Fire*, compounded as that book is of so many allusions to other works of literature. And it is no accident that his theory of the university as a social contract, the study of the arts and sciences as society's gauge of idealism, can remind us of some lines from *Pale Fire*.

> But who can teach the thoughts we should roll-call
> When morning finds us marching to the wall
> Under the stage direction of some goon
> Political, some uniformed baboon?
> We'll think of matters only known to us—
> Empires of rhyme, Indies of calculus. . . .

While a few more lines from the same passage suggest the tendency of Frye's tone at its liveliest.

> And while our royal hands are being tied,
> Taunt our inferiors, cheerfully deride
> The dedicated imbeciles, and spit
> Into their eyes just for the fun of it.

However, Frye is to be treated so dismissively only when he is dealing with the complex interactions of literature and society. When he talks about the latter by itself, as for instance in that theory of the university, he deserves our attention; he finds a new and interesting route to Matthew Arnold's conclusions. When he talks about literature by itself he nearly always commands respect, except when he attacks value-judgments. (His treatment of *that* question is exemplified by remarks in his 1951 essay, "The Archetypes of Literature," 1951, where he says that casual value judgments, based on sentiment or prejudice, belong to the history of taste. He says nothing about non-casual judgments, those not based on sentiment or prejudice—*all* judgments are implicitly subsumed under this category in order to be dismissed. It is hard to believe that this is the same man who on other topics can argue so carefully and be so serious.) For instance, his theory of a man's reading experience as something essential, independent of the individual books he has read and of his existential experiences in reading them, seems to me very suggestive. But the complex subject of the relations of literature and society throws his mind out of gear; which seems to me to demonstrate the value of that "cultural" study of literature he so long flouted, the study I call criticism.

What all three books taken together demonstrate is what used to be called the "grandeur and misery" of criticism; the pride and ambition which criticism wonderfully sustains in its adherents, and the shock they feel on meeting (as they did in the late 1960's) its limitations. *Cities of Light* is the book that most directly and consciously confronts these questions and records this shock; because I was brought up in a highly self-conscious and self-confident tradition of criticism. But Trilling's book, and whole career, indirectly illuminates that grandeur and misery, too. Trilling has been anti-heroic—taking a cue from Wordsworth and the Rabbis, it seems—but what he has taken from Freud all these years has been the doctrine of criticism. As he says in an essay, "Freud: Within and Beyond Culture," 1955, Freud felt his immediate cultural environment, as a Viennese Jew, to be hostile, oppressive, unworthy of his allegiance. But he accepted and cultivated ideal forms of culture (including something so substantial though remote as contemporary England) and gave his allegiance through them to the best potentialities of civilized life. Thus he criticized and protested that life, in his measure changed it, but without recourse to direct revolt. Trilling too has brought ideal culture as a remedy to actual culture—that is the theory of *The Liberal Imagination*—and his best work is a proud achievement of criticism. But during the last ten years, he has seen the men of intensest sensibility, who should have been his disciples, repudiate everything he stood for. He has felt the misery of criticism.

Frye, on the other hand, began his career in triumphant scorn of criticism, and defiant assertion of aesthetic scholarship. He thrived in the cultural climate produced by America's post-war prosperity, in which the universities formed a society of their own, each university a city—in some cases a nation-state—of its own, with scholarly industries booming in seeming independence of their political protectors. In those circumstances, the hero with a thousand faces came to look like Frye, a massively abstract intellect, in command of all the toughest intellectual cyphers, and forearmed against the reproaches of moral and political engagement. He combined a totalitarian system with an elegant eclecticism, so that he was able to touch on everything he chose and to make brilliant paradoxical connections without renouncing seriousness. (And he had of course a great deal of taste and knowledge—anyone can learn a lot from Frye.) The fate the last ten years have brought *him* has been to make him acknowledge the grandeur of criticism—in part explicitly, but even more implicitly, by his vain search for an alternative way to discuss literature-and-society.

Despite these differences, the three books have a good deal in common, and can be taken to add up to a single statement (description and prescription) about criticism today—a statement of the close connections between criticism and liberalism. All three are liberal, in that their political tendencies turn away equally from revolution and from reaction, and their immediate attention turns away from all action, all politics. If that is explicit only in *Cities of Light*, it is implicit in Frye's definition of "revolutionary" and in Trilling's sense of the current threat to mind. All three set great store by universities and all that they represent in society. And all three owe a great debt to Matthew Arnold—*Cities of Light* via Leavis, the other two more directly. It is quite striking to see such opposites as Frye and Leavis owing so much to the same precursor. (It is the Hebraic and Hellenic side of Arnold that is most felt, the German-style analysis of a cultural situation by means of two hypostatized ideas, that are dialectically inter-related.) And both Frye and Trilling discuss—as an alternative to their own positions—Morris's idea of a culture of crafts, with no fine arts, no geniuses, no great achievements of individual will and desire. They see this as the aesthetic policy appropriate to radicals; which of course fits well with the idea of the Calvinist temperament discussed in *Cities of Light*.

Such divisions of function between liberal and radical imply a special affinity between liberals and the great works of art and the high culture that centers around them. Liberals are the natural interpreters (conservatives the natural *guardians*) of that high culture. But they are also its critics. For what gives criticism and liberalism their vitality is that they involve more than guardianship and interpretation. They involve working out new ideas, new modes of thought, new modes of action, new identities.

Bibliography

Lionel Trilling: *The Opposing Self*, New York, 1955. (Essay on Keats.)

The Liberal Imagination, New York, 1950. (Essay on Freud.)

Beyond Culture, New York, 1965. (Essays on Freud, and Babel.)

Sincerity and Authenticity, Cambridge, 1972.

Northrop Frye: *Fables of Identity*, New York, 1963.

The Stubborn Structure, Cornell, 1970.

The Educated Imagination, Indiana, 1969.

The Critical Path, Indiana University Press, 1973.

Northrop Frye in Modern Criticism, ed. Murray Krieger, N.Y., 1966. (Frye's essay, "Reflections in a Mirror.")

Chapter 16

BRITISH NOVELISTS
WRITING ABOUT AMERICA
AND VICE VERSA*

The first point to make is that there is not much vice versa. American novelists have written very little about Britain in the last twenty years, and when one adds the limitation of significance—limits the showing to significant novelists, making significant statements—one can almost say there is nothing. But this is itself a significant statement, of course. It tells us that our climate of ideas is such that there seems to be nothing exciting to say about the English experience for Americans. There *is* such an experience, after all; the sort of Americans who write novels are to be found in England, in university teaching, in publishing, in writing; there may be as many of them as there are Englishmen in America. But only the latter's experience, and not the former's, expresses itself in novel-form, or essay-form.

The Americans come to England for a quiet life—at the varying levels of dignity which that phrase can be made to carry. There is a good deal of nostalgia, of conservatism, of retreat, in their journey, though of course one must not equate retreat

* This chapter appeared in *Old Lines, New Forces* (Cranbury, N.J.: Associated University Presses, 1977), pp. 53, 67, R.K. Morris, ed. Reprinted by permission.

with cowardice. For that reason, their London tends to be the old London of the Duke's Hotel and the London Library, the London S. J. Perelman used to write about and finally retreated to, an almost Edwardian London still. The other city that is written about in the magazines, swinging London, does not seem to engage their attention. That is not what they came for, the King's Road, the Beatles, "Blow-up," or even R. D. Laing. Obviously, my "they" derives from one group of American writers, those New York Jewish intellectuals who do have an attraction to London. The wilder radicals, in flight from America, seem to feel that however long they stay, they are just passing through, on their way to Algiers.

The main case I can think of, where a significant American novelist makes use of London, is Saul Bellow in *Mr. Sammler's Planet*, and it is typically nostalgic. Arthur Sammler, a Polish-born intellectual, refers back to the London he knew when he was a friend of H. G. Wells. This was the happiest time of his life, and he looks back to it for consolation in the period of violence and anti-intellectual insurrection that he is enduring in New York in 1969. In Wells's London the formalities of life, social and intellectual, were observed even while the most revolutionary plans were being drawn up for changing human society and even human nature.

Bellow is expressing the anguish of his whole generation of radicals, and London is an important reference point in his discourse. But there is no other use for it in the American adventure of ideas. We had, in the Fulbright period, lots of novels about Italy and France (Fiedler and Styron, for instance) and Bellow on Africa, but of recent years American novelists have felt that the action was at home and that of all places it was not in England.

By and large, the English novelists have agreed. There are lots of novels by Englishmen about Americans in England, and the American is usually granted more size than the other characters, including the English. And there are lots of novels, like *Gumshoe*, about Englishmen trying to make themselves into Americans. But the most significant group, or subgenre, is of novels about Englishmen visiting America. Since they all have a lot in common, I propose to describe one of them, and then point out the similarity between that and the others.

Malcolm Bradbury's Stepping Westward

Stepping Westward is a great advance over Bradbury's first novel, *Eating People Is Wrong*; in fact, it shows a really significant comic talent; let us take as an example this passage describing the hero's arrival in New York. He takes a cab from the dock to his hotel with the all-too-English girl he has become involved with on board.

> "Okay, let's move," said the cabbie, lighting a cigar with a book-match, and between them Miss Marrow and Walker strove manfully with the heavy luggage, finally getting it all into the passenger area and retaining a tiny intimate spot for themselves. "You just made it, don't you?" said the cabbie, turning round at last. "Where to?" Walker gave the name of Miss Marrow's hotel off Times Square, and his own in Brooklyn Heights. "You two not staying at the same place?" said the cabbie. "Come on, why not shack up together, make things easier for all of us. I don't got to drive so far, you got fun. How's that for a suggestion?" He pushed in his gear-lever and they swept under the expressway, over the cobbles and rail-tracks. "Whadya say, lady?" They turned up one of the crosstown streets, past the unmistakable odour of the abattoir, towards the centre of the island. Dust and paper blew out of lidless garbage cans on the kerbside and iron fire-escapes staggered down the sides of ancient buildings, falling into decay. People sat on stoops, white, coloured. Sun glinted on windows, the city looked dark and hostile, and Walker felt defeated and confused, an animal without a soul, a dead thing. "No," said Miss Marrow, winking coyly at Walker.

A great deal, about the three people involved and about the two environments they represent, is said there with the crispness of expert comedy.

But I don't want primarily to appraise the novel here. I want to reflect on some of its themes, both as Bradbury handles them and as they exist (in the reader's mind) outside his handling of them. It is just what makes him a significant comic talent, of course, that he puts his finger on material in the reader's mind which stimulates one to this sort of thinking. Those themes may be described as some American psychological types and their environment, or the differences between all that and the English equivalent. But in fact, as Bradbury fictionally defines those types, they are something much more sharply challenging and richly suggestive than "types"; they are a discovery of his own, and a discovery for us of our own experience.

The story tells how James Walker, a literary married Englishman, comes to America on a creative writing fellowship to a Western university, and there encounters a different idea of being a writer and being married. This idea, which is essentially the same mode of being in two different contexts, is in fact his "America." He finds it very exciting and very inviting, and much larger than the English equivalents. But he himself does not measure up to it, and at the end of the book he goes back to England, which means his "large domestic wife" and his writing of querulous comic novels.

The American idea or mode of being is embodied first in Julie Snowflake, a student at somewhere like Wellesley, who meets Walker on the ship from England, visits him during the Christmas vacation, takes him off with her to California, and finally rejects him. This is the sexual, would-be-marital, mode of the idea. In its literary-intellectual version, the American idea is embodied in Bernard Froelich, a member of the English faculty at Benedict Arnold University, who gets Walker the fellowship, who persuades him to refuse the loyalty oath the university imposes, and who exploits the resultant scandal to advance his own interests.

Bradbury has drawn both these figures very well, it seems to me. It is the things they say which are best—very accurate, very funny, very interesting and impressive bits of behavior— but he also knows the houses they live in, the books they read, the food they eat, and so on. The writing about them is on a different level from the straight satirical description of institutions and streets and Americana. Bradbury is always sharp in his observation, but when he deals with Julie Snowflake and

Bernard Froelich he is doing more than observe. He is responding to an idea, and the surface reality interests him also as the
expression of something within, about which he has many,
powerful, and conflicting, feelings.

There is an important difference between the two major
manifestations of the American idea. Froelich condemns himself
finally as a bully, a careerist, and a manipulator, while Julie is
none of these things, and remains essentially incriticizable. She
seems to Walker more "beautiful and human" than anyone he
has ever met, and she is presented to us for much the same
response. She deserves to be compared with Margot Beste-
Chetwynde in *Decline and Fall*, and though Bradbury does
not yet have Waugh's dazzling incisiveness and economy in
designing a novel as a whole, his idea of his heroine is really
the more interesting of the two. Julie and Margot both represent "calmness, coolness, freshness" (Bradbury's phrase) to
the young men at the center of the two novels. They are both
quicker, cleverer, gayer, bolder, *freer*—their physical beauty is
supererogatory—than the young men themselves or than anyone else. Above all, they have style; in everything they say and
do they achieve themselves; their behavior is a creation, a
work of art. Their moments of self-doubt, the tremors that
mar their style momentarily, only make that style more humanly authentic and valuable, more really triumphant.

The fact that Julie is an American undergraduate while
Margot is a Mayfair hostess—and white-slave-trader—vividly
shows us the way the British literary imagination has changed
in thirty-five years. It has changed not merely in its attitudes
to America and to the British upper classes but also in its modern preference for "life"-values. But what makes Julie a more
interesting heroine, and is Bradbury's achievement, is that he
has taken his idea more seriously than Waugh or than most
comic novelists. We know more about Julie; she is real as
much as ideal. When Waugh tried to take Margot seriously we
got something like Julia in *Brideshead Revisited*, something
faintly caricatural. Waugh's mind was too powerfully sardonic
to leave a heroine free to be herself. Bradbury's mind is looser,
more fragmentary, more compelled by things outside itself.

So Julie Snowflake is a much finer manifestation of "America" than Froelich; in fact it is she who finally judges and condemns Froelich for Walker. But they are still versions of the same idea, only of differing moral quality. For the point about Froelich too is the forcefulness and authenticity of his style; he too achieves himself in everything he says and does. He is aggressive all the time, throwing any onus of embarrassment, anxiety, uncertainty, guilt, on to the other person; but wittily and even winsomely—with style. When we first meet him he quite stupidly damages the car he is driving—which belongs to the chairman of his department—by reversing into a fence.

> "Oh dear," said Walker, coming round the other side of the car.
> "Well, that's how it is," said Froelich, "no matter how careful you are, there's always the other fellow."
> "Bit of a mess, isn't it?"
> "Isn't it?" said Froelich.
> "You must have been in reverse," said Walker, his longish, roundish English face peering seriously into the damage, as if a word or two from him might rectify the situation.
> "Well," said Froelich, "don't just do something, stand there. . . ."

This, especially with the contrast of Walker's anxious, guiltridden negativeness, is more than mere aggression. But it is still aggression, and in Froelich's relations with his wife, in his career, in his literary and political opinions, he is always similarly asserting himself; provoking quarrels, taking over other people's affairs, ministering to their troubles, challenging any cool remoteness or mere politeness, any retirement or reliance on conventions.

But this assertiveness, even this aggressiveness, is true of Julie, too. It is perhaps clearest in the scene in which she dismisses Walker, but all the way through it is really unimaginable that she should be ever at a disadvantage. She must always be 'cool'; the moment she ceased to be "cool" she would cease to be Julie Snowflake. She must always assert herself; behavior which involved no risk, which merely followed convention, would not be a mode of achieving herself, a selfcreation. On the whole, this quality in her is shown always in its attractive aspects, but I think most readers will feel surprised, at one moment or another in the action, that the novel is finding her (or Froelich) quite so impressive as it is. The explanation lies of course in the character of Walker, who is so remarkably negative and passive, scrupulous and uneasy, physically and psychologically uncoordinated, *unstylish.* He has never achieved himself in a piece of behavior in his life. He is necessarily fascinated by even the worst sides of this American type, hypnotized by even Froelich's aggressiveness.

Walker represents England and English liberalism, we are told. Bradbury offers us some quite elaborate analyses of those concepts. I am unconvinced. Politically, Walker is a lower middle-class conservative, it seems to me; ideologically, he is a Romantic pessimist, with a horror of the technological future; and I don't see anything valuably English about those categories. (I mean, of course, that *his* England does not impose itself on me as being even comically authentic.) But Walker does represent his kind of negativeness quite vividly, and thereby gives full value to the American positiveness. He "brings out" the other characters. And since this American quality is so powerful even when not brought out, is so much a feature of the cultural scene, Walker's experience does represent that of Englishmen (among others) when in America.

That quality we can perhaps analyze a bit further by starting from a remark about Froelich by his wife, Patrice—that he is a hundred percent ego. It is the first part of the phrase which is the more important, that he—like Julie—gives the sense of being *fully* expressed in every gesture, and every silence, every action and reaction. The word ego should not be taken to mean selfishness, in the old-fashioned moralizing sense. In that sense, Walker could be condemned as being just as egotistic, and in a meaner style. What ego means here can best be explained by reference to Norman O. Brown's book, *Life Against Death.* He there sets the human body, including the instinctual drives and premental responses, in opposition to the cultural abstractions that derive ultimately from instinctual repression. What Froelich has, what "America" has, and what Walker has not, is an egotism of the body. This American type, though involved so much in intellectual activities, is dedicated to self-expression and self-enforcement in immediate relationships, tests of strength, and direct sensual-emotional contacts. The English equivalent expresses himself and enforces himself much more through his identification with cultural abstractions—in Walker's case, through his writing.

One of the puzzling things about Walker, as a person, is the completeness (the hundred percent quality) of his self-negation. He has *no* convictions, *no* opinions, no power to assert himself, no power to cope with the world or with other people; the reader wonders how he holds together. And yet we are told that Froelich "envies and admires" him; and Julie seeks him out and gives herself to him. Why? Because of what he has written, in both cases. And that is obviously not a matter of mere talent, if we separate that off from the personality it expresses. We need only turn to the book-flap to remind ourselves, with a glance at Bradbury's own career-history, how much seriousness, industry, energy, ambition, and sheer force of will, go into becoming what James Walker is. This too is self-creation, and of a kind which impresses the other two.

Julie and Froelich, though so much more impressive in their social performances, even as people of intelligence, are probably not going to achieve anything in the world of literature, or of any other kind of "abstract" activity. They put a lot of their energy into such activities, but not of the best *kind* of energy. Froelich is going to be chairman of his department. He is writing a book on the plight of the twentieth-century writer, and we are given to understand that it will be just another such book. All that inventiveness in immediate contacts becomes sterile academicism in the world of thought. And I think the reader knows instinctively that Julie too will always be able to express herself in the world of immediate contacts too completely to need, or be capable of, any large-scale venture into "abstractions." People like her have great psychological trouble with their Ph.D. theses just because they can't achieve themselves in those terms, and can't bear to do anything that is not a self-achievement.

It seems to me worth bringing in *Life Against Death* here because the fullness of the ego is linked with "the body" in so many ways in *Stepping Westward*. There is much stress on Walker's paleness, flabbiness, paunchiness, physical uninterestingness, and on these being English qualities in him. The attractiveness of Julie and of American girls in general is located in their physical firmness, litheness, springiness. Much is made also of his clumsiness, his gracelessness, his lack of physical coordination, and his ineptitude in the swimming pool and at changing a tire. Julie's first attempt to reform him is an attempt to teach him to "relax physically." And after his few months in America, Walker does become browner, leaner, fitter, more interesting physically, and the mere approach to the boat home sets him sneezing again. America is the land of bodies, as Dr. Jochum, a European wise-man, tells Walker.

It is also and relatedly the land of intense emotional relationships. Walker finds America very confusing because he cannot tell whether people are being friendly or hostile. "Most of the time they seem to be both simultaneously." Froelich embodies this trait. As Patrice says, being liked by Bernie is a full-time job. He is so hostile to the people he likes. She also says that when you see two Americans quarrelling, you know they are preparing to go to bed together. "It's a relationship. Hostility is so much more friendly than total indifference." And she complains of Walker's English comic novels that they hadn't enough affection in them; the characters were too rational, not intuitive enough. The lines of contrast between the two countries are therefore clearly drawn.

America is finally the land of freedom, of anarchy, in every cultural, moral, and sexual way. The campus buildings are a riot of architectural styles, the students are extravagantly sophisticated and extravagantly naïve, the married couples on the faculty swap partners for the night. A part of Walker's fascination with America is his sense that anything goes; right and wrong are irrelevant there. And this too is an important element in Brown's complex of ideas in *Life Against Death*; this full free sensual and emotional life of the body demands a breaking down of moral and intellectual categories.

Not that Julie Snowflake and Froelich represent moral and intellectual breakdown—quite the reverse, and it is the novel's generosity and justice toward them in this way that is one of its best features. Both are keenly interested in ideas and in making sense of life; both are full of that self-respect which derives from embodying the principles one believes in. But there are one or two qualifications to make to that. Both are in a sense childish, compared with Walker. They reach out for everything they want, rather poutingly; they expect an amused, admiring indulgence from everyone else, from the universe. And it is notable that Froelich, by the end, has used the loyalty oath issue to make himself chairman, and is using his new power to abolish the writing fellowship and establish a magazine that will publish his own articles. This is notable because it *isn't* a dramatic betrayal of his old standards. It is more like a translation of them into action. For his old standards were that one should get the power into the right hands. His hands are the right ones because they are alive, able to touch, full of love and anger; and they are alive because he believes in himself. This does involve a certain betrayal of abstract principle. When Froelich is getting Walker to refuse the loyalty oath, Patrice says, "You didn't stand. Why should he?" "I did stand. I crossed my fingers when I signed it," said Froelich. "No, look, this is the point, friends." He is quite in earnest when he says that, and perhaps for him "standing" means being able to say that—being able to take the moral tone so fully even when one's actions have not entitled one to it; his moral *personality* triumphs.

If we may call the cultural abstraction of the personality the mind, then what we have in Julie and Froelich is a marriage of body and mind that allows the body a decisively larger role than it has in that marriage in Walker's type. Their interest in ideas, without being insincere in the ordinary sense, is at the service of their "bodily" selves. Walker has a very uncertain sense of that self in him. The ideas he deals with loom much larger in his life—which is not to say that he takes them more seriously in the old-fashioned moralizing sense. This is a contrast in personality structure. Froelich establishes himself in terms of immediate power—confrontations, tests of strength, embraces, alliances, defeats, triumphs—while Walker establishes himself in terms of impersonal cultural performances—lists of publications, invitations to speak, impartial surveys of other people's books, comic novels. After his loyalty oath stand, Walker finds that in his creative writing class, he is "freely spoken of as a 'genius'. It struck him as odd, yet not inconsistent, that this praise came, not because he wrote like a writer, but because he had spoken like one." This is the American idea as contrasted with the British.

The Americans Julie and Froelich can be said to represent must be primarily the intellectuals. But in a longer perspective, surely a great deal of the country can be said to be, as it were, focused through them. They are experimenters, morally, socially, intellectually. Their personality style promises to be able to handle difficult and unconventional situations—to be able to establish them with total strangers as what they are in ten minutes, unprotected and unsponsored—to be able to sell themselves. And this is what non-academic America seems to Walker, a series of alarmingly difficult and unconventional situations. His two great failures with women are over car breakdowns—the classic American situation. Froelich would not have so failed, neither because he has any mechanical aptitude nor because he has any considerateness for the women, but because the personal-social problem of getting the car fixed is just the kind of thing he is organized to do.

And surely Bradbury has the right to identify America with this kind of personality structure in which the ego is located much more in the area of direct emotional-sensual relations, direct and "childish" affections and hostilities, and every kind of cultural abstraction is distrusted, from formal manners to state socialism. It presumably has something to do with the much more permissive system of child-rearing in America. This is the America that erupted in the Berkeley student's movement, and this is the America we can place in opposition to the official personality of Communist Russia.

One of the reasons Froelich seems so interesting and representative to me is that through his voice I hear that of Henderson the Rain-King and other of Saul Bellow's heroes. Henderson, Herzog, Tommy Wilhelm, all have the same interest in their own bodies, the same emotional fullness, the same organizational anarchy, the same intellectual looseness.

Even the writing of these novels gives the same impression of a man very interested in thinking, in working out the truth, but a good deal more interested in himself in the act of thinking—never quite able to forget himself and so always comic and childish; a man pointing fervently at some saving truth about the human condition, but with his eye on himself in the mirror, so that the finger is not pointing at anything in particular, after all. And Bellow is, as we know, a great representative figure for intellectual Americans. Moreover, if Froelich's book were better than it is promised to be, it would perhaps be *Love and Death in the American Novel*. For of course people like Froelich do sometimes write books, and they are sometimes very good books, full of a sense of the author as a big personality, mischievous, unpredictable, and brilliant. (Froelich and Julie are almost certainly Jewish, incidentally, but that fact has only representative significance. The point is that they are American.)

Walker represents an opposite type at least half against his own will. He believes in American-style "freedom" before he comes to America, despises his own domesticity, and is only half hearted about the English virtues of politeness, detachment, not hurting people, and so forth. He sees England much as his American friends see it, as a damp dugout for the damp of soul, a national funk-hole. And at the end he completely accepts Julie's indictment and dismissal of him. And it is in the completeness of his failure that the punch of Bradbury's story lies.

Julie and Froelich were attracted to Walker partly *by* his negativeness; in their world he is a curiosity of almost pornographic interest; he is a nudist among knights in armor. They took him into their favor, offered to play the games of life with him, promoting him over the heads of a hundred other people nearer their own size and weight. The moment they forgot to give him extra advantages, the moment they began to use both hands, he was hopelessly outclassed. He was knocked to the floor and trampled under foot. Bradbury is saying that this is likely to happen every time between an Englishman and an American, at least, as long as the Englishman accepts the American standards, the superiority of the psychological structure which we described as 'American'. And that Englishmen should do that seems to be part of American cultural dominance today.

I wrote the preceding remarks in 1965, immediately after reading *Stepping Westward*. Now, in 1972, it seems worth adding a few more, which derive from the events of the seven years which have passed since then. It is now *not* true that Englishmen "must" accept American cultural standards or psychological structures.

In America, a great deal has happened which can be summed up by saying that we have entered upon an age of revolution. A considerable number of bright young people have made up their minds that a revolution must happen, and everyone who thinks has been forced to declare himself for or against the idea, and to say why. The American personality type which Bradbury presents as material for comedy has begun to deal in death. Its love of freedom has ceased to mean mostly sexual license. It has taken on political functions.

If Julie Snowflake were created today, she would perhaps be called Firebrand. She would certainly be a much more extremist personality than the one Bradbury describes, both in political ideology and in life-style. She might either have gone underground into some Weatherwoman group or to live in a commune. Froelich would not be involved in loyalty oaths and wife-swappings, but in trashings and bombings, draft-office raids and prison-terms. Moreover, though the two personalities might be in some sense the same despite the change in their activities—the same as far as their contrast with Walker goes—their whole environment, and so their meaning, has changed. America is no longer the land of comedy. It is a land of tragedy now, and Julie and Froelich, even seen from this book's angle, would not be comic characters. Of course, they *could* be seen as comic again, but that would need a new angle of vision, which has yet to be fixed.

For perhaps the most interesting thing which the seven-year lapse measures is the way "reality" has changed while the literary conventions have not. (By "reality" I mean that consensus view of America which is powerful and general enough to force itself on a writer as much in touch as Bradbury.) I have read several other British comic novels since 1965 which took the same angle on America as *Stepping Westward* did. Some of them were published slightly before, but essentially they were contemporary with it, and David Lodge's *Out of the Shelter* was considerably later. Two of them, Julian Mitchell's *As Far As You Can Go* and Kingsley Amis's *One Fat Englishman* were of comparable literary interest with *Stepping Westward*, and Andrew Sinclair's *The Hallelujah Bum* was at least lively. In all of them—they form a distinct genre of modern British fiction —the view of America and the way its idea contrasts with the English idea is the same. In them all, the central character, who represents the novelist, comes to the United States, responds reluctantly to its various challenges and invitations, gradually makes up his mind for it as opposed to England, but usually returns home nevertheless, feeling unable to meet those challenges adequately. And though they do not deny the tragic elements in the American situation, they respond more to the comic elements. They see even the tragic as comic, in the sense that it is another manifestation of the whole country's size and vitality, its oppositeness to the smallness and claustrophobia of Britain.

Of course, the heroes do not all represent the same England as Bradbury's Walker does. Amis's hero is more like Evelyn Waugh's early figure, Basil Seal, and his novel might be given the title which Waugh gave to a late story, "Basil Seal Rides Again," since Amis also is confronting Tory amoralism with the challenge of young America. This marks Amis's definitive affiliation to Waugh—his turn away from the "British decency" of *Lucky Jim*. It thus marks his self-affiliation to that earlier mode of British sensibility, which was much more aggressively anti-modern and anti-American than Bradbury's. But even Amis's hero is morally intimidated by America, in the same way as Walker. The differences between the heroes illustrate the range of British types involved in this imaginative encounter with "America" during the 1960's.

Moreover, during these years we also saw America produce comic work which corresponds to the British, in the sense that it issues from the identity which Bradbury attributes to Froe-lich—I mean the comedy of Heller and Pynchon and *M.A.S.H.* and above all John Barth. *Giles Goat-Boy* is surely the supreme manifestation of that aggressive extrovert ebul-lience, that harsh gross body-humor, which Bradbury de-scribes as "America."

But both these styles seem to have been by-passed by events. America is no longer triumphantly comic for either its citizens or for its visitors. It is perhaps a sign of the times that John Wain, one of the first Angry Young Novel-ists, published a novel in which another British anti-hero is humiliated by a golden American girl in the first episode; but this one goes on to retrieve himself by rooting himself in a Welsh village. In *A Winter in the Hills* the hero (who like others of his type has become dangerously dessicated by academic life) does *not* leave England for America to find re-generation. He goes back to the world of *Lucky Jim*, and to the virtues of the working class and the trade union, to com-radeship and decency. He learns again to be the kind of Eng-lishman I described in *Mirror for Anglo-Saxons*, to practice the sort of style which Richard Hoggart has represented in British public life.

Moreover, among the Englishmen I have recently met over here, more and more seem to have that sense of themselves, and of their style as Englishmen in America. They move through the thundering ruins of this great gaudy wicked Hollywood set, this *Day of the Locust* scenario, openly keep-ing a tight hold on their integrity—publishing a sense that they belong to a tight little tradition, unambitious and un-triumphant, but simple, solid, cautious, durable. It is a vastly more attractive posture than that of James Walker. Morally they have every advantage. Imaginatively, however, I suspect that the disintegrated looseness and openness of the comic heroes of the 1960's promised more in the way of new life for British comedy.

Chapter 17

BRITISH MARXISTS AND
AMERICAN FREUDIANS*

The circumstances of my life have forced me to compare
England with America more than most people do; not so
much in formal, large-scale comparisons, with each country
taken as a whole, as in involuntary acknowledgments that
my life on one side of the Atlantic was different in some way
from what it was on the other, and speculations as to why.
Such comparisons are necessarily limited to those parts of the
two environments that impinge on me, as I am defined by my
vocations and professions—for instance, as a teacher of literature—and even as defined by my temperament. These are
large limitations. They mean that the comparisons must be
very partial, very personal. The only compensation there can
be for those limitations is some equivalent of personal sincerity that may at best go with them. The intentions that
shape and limit such comparisons are at their best existential
—intentions deriving from the struggle to make sense of one
person's experience, and therefore (at their best) deriving
personal good faith from that struggle. But such good faith
is no guarantee against distortion of vision, especially when
both ideas to be compared involve oneself.

This comparison is not personal in any ordinary sense,

* This chapter appeared in *Innovations* (London: Macmillans, 1968),
ed. Bernard Bergonzi. Reprinted by permission of A. D. Peters & Co., Ltd.

but it is so wide-ranging in its implications that I must remind myself how much it derives from me, from my experience, from my being who I am; for instance, from my interest in literature-and-other-things, but also from my preference for seeing situations in patterns of brightly colored, simply labeled, alternative choices. However, having reminded myself of that, I still want to offer other people my comparison, for them to make of it what they can.

Since I last returned to live in England, I've been struck by how often the name of Marx has turned up in contexts not just of political philosophy, but of cultural criticism, of literary criticism, and even within the arts themselves. Marx and Marxism are a pervasive presence in the plays of John Arden and Arnold Wesker, for instance, in the history of Edward Thompson and E. H. Carr, in the novels of Doris Lessing; while the liveliest new theatrical methods, like those in *US*, derive a lot from Brecht.

Marx and Marxism are in the air generally, then; and seriously so in matters of literary-cultural discussion. Moreover, in that area they mean something different from what they used to. When I was an undergraduate, the Communist party was a possibility for us in British politics, but Marx himself was not a force in our thinking. He figured there as an outdated economist and a rather crude political philosopher, and not as a cultural philosopher. Nowadays the Communist party counts for less, but Marx as a cultural philosopher counts for much more. To people who want to connect their study of literature with a general understanding of the world and responsibility for society, I would say he is the most important of all figures today. Englishmen who are *not* influenced by Marx, and who have some liveliness and scope of mind in literary matters, are people resistant to *all* ideological affiliation. Simplifying radically, I'd say that a literary Englishman today either engages with Marx, or settles for aestheticism and scholarship. Whereas in America, as it seems to me, there are many people interested in literature-and-other-things who are strongly influenced by Freud, and the people who aren't influenced by him tend to be ideologically indeterminate or scattered.

I'm talking, I should say, about emergent movements and new voices. Of course in America there are still the New Critics and the Southern Gothic writers, and in England there are still the Leavisites and the Angry Young Men. But if these are still forces on the scene in one sense, then there is another sense in which they are not. I am talking about movements visibly growing and increasing in vitality over the last ten years.

This is an enormous simplification. Because both names are only representative; the line of thought I associate with each of them derives from many thinkers; for instance, from some points of view Freud is less important than Nietzsche to the movement I've labeled post-Freudian. Also because both movements make much the same protests against genteel acceptance culture, against conservatism-reaction, and even against conscientious liberalism-individualism. Both stand for a kind of radicalism. And I'm not talking about movements that are conscious of themselves as limited and organized wholes, much less of each other as alternative movements. I'm talking about tendencies in nearly all the people who react to the current cultural situation in intellectually adventurous and morally indignant ways. There are many places therefore where these two tendencies come together inextricably—in art like *Marat/Sade* and *US*, and in thought like Marcuse's and R. D. Laing's. In such places it is not very profitable to disentangle the two strands and argue that they are mutually hostile—though I think that can be done. But my claim, my defence of this reductive simplification, is that there are a fair number of places where there is no need to disentangle, where people and books are clearly aligned with the one tendency and aimed against the other.

Some of the exceptions will be worth discussing, but most will not, because the value of such generalizations is not to account for the exact position of all the items involved, but to indicate the direction in which they are mostly tending to move. The fact that some of the dots on the graph don't fit into the curve doesn't matter so long as there clearly is a curve. And as well as exceptions there must need be conclusions; some sense of what this means; from what causes this difference derives, and with what consequences. These I will consider at the end. But conclusions are as extraneous as exceptions to the main proposition I am going to try to establish; which is simply that these two movements, in these two countries, do exist, and are interesting, and do, in tendency, contradict each other.

Of the two, let us consider first the British Marxists. The first thing to say is that these are post-Marxists (and the American Freudians we shall come to are post-Freudians). That is, these Marxists take Marx's thought at its roots, and are interested in what they can make of its largest philosophical implications, and quite uninterested in what most of his political disciples, between then and now, have made of it. There were literary Marxists in the 1930's; and being a Marxist seems to have meant most typically the process of belonging to the party and obeying the party, and, in literary matters, haggling over the difference between what Engels wrote to Minna Kautsky in 1885, and what Lenin said, or meant, in "Party Organization and Party Literature" in 1905. Being a post-Marxist means something different. These people are not concerned with the party, they are not concerned with Russia, they are not primarily concerned with China; it is the Third World on which their gaze is concentrated. And in literary matters they haggle over what Leavis said and what Lawrence said.

Theirs is not the Marx of Lenin, much less of Stalin. It is not even primarily the Marx of *Capital*; it is mostly the early Marx of *Economic and Philosophical Manuscripts*, the philosopher of alienation and dehumanization. In what follows I am reporting (to the best of my ability) what the post-Marxists say of Marx and Hegel, Sartre and Lukacs. I have not read Hegel, and I have not really understood the others. The leading concepts of this line of thought Marx took over from Hegel; self-estrangement or alienation is a result of objectification, the externalization of what man has produced; and the way back to cultural unity is through the re-appropriation of man's productivity—that is, through seeing all man makes as under his own control, a part of his self-expression, and therefore a part of his responsibility and not a thing independent of him.

The early Marx blamed Christianity for alienation. He saw Christendom as a fragmented and individualistic culture, in contrast with the unity of the Greek city, which was a political and religious whole; individual and social experience, divine and secular, fitting together. In the Greek city all of man's life was felt as his responsibility, his creation, and so was made beautiful. The religious was integrated with the rest. Christianity, on the other hand, derived from Judaism, which had externalized its religion into the Law. The Jews had reified their religion, made it a thing outside themselves. Christ then re-appropriated religious experience, but only individualistically. He made it each man's responsibility to work out his own salvation as an individual, but not the race's as a collectivity. Thus he left the experience of the divine outside the area of man's political life, and created a religion of otherworldliness.

From this, Marx thought, derived a hundred other kinds of alienation. Thus, in "On the Jewish Question," (1843) he wrote:

> Only under the sway of Christianity, which objectifies all national, natural, moral, and theoretical relationships, could civil society separate itself completely from the life of the state, sever all the species-bonds of man, establish egoism and selfish need in their place, and dissolve the human world into a world of atomistic, antagonistic individuals.

In *Economic and Philosophical Manuscripts* (1844), he argued that this religious alienation was only an expression of a political alienation, which derived from the contradictions between private and social life in the bourgeois state. And later he found the source of those political contradictions in an economic alienation. Indeed, in *The German Ideology* and *The Communist Manifesto* Marx rejected the idea of alienation as the *source* of evil. But the post-Marxists claim that this was only Hegelian-idealist alienation he rejected; for alienation proper is fundamental to their idea of Marxism.

Although Marx in this phase was obviously hostile to Christianity, he was very interested in it, and his own philosophy was both more "religious" and more compatible with religion, than it was later represented to be. The Christians among the post-Marxists not only accept his strictures on Christianity, but rejoice in them as a programme for church reform. One of the striking features of the movement is this combination of Marxist with Christian, even Catholic, categories.

The key idea, then, is that man is a species, and that to be a man is to acknowledge membership of that species; to cease to be a merely individual entity. A man is a universal being because he can represent his species, and he can represent it because he can grasp the idea of it, can think it. An animal is inseparable from its life-activity; it exists *an-sich* or *en-soi*; Sartre's phrase is cited as often as Hegel's. A man makes his life-activity the object of his consciousness and will-power; he exists *pour-soi*. But this *pour-soi* cannot be said of the naked individual; for Marx there is no such thing among humans; man is constituted by his relations to other men. It is society which creates, through language and through work, through participation in common activities, man as man. That is, society enables man to treat himself as the species; the individual becomes universal, and potentially free. Material scarcities restricted that freedom temporarily, and the alienation of labor did so essentially, reversing the whole movement of history. But under communism, and with the abundance made possible by automation, man would become entirely free, purely *pour-soi*.

These Marxist ideas have been developed towards their post-Marxist form by European rather than by Russian thinkers. It is Sartre and Lukacs rather than Lenin and Trotsky whom British critics cite. There seems to be general agreement that the two most important books since Marx's themselves are Lukacs's *History and Class Consciousness* (1923), which was condemned in Moscow for its semi-subjectivist interpretation of history and Sartre's *Critique of Dialectical Reason* (1960), which is openly contemptuous of Moscow Marxism. Sartre adds to Marx what he feels is lacking in orthodox Marxism, a hierarchy of mediations; to make it possible to grasp just how a person and his work are produced by a given class at a given moment in history. For instance, to show how Flaubert came to choose to be a bourgeois writer rather than doctor, and how he came to write *Madame Bovary*, rather than some other equally bourgeois form of literature, like the Goncourts' books. Sartre sees contemporary sociology and psychoanalysis as realizations of moments in the dialectic, finding their proper shape when incorporated into the Marxist theory of history. Psychoanalysis, for instance, discovers the point of insertion of a man in his class; it helps us understand the family as a mediation between the individual and society; an individual experiences alienation first, and crucially, as a child, through his parents' being exploited as alienated labor, through their experience passed on to him as an infant, not through his own first job.

So much for the general ideas of post-Marxism. In Sartre and Lukacs we begin to approach the specifically literary attitudes that go with this philosophy in England. But strikingly enough, though both of them are literary critics, neither have had much direct influence here in literary matters. The probable reasons are various. In *Theory of the Novel* (1916), Lukacs said that in nineteenth-century novels the heroes had souls larger than the destinies life offered them, and the problem they all reflected was that of how to be reconciled to an inadequate world; and he saw Dostoevski as pointing the way to a solution. But after he became a Communist his literary sympathies were much narrowed, and he has had little sympathy since with Dostoevski or with most modernist writers. D. H. Lawrence and Samuel Beckett he has dismissed as decadent; *Ulysses* he has described as merely "a tape-recorded sequence of a number of associations"; Roger Martin du Gard is preferred to Kafka. It requires no explaining why such judgments should have little influence even among the post-Marxists in England, which has its own lively literary criticism. But neither, so far, have Sartre's huge study of Genet or his lengthy analyses of Flaubert. The biggest reason in this case is probably something within that native tradition of literary criticism. While Lukacs's mind is rigid in ways which Sartre himself has sufficiently exposed, Sartre's criticism is unpalatable to native British taste for its implicit hostility to decent averageness.

This English literary and cultural criticism has a powerful

tradition of faith in the values of simple ordinary community life even under capitalism. This no doubt goes back as far as Carlyle, with his faith in work and moral duty and the native grandeur of character of the Scottish Presbyterian crofter. Perhaps the icon of that faith most people refer to nowadays is D. H. Lawrence's picture of his own home and others like it in *Sons and Lovers*, which shows those simple values surviving the Industrial Revolution. And both the fiction and the criticism of Raymond Williams clearly draw on his own experience of Welsh village life. When Williams says, "Culture is ordinary," he quite explicitly relies on that experience and our response to it.

Sartre belongs to a very different tradition, and when he describes simple ordinary community life it is not to praise it. The peasant family in the Morvan, with whom Genet was boarded out as a child, and who sent him to the reformatory when they caught him stealing, is implicitly blamed for much of Genet's trouble. The badness attributed to the boy and introjected by him was a projection of these good, self-respecting people, a product of their goodness. And these were people who, objectively described, might not be easy to distinguish from Carlyle's crofters and Williams's villagers. Sartre's sympathies, in a major French tradition, are with the anti-social intellectual, with Genet himself; liar, thief, homosexual prostitute, pornographic fantasist. Readers are warned against thinking themselves any "healthier" or more normal than Genet. When Sartre hears a man saying "We doctors," he knows that that man is morally and psychologically a slave, with no identity of his own. This socially accepted alienation of the psyche he calls a "legitimate hell," and he expresses a fierce distaste for these "inhabited souls."

This difference in fundamental sympathy divides Sartre from the English post-Marxists in literary sensibility. They acknowledge, of course, the truth that a sick society infects its members, but they tend to associate social sickness with ultra-modern, big-city life, or with the new mass-media, and to imply that the older and smaller forms of social organization still have a life that fosters health in the individual. Their primary stress is on that other truth, that an individual cannot be healthy unless he accepts his being part of a community. They barely at all acknowledge the heroism or the sanctity of a Genet, achieved over and against his society. The native English literary tradition, mediated to the present in the work of Leavis, has been as powerful an influence on the literary men among them as Marx himself. Raymond Williams for instance describes his life as affected by two major sources of cultural thought, Leavis and Marx; and all these people, in their literary criticism, plainly start from *Scrutiny*. And one can see good historical reasons for this conjunction. This English tradition, with its strongly normative stresses and its sense of responsibility for national culture, derives from Coleridge and Carlyle, who drew on the same stock of German Idealist ideas as Marx did. Leavis himself, when he began *Scrutiny*, declared himself friendly to Marxism, and a believer in "some form of economic communism;" his roots are in Ruskin and Morris, with their anti-capitalist vision of an England of arts and crafts communities. His literary criticism has always been preoccupied with the relation of the particular work of art to the cultural life it derives from. It has therefore been easy for our modern post-Marxists to take over his judgments and his methods.

Raymond Williams is pre-eminent among them, and his two books on drama are among the few pieces of straight literary study these people have produced so far. There is however a good deal of literary criticism in Edward Thompson's histories; least surprisingly, in his book on William Morris, but also in *The Making of the English Working Class*, and in unpublished essays on Wordsworth and Marx. There is more in two books of cultural thought by Roman Catholics: Terence Eagleton's *The New Left Church*; and *Catholics and the Left*, by a group of writers. The first section of the latter book is called "Christians against Capitalism," and the whole is essentially literary, for the writers use poetry and novels as crucial evidence for their social arguments.

We might describe in a little more detail three books; Williams's *Modern Tragedy*, Brian Wicker's *Culture and Theology*, and Terence Eagleton's *Shakespeare and Society*. The first argues—against books like Steiner's *The Death of Tragedy*

—that tragic writing *is* possible in our time, because the contemporary experience of political revolution is highly appropriate subject-matter for a tragic writer. We have all shared, publicly, just the kind of experience that demands the tragic form. The last section of the book, Williams's own attempt at such a tragedy, uses the events of the Russian Revolution and the history of the Communist state in Russia. The book also contains a long interpretation of *Doctor Zhivago*, and a contrasting of it with *The Cocktail Party*, as two ways of dealing with the themes of sacrifice and resignation. Williams interprets *Doctor Zhivago* as expressing a painful, a tragic, acceptance of the Revolution, with all the sacrifice it involved of private happiness. Interpreting it this way, he finds it infinitely superior to Eliot's play, which has so little sense of the value of human experience, once we define human as deriving from community life. The book as a whole is a survey of the various modern approaches to tragedy, and the titles of some of its main sections outline its analytic method. "Liberal Tragedy" includes Ibsen and Arthur Miller; "Tragic Deadlock" includes Ionesco, Beckett, and Pinter; "Private Tragedy" includes Strindberg, O'Neill, Tennessee Williams. All of these are found radically unsatisfactory, deriving as they do from the bourgeois-individualist mind at one or other stage of its development; even *Women in Love* betrays an incomplete understanding of community; the only satisfactory modern artist, apart from Pasternak, is Brecht, who also draws on public, political experience as his subject matter.

Brian Wicker's book has sections on philosophy, and anthropology, and literature. There are critical essays on Dickens and George Eliot, whose novels are taken to represent respectively a sacral and a secularist understanding of life. Secularism is identified with Locke, private citizenship and private consciousness, and the possessive individualism of capitalism; and thus is at an opposite extreme from Marxism. Marx's view of life Wicker calls sacral. Dickens's novels are sacral because they represent both nature and society as possessing a life of their own—Dickens's London, for instance, is an organic entity, an active force acting on its citizens—

rather than a merely objective background to the subjective drama of individual consciousnesses, as nature and society are in *Middlemarch*. Dickens's art breaks down that antithesis between the subjective and objective which Wicker regards as a major fallacy of thought since Locke, and the source of "secularism." And there is another emblematic contrast, between Orwell and William Golding, with a similar point. Wicker defines Orwell as a contemporary writer, as opposed to a modernist one; and contemporaneity he relates to secularism. Golding he calls an allegorist, using Lukacs's opposition of traditional realism to modernist allegory. He then traces both these writers' artistic failures, in different ways, to the power of the secularist view of life in the culture they work in; and in the philosophical and anthropological sections of the book he tries to refute that view. Secularism derives from, and makes permanent, the failure of western man to achieve community.

In Eagleton's *Shakespeare and Society* the central concern is to find in the plays evidence of both the playwright's interest in conflicts between the individual and society, and his sense that the only solution must be a fusion of the two. Our own age, we are told, is approaching this solution via an abandonment of the old distinctions between the two categories. "The converging experience of a number of thinkers, in culture and psychology, politics and philosophy, has given us definitions of person and society which make any straight division between individual life, and the social forms within which this is available, unthinkable." Reason and law and society are shown as opposed to spontaneity and authenticity and individuality, in *Troilus and Cressida*, *Hamlet*, and *Measure for Measure*; and as fused in the last comedies. Hamlet Eagleton describes in terms very like those Richard Poirier used to praise Emerson (see the second half of this essay), as a man refusing to accept self-definition in any of the roles society offers him; but the "point," for Eagleton, is that such a man destroys himself; a man who preserves his sense of identity only in opposition to formal social patterns finds that this identity becomes unreal, negative. Hamlet exemplifies a life-pattern we should avoid. (The "point" of Cleopatra is even more strikingly moralistic. She is "Shakespeare's most complete image of fully authentic life; she cancels and recreates all values in herself;" but therefore the "result" of the play is "a new insight into the depth of authentic life which will have to be part of any attempt to make this life responsible, to put it back within society." How to turn Cleopatras into bigger and better Octavias.) *Measure for Measure* Eagleton reads as showing that marriage and law must be understood as equally individual and social realities, to be taken as neither merely personal nor merely impersonal, nor as something combining those two kinds of elements, but as a fusion of them. This is the only way we can give our values constancy. The whole book is an attempt to find in Shakespeare illustrations of a society that has lost its values because it cannot make its members still believe in it as a society; they set up an opposition between themselves and it, between spontaneity and social duty; this is the source of both situation ethics and existential authenticity, Eagleton thinks, and the only answer to them is a reconciliation of individual to society, a reconstitution of community.

The post-Marxists are significant in part because they are in natural alliance with other forces in British intellectual life which are not Marxist at all. For instance, the people who write for the *Cambridge Quarterly* and *The Use of English*; and the people at the Center for Contemporary Studies at Birmingham; and, as I have pointed out, some of the most committed among the post-Marxists are Roman Catholics, laymen and priests. All these people, disparate as they are, belong together in their contrast with the other large literary-cultural tendency in England now, which is much more purely aesthetic and anti-ideological. We might identify this with the names of Frank Kermode and Christopher Ricks, John Gross and Tony Tanner. In many ways this cultural split follows the lines of a traditional British opposition, between Oxford and Cambridge. Cambridge being the home of the more austere and strenuous, Puritanical and radical mind; Oxford the more elegant and playful, sophisticated and nostalgic. Oxford in one sense of the word right wing, Cambridge left wing. In literary matters Cambridge sees art in relation to society, and in relation to right and wrong. Within the congeries of groups united by this Cambridge tendency, the post-Marxists seem to me the most highly charged with intellectual life, and potentially of great significance.

I said at the beginning that they were anti-Freudian in tendency, but I have no texts to cite to prove that. Except, paradoxically, Sartre. This is a paradox because Sartre *is* profoundly indebted to Freud. Indeed, he is Freudian, in his full acceptance of and use of psychoanalysis. But he is not post-Freudian, because he dismisses as quaint mythologizing those late works of Freud in which we get theories of world history; and it is from those works that the post-Freudians start. Psychoanalysis itself they are not much interested in; indeed they are often contemptuous of it. Being analysed, for the post-Freudian, is as irrelevant as belonging to the national party is to the post-Marxist.

The English post-Marxists, so far as I am aware, have not committed themselves on the issue at all, explicitly. Implicitly, as it seems to me, they are anti-post-Freudian; because they believe in the regeneration of the individual sensibility through the regeneration of community life, through retightening the social bonds between men. Whereas the post-Freudians believe in loosening those social bonds, and in a sense in the degeneration of community life, and the renewing of individual life as a consequence of that. The post-Marxists insist that an individual derives everything that makes him human from his society, from his community; the post-Freudians see the self achieving itself in struggles against system, in the family, the school, the whole culture. It seems to me significant that the one Fabian pamphlet written in protest against Raymond Williams' theory of culture was written by a Freudian, who spoke for a more pluralistic theory, with less insistence on unity of belief and purpose (Richard Wollheim, *Socialism and Culture*, 1961).

Again let me say I realize how many shades of each opinion there are; how possible it is to share some of them without being significantly post-Marxist or post-Freudian; how possible to combine some varieties of one tendency with some varieties of the other without feeling torn apart. But there remain two tendencies. There are people and books who belong clearly in one and not in the other, whose fundamental energies and aims are aligned with the one and against the other; or in whom the two obviously fight against each other. And these include people who are thinking strenuously about literature and culture today.

The post-Freudians, as I understand them, start from late Freud, speculative Freud. Just as the post-Marxists start not from *Capital* but from *Economic and Philosophical Manuscripts*, so the post-Freudians start not from *The Interpretation of Dreams* but from *Civilization and Its Discontents*. Both groups take their masters' largest world-view statements, and interpret them in the largest style, with vivid implications for literature, past, present, and to come.

The writers I'll briefly mention are Norman Brown, in *Life Against Death* and *Love's Body*, Herbert Marcuse in *Eros and Civilization*, Philip Rieff in *The Triumph of the Therapeutic*, Susan Sontag in *Against Interpretation*, and Norman Mailer in *Advertisements for Myself*. In Norman Brown's work what we begin with are basic Freudian ideas, comparable with the basic Marxist ideas. "Sexual instinct is the energy or desire with which the human being pursues pleasure, with the further specification that the pleasure sought is the pleasurable activity of an organ of the human body." And that energy however disguised or transmuted, is in fact the only human energy. So that philosophy and religion and history, whether as subjects of study or as states of consciousness in the individual or as the activities of parliament or congresses, are all produced by the same instinct. "The special contribution of psychoanalysis is to trace religious and philosophic problems to their roots in the concrete human body." And "Man, the discontented animal, unconsciously seeking the life proper to his species, is man in history; repression and the repetition compulsion generate historical time." We ought in fact to live outside time; and we would if we were not discontented but contented animals. Infants are naturally absorbed in themselves and their own bodies; they are in love with themselves, and their sexuality is polymorphously perverse. But civilization interferes with their development, in the form, for instance, of toilet-training and the prohibition against masturbation; their sexuality is genitally organized, and the result is repression and neurosis.

But these simply Freudian ideas lead Brown on to a strikingly post-Freudian interpretation of culture and of world history. He asserts a profound opposition within every personality between the interests of the body, including in that all of pre-mental life, the instincts as well as the senses, and the interests of the mind, that is of civilization representing itself inside the personality as morality, productivity, systematic thought, patriotism, religious duty, and so forth. The spokesman of the body in literature is Blake, "Energy is the only life, and is from the body," and "Energy is eternal delight." Typical spokesmen of the mind are Plato and Descartes, with their worship of the abstract, the ideal, the disembodied, the sublimated.

We are most concerned with the theory of art and literature within this theory of culture, so here are some representative quotations. "The function of art is to help us find our way back to the sources of pleasure that have been rendered inaccessible by that capitulation to the reality principle which we call education or maturity—in other words, to recapture the lost laughter of infancy. . . . Art, if its object is to undo repressions, and if civilization is essentially repressive, is in this sense subversive of civilization." These ideas, obviously, are very alien to Eagleton's view of literature, and it is because Sartre is not so far from this point of view—that art is subversive of civilization—that he is so different from his English disciples.

In *Love's Body* Brown is more explicit about what we ought to do here and now as a consequence of this understanding of our situation. Salvation lies only in the resurrected body; that is, in a sensuality not genitally organized. And the giving up of genitality will include giving up all heroic individualism, all politics, and indeed all personality. The sign of man's fallen state is the boundaries he draws; the distinction he makes between good and bad, that between me and thee, that between mine and thine. These are the death-breeding boundaries, between persons, between emotions, between items of property, and they are all essentially the same. To have a personality is to have property. The only way out is to give up personality. Then one can escape from the domination of the reality principle and of the mind and morality. Freud, rightly used, can lead one out into the world of free speech, free associations, random thoughts, spontaneous movements. Clearly, this is very bold thinking; and however often Brown may invoke Marx, it recommends a disengagement from community and culture which no loyal interpretation of Marx could encompass.

Herbert Marcuse, in *Eros and Civilization*, combines Freud's account of the repressive civilization he knew—that is, nineteenth-century civilization—with Schiller's theory of what a non-repressive civilization might be. In the organized society of the past, happiness had to be subordinated to, for instance, the discipline of monogamic reproduction, and all the systems of established law and order. The methodical sacrifice of libido, its rigidly enforced deflection to socially useful activities and expressions, all this *was*—for Freud—culture. But in a society of abundance and leisure, such as was hypothesized by Schiller and such as is now foreseeable as a result of modern technology, it will be possible to have, in Schiller's words, an indifference to reality, and an interest in "show," in appearances, in the aesthetic aspect of everything, and an interest in play, in the non-serious, in mere self-expression, which will be a "true enlargement of humanity."

Moreover, it is art which has expressed these interests in the past, and so it is art which will be, in the present, our guide in constructing the culture of the future. Orpheus and Narcissus are the mythological representatives of art, and they stand in opposition to Prometheus, who represents competitive economic performance and productiveness, the old reality principle, the unceasing effort to master life. Orpheus and Narcissus, the artist figure and the figure of self-delighting, self-sufficient beauty, stand beside Dionysus, the figure of lawless instinctual energy, in opposition to Apollo and the realm of reason and organization and morality.

But Marcuse is a difficult person to fit into these categories, because in most of his books he is clearly a Marxist or Hegelian thinker, and in all of them he shows a strong political consciousness of a non-Freudian kind. But in *Eros and Civilization* it seems to me that he is post-Freudian in the sense described. He does there proclaim the possibility of a non-repressive civilization in which Eros would replace Logos, and the reality-principle Freud spoke of would be defeated, and the play impulse would abolish time. Six years later, it is true, in the preface to the Vintage edition of the book, he introduced the idea of repressive de-sublimation; the release of sexuality in modes which reduce erotic energy; making a big distinction between Eros and sexuality, of a surely non-Freudian kind, by means of which he could say something quite different from what he had said in the book itself. He could warn us that in present political conditions the spread of non-repressiveness might be politically stabilizing and indeed culturally regressive. The years between the book and the preface, he said, had refuted all optimism; he had sufficiently (perhaps unduly) stressed the progressive and promising aspects of this development, to be able here in 1961 to accentuate the negative. To put it crudely, he had changed his mind. And in *One-Dimensional Man* it is the second line of thought he follows up. Non-repressiveness in our present society produces the Happy Consciousness, which invalidates Art; for art has traditionally spoken the Great Refusal, the protest against that which is. This idea of art is of course compatible enough with Marxism. I don't myself see that it is compatible with the Freudian Orphic-Narcissist idea of *Eros and Civilization*. And even those who think that it is should be able to agree that the combining of the two is a unique achievement, fairly special to Marcuse. In most people you find one or the other, but not both.

This theoretical position I've described, in Norman Brown and Marcuse, seems to me vitally related to a contemporary set of attitudes to cultural problems and a contemporary literary sensibility which one finds expressed in, to take some striking examples, Susan Sontag, Philip Rieff, and Norman Mailer.

Norman Mailer predicts that the revolutionary vision of our age will not follow Marx into political economy but will en-

gage the mass media. This sounds like a foretelling of Mc-
Luhan, and Susan Sontag remarks that "such strongly apolitical critics as Marshall McLuhan have got so much better
grasp on the texture of contemporary reality . . . than the
Marxist critics." In fact McLuhan is as much the natural ally
of the post-Freudian writers in America, as the orthodox
Leavisites are of the post-Marxists in England. He is instinctively apolitical and implicitly on the side of all new, free,
sensory mixes and psychological novelties. The artist's job,
for him, is to correct the sense ratios before the blow of new
technology has numbed conscious procedures. Art *is* precise
advance knowledge of how to cope in this way with the
psychic and social consequences of the next technology. But
it is above all McLuhan's way of writing, his persona as a
writer, his defiant gaiety and joking, his evasion of normal
seriousness and connectedness, his commitment to aphorism,
which seem to me to place him. The post-Freudian creed
demands, or at least invites, the aphoristic manner. One cannot
go on calling for the end of the old seriousness in the old
serious and systematic manner. Aphorism is exaggeration, as
Norman Brown tells us in *Love's Body*; it is the road of
excess which leads to the palace of wisdom. Intellect *is* courage;
the courage to risk its own life, to play with madness. Intellect
is the sacrifice of intellect, or fire; which burns up as it gives
light. This is truth as fragments, as opposed to systematic
forms or methods. *Love's Body* quotes a good deal from
McLuhan, and borrows even more in direct imitation.

Other major allies of the post-Freudians are the formal
aestheticians of symbolism. Susan Sontag calls her book of
criticism *Against Interpretation* because she thinks the interpretation of art derives from an over-emphasis on its content.
When she says we need to recover our senses, one thing she
means is that we need to appreciate art formally. "In place
of a hermeneutics we need an erotics of art;" and we note
the continual equating of sensuality with formalism. This
seems to me arbitrary, for the formal approach to art, especially art in the intellectualized forms Sontag likes, is as abstract an activity as anything human. But in Norman Brown,
too, we find a constant reference to such formally self-con-

scious poets as Rilke and Yeats, and a recommendation specifically of Symbolist methods. And I suspect that McLuhan's formula, the medium is the message, is understood—even by McLuhan himself—as among other things a formalist slogan. Certainly Sontag sees her formalism as what sets her apart from Marxist criticism. "What all the culture critics who descend from Hegel and Marx have been unwilling to admit is the notion of art as autonomous form. And the peculiar spirit which animates the modern movement in the arts is based on, precisely, the rediscovery of the power (including the emotional power) of the formal properties of art. . . ." And the Marxists on their side accept the same distinction, putting their own stress on content. Ernst Fischer's *The Necessity of Art* gives eighty pages to a chapter called "Content and Form" which is an attack on formalism. And the post-Freudians' formalism goes along with aestheticism in the vulgar sense, to some degree. "The world *is*, ultimately, an aesthetic phenomenon," says Sontag, "That is to say, the world (all there is) cannot, ultimately, be justified." She explicitly rejects humanism for being an attempt to justify the world, to make sense of experience.

Another phenomenon of our times, Northrop Frye, is in effect allied with this tendency. Murray Krieger explains him by referring us to two great models, of whom the second is Freud; and historically Blake was the great focus of literary and cultural ideas for him, the great catalyst of his poetic theorizing. For him the individual book is to be related to the whole world of literature, which is a part of the whole world of culture, which is part of the world of dreams. His systems of archetypes and modes are described by his admirers as "charting the galaxies dreamed of by human desire," "galaxies whose centers and axes are constantly shifting." In other words, you can't understand what he means, or you can't understand it rationally. As they say, he has freed the critic from the stringent procedures of critical discourse, as well as the poet from the bondage of sublunary language. This must remind us of McLuhan and Brown, and indeed his taste is, like theirs, for romanticism, transcendentalism, classless democratic individualism, the future. Like McLuhan's, his schemes of thought are an attempt to meet the challenge of tomorrow's conditions—our immensely increased knowledge of so many literatures from so many points of view—by abandoning yesterday's procedures. He is an antithesis to the New Criticism, and most of all to Leavis. He is not concerned with close reading or with evaluation, or with any total encounter with individual works, and he has little interest in irony, realism, tensions of opposite tendencies, or tragedy. Like Brown, his central myth is one of rebirth, his central modes comedy and romance. And all this derives from his association of art with dream, with the transcendence of individual desire over social conditions. (Frye's novelist is John Barth. Barth's "anatomy," *Giles Goat-Boy*, exemplifies nearly all Frye's enthusiasms, combined in Frye's kind of synthesis.)

The same emphasis can be seen in the work of two critics who represent the best fruitfulness the post-Freudians can bring to literary studies. I mean Robert Garis in *The Dickens Theatre* and Richard Poirier in *A World Elsewhere*. The second is subtitled *The Place of Style in American Literature*, and its argument is that style has a special place there, because major American writers have used style as a means of self-assertion, and because the self thus asserted has not been the sordid sublunary competitive ego, but the transcendental and ideal self; the self Emerson bade us be. The argument is perhaps clearest as it applies to Emerson, whose style is itelf an exhortation to freedom, to the defying of traditional limitations, to the imaginative mastery of the universe. And what is granted about Emerson may be taken as proved about Thoreau and Whitman. But Poirier is most interested in fiction, and applies his theory to James, whose style, especially in the late novels, dominates everything it describes, transforming it from that "real-life" form which is in fact dictated by society into an environment of freedom for the novels' heroes; who, for instance Strether, themselves "imagine" their experience in defiance of reality. They are in a sense dreaming their lives, and James, Poirier says, is in collusion with them. He makes similar points about Melville and Faulkner, and indeed extends his argument to cover

Cooper, Hawthorne, and Twain. But what I have already reported makes it clear how much this depends on the idea of literature as dream, the product of a triumph of self over system. It is worth noting, too, that Poirier thinks that in British literature the self is not always presented as in conflict with society—that the writer's interest is often in the ways the one can enrich and extend the other—but that in American literature you don't find this.

I'll conclude with two quotations from Norman Mailer's "The White Negro: Superficial Reflections on the Hipster," which demonstrate, I think, an extreme version of post-Freudian sensibility working itself out spontaneously, in independence of its intellectual origins:

> Knowing in the cells of his existence that life was war, nothing but war, the Negro (all exceptions admitted) could rarely afford the sophisticated inhibitions of civilization, and so he kept for his survival the art of the primitive, he lived in the enormous present . . . relinquishing the pleasures of the mind for the more obligatory pleasures of the body. . . . For jazz is orgasm, it is the music of orgasm. . . . If the fate of twentieth century man is to live with death from adolescence to premature senescence, why then the only life-giving answer is to accept the terms of death, to live with death as immediate danger, to divorce oneself from society, to exist without roots, to set out on that uncharted journey into the rebellious imperatives of the self. In short, whether the life is criminal or not, to encourage the psychopath in oneself, to explore that domain of experience where security is boredom and therefore sickness, and one exists in the present, in that enormous present which is without past or future, memory or planned intention . . . the psychopath may indeed be the perverted and dangerous front-runner of a new kind of personality which could become the central expression of human nature before the twentieth century is over.

That I take to be a pretty striking statement of the post-Freudian readiness to recommend disengagement from society and the pursuit of individual salvation. It is impossible to imagine anything like that being said in England in that post-Marxist movement which seems to me its equivalent for intellectual excitement and intensity. And with that I want to ask what conclusions can be drawn from this differentness between the two countries.

In one way it is easy enough to see why the two countries should be so different now, by considering their two histories of cultural thought. England had, as I said, a powerful tradition of cultural criticism all through the nineteenth and twentieth centuries. This was a tradition of speculative thought and aesthetic criticism, but not without a practical social effectiveness, which rooted it in objective social realism and activism. The national education system, for instance, is powerfully influenced by it; the teaching of English in particular is very much in touch with the whole Leavis movement. The teacher training colleges are full of Leavis disciples. So neither literature itself nor literary comment has been presented as the arena of a merely hostile struggle between the individual and society. The stress has been on that fruitful interaction between the two ideally possible. Whereas in America, even that same tradition of cultural thought, in its native manifestations in Emerson and Whitman, has laid much more stress on self-reliance, on the individual's wonderful and sufficient possession of a private self. The individual has not so much defied society, as in one French tradition, or redrawn his contract with it, as in the British, as transcendently evaded it. Philip Rieff, describing psychological man as a new form of humanity only just being born, admits that in America he may have a history, even a nineteenth-century manifestation.

This contrast was obscured in the recent past because of the New Critics' hostility to transcendentalism, and because of the interpretation those critics therefore gave to even nineteenth-century classics of American literature like Hawthorne and Melville. But nowadays we have something of a new Romanticism in America, in criticism and cultural theory as well as in creative art, and the old version of the national identity, the pre-eminent interest of Emerson, for instance, as an American mind, is re-established. If America is again seen as the land of individualism and transcendentalism, albeit re-interpreted in a post-Freudian way, then a contrast with England very relevant to our problem becomes 'clear' again. In fact, however, to focus on this contrast, to revive this tradition, is itself an act of interpretation, which does not derive from evidence alone, nor can be justified by evidence alone, so its "clarity" or its "obscurity" are themselves tendentious terms. And I have no theory better based on evidence, no explanation worthy of the name, to offer.

But I have one comment. Putting the two movements face to face mostly makes us aware of the weaknesses of both. Each makes an implicit comment on the other which seems pretty pertinent. (In all that follows I use my key terms to refer to the figures I have called representative of those movements, not to those I have called their allies. For example, I do not here include Garis or Poirier as post-Freudians, because they draw on other sources of strength which save them from the weaknesses I ascribe to the movement.) Seen from the post-Freudian point of view, the post-Marxists are aridly theoretical and out of touch with the majority of people writing or composing today, with the processes of composition, and all too often with processes of reading. The way the post-Freudians talk about the modern situation bears some obvious relation to the way most people in the arts feel and behave. The way the post-Marxists talk relates to that condition only as to something to be cured in other people. They are prescribing an art which ought to exist, and with what does exist they deal rather stiffly, primly, deadly. Raymond Williams's exemplary tragedy, *Koba*, seems to me a non-play.

Conversely, the post-Freudians, once seen from their rivals' point of view, are surely childish in their idea of what culture is. If affluence and automation are making possible a world in which repression will no longer be necessary, first of all the bulk of the world is not sharing in this affluence. Secondly, this affluence even in a rich country is being achieved and maintained by an elaborate technology and elaborate systems of human controls. Power is remaining with those who have sublimated their energies—by repression—into formidable weapons of intelligence and will-power; just as before; not with the self-delighting heroes of Eros. The future the post-Freudians talk of is only a possibility—and only that—in one part of one country; in an America without a Pentagon and without General Motors and without universities. There is no such country. In effect, this theory identifies a culture with its Bohemia.

Both ideas seem to me, for all their energy, strangely incomplete. Or perhaps it is not strange, since they are still young, but signally incomplete. Neither has, for instance, worked out its own literary taste or critical vocabulary. In literary matters the post-Marxists are still Leavisite, and the post-Freudians are still modernist. The artists Susan Sontag recommends to us are Artaud, Rimbaud, Kafka, Bosch; and the artistic virtues, derangement, anguish, distortion, ugliness. Both groups are living on their inheritances—if indeed they may not be said to be usurping those inheritances. First-class literary work is likely to come from their allies, their collateral branches, rather than from them.

However, their mutual criticism does not amount to a canceling out of either, to my sense. I don't want to feel either set of ideas muzzled and made harmless, for each is valuable in its way. The setting of the two in opposition satisfies me, I think, not because they destroy each other, but because they work out a vivid dialectic between them. And if saying that reveals a personal motive behind the pattern of comparison I've made, I've said plenty of other things which surely bear witness to there being something there which demands patterning.

Chapter 18

REFLECTIONS OF
1972

I happen to be living this year in London, while still teaching for Tufts, my university in America. Tufts rents a hotel in Stanhope Gardens and sends about fifty students there every September for a year's study of drama and literature. I find myself therefore living in America in Stanhope Gardens, and in England in Cheltenham Terrace, twenty minutes walk away. It is of course academic America I live in (or rather student-dormitory America, for there are no other teachers) and it is elegant England; the terraces and gardens of Chelsea, with the people all prosperous, and either dashing or retired. (Its rectangular plan is given by the King's Road on one side, and the Chelsea Hospital on the other, Ranelagh Gardens and Tite Street.) But the ideological atmosphere of the two places, which differ sharply, do so in ways that relate to the larger differences between the two countries. In the hotel we talk about revolution. There is in fact a course in "Ages of Revolution," but apart from that, the idea is alive in the students' minds. While in Cheltenham Terrace and the park beyond, one thinks of stability, recurrence, continuity, and elegance.

I in fact think of one special kind of elegance, or *raffinement*. Because of my current reading, for me Chelsea is the home of a certain kind of twentieth-century artist and intellectual. I know that Logan Pearsall Smith lived on St. Leonard's Terrace, and that Cyril Connolly was his secretary there, when he first came down from Oxford in the 1920's. I know that Oscar Wilde and Whistler lived on Tite Street. So did William Acton the painter, brother of Harold Acton, who wrote *Memoirs of an Aesthete*, and who, like their friend, Brian Howard, used to stay with William there. The Sitwells lived in Carlyle Square, Ronald Firbank in Sloane Square, and Aubrey Beardsley worshipped in St. Barnabas' Church on Pimlico Road. These men were all dandies of one kind or another, and the tall painted Regency facades and studio windows of these streets are still, for me, the back-drop to their life-style.

In the 1920's this was a very *literary* kind of dandyism, and a *somewhat* tame and dowdy kind. Cyril Connolly, who has reflected a lot on dandyism and his own generation, associated Chelsea with fogs as much as with dandies, and both of those with prose as opposed to verse. For him, London is *the* capital of prose. And indeed, though there were some fine sartorial elegancies among these men, the questions of prose style were central—certainly meant more to them than to, say, Brummell and his friends. They could perhaps be called men fascinated *by* dandyism, and hoping to achieve some measure of its elegance by safe and literary means. Anyway, I found my thoughts about Chelsea, my sense of its atmosphere, continued quite naturally at the London Library, in St. James's Square. This is a quite dowdy institution, containing many symbols of the Victorian past and many symbols of continuance in service, like a photograph of an assistant librarian who spent seventy years there from 1882 to 1952. And the young people who work there now seem to come out of that past, with their short hair, neat suits, Northern accents, soft-voiced politeness, eagerness to serve. There is nothing dandified about them. By the standards of the King's Road, they are definitely dowdies. But the talents they have served, the writers who have belonged to the library, have written dandy books there. And those books have been England's intellectual profile in this century.

Stylistically elegant, intellectually these books have been in some sense adolescent. This is not a scholar's library, in the

German-American sense of full-scale scholarship. It is an Oxbridge undergraduate library, serving the Oxbridge amateur's literary humanism, which has been transplanted to London for the use of undergraduates gone down. One expects to meet Evelyn Waugh, Nancy Mitford, Cyril Connolly, Harold Acton, Harold Nicolson, round every corner. The good prose written there has been of that English kind, that dandy-cum-country-gentleman kind, which is part adolescent and part provincial by twentieth-century intellectual and artistic standards—the standards of major modern adventures of the mind.

And it is a striking feature of the literary England of 1972 that that prose and the mind behind it is still so much in evidence. In the "cultural" pages of the good Sunday papers Cyril Connolly and Maurice Richardson and Raymond Mortimer and Philip Toynbee and Angus Wilson and Malcolm Muggeridge still account for a high proportion of the space covered with print, and still establish a dominant tone for the rest. In the *Daily Express* the William Hickey gossip column and Beachcomber and the Osbert Lancaster Littlehampton cartoons are still full of the atmosphere of the 1920's. Among paperbacks, Evelyn Waugh's novels are still among the very highest sellers, and so forth.

There are of course other sectors of our culture where the dandy influence is minimal, or is present only as The Enemy. At the level of high culture, these sectors are emblemized if not dominated by the names of Lawrence and Leavis and their disciples and successors. They have constituted the great alternative to dandyism within British intellectual life—the fresh air and new nourishment. But they don't do so any longer, at least for me. What has struck me since I came back about those elements of the English imagination has been their continuance rather than their innovation or development. There don't seem to be any new ideas burgeoning on those stems. Just as in the dandy sectors, the same names and terms as thirty years ago define the situation. There *are* new achievements, and so in some sense developments, but they are modest in scope and even provincial. I was struck by this in, for instance, the Nottingham Castle Exhibition of D. H.

Lawrence's early years, "Young Bert." This was in the spirit of Leavis's Lawrence, both by its "statement"—that Lawrence drew great strength from being a member of Eastwood culture before the War—and by its application of that statement, its attempt to reconcile Nottingham to its famous son, to re-integrate that genius into the common culture.

The exhibition said these things with real inventiveness and style, of a modest and provincial kind. The mixture of realism and fantasy in the presentation, the appeal to the viewers' imagination, the appeal to their memories, the *Biedermeier* evocation of miners' kitchens, the home-made schoolroom quality of some of the effects—the very home-made giant Rainbow, for instance—these were provincial achievements. But seen in the larger scene of the *national* life, the exhibition was stating platitudes, truisms, dying dulling truths. We have heard too much about Young Bert, the Eastwood boy, and about the rich content of Eastwood culture. Intellectual sincerity now demands that we name Lawrence Lorenzo. It was Lorenzo who wrote the books we admire. If Lawrence had stayed Young Bert, or stayed true to Eastwood, we should have had the author of *The White Peacock* and *The Trespassers*. He would certainly have written better in *some* ways as he grew older. But he had to remake himself, and Frieda's help in this was crucial, before he could write *The Rainbow* or even *Sons and Lovers*. The exhibition was admirable in its own provincial terms, but by being so good it assumed a national character in Lawrence studies or called attention to the lack of anything national to compete with it and invited judgment by national standards. And by those standards its intellectual quality was cosy.

That is the feeling that has imposed itself on me most since I came home, the cosiness of the intellectual and imaginative scene here. That is why Chelsea could seem typically English to me, even though I knew how much of England was unlike Chelsea. In all England there is no real space between the major people and their ideas, no resonance among the dandies and among their opponents. One example of this was a satirical TV programme in which Auberon Waugh described and presented to us a shoot at the Earl of Onslow's estate. The programme was openly satirical, and mocked the members of the shoot for destroying harmless birds and for being rich and upper class. But Waugh was himself clearly just as upper class as they, and clearly those on the screen shared his sense of the joke. The Earl of Onslow is his brother-in-law, and when Waugh said, stressing the cruelty to animals, "Only the *brave* deserve the fair; and here comes the lovely young Countess of Onslow," it is his sister who appears bashfully before the camera, and one knows that one is at a family party. This is not satire, because there is no distance, personal or ideological, between mocker and mocked. He pointed to his three or four year old nephew, who was running along behind the adults, learning the ways of the shoot, and said, "Here is little Lord Something, *plucky* little fellow." To be satirical, that line would have to be savage. Clearly it wasn't savage, but humorous, and so it wasn't satirical. This was rather satire *of* satire. And English TV is like that. To turn on the set is to clamp down over one's head a world as small and shiny as a hair-drier.

At the hotel, discussing ideas with my students, there is all the space and resonance in the world. We read Blake, and compare him with Mailer, read Mary Wollstonecraft and compare her with Doris Lessing, read Godwin and compare him with Paul Goodman, and so on. Paine's essays lead us to reflect on the absence of any equivalent in the McGovern campaign. On the American intellectual scene such sweeps of perspective come more naturally than they do on the British scene.

Of course, they come so easily because of all the anger and violence on the American scene. And the end to that violence is likely to be found, or sought, by means of reaction. The signs are set for a decline of radicalism and even of liberalism, and a rise of conservatism. I had five American books to review together for the *Guardian*, and I found that they delivered a common message. And the massive vote for Nixon seemed to corroborate that message; that the conservative mind in America was recovering its courage, and the radical mind was running out of conviction. These were books about ideas, so their message was not a close equivalent to the election vote. But it was parallel in tendency, and the distance between the two made their parallelism the more impressive—this was a general reaction, running at different levels of culture.

Reading those books was an occasion for me to reflect on "America"; on my part of it—intellectual America—and my part in it—my duties toward it and expectations from it and fears of it. The country had meant such various things, and such powerful things, to me, and these books were recording the deaths of so many of them.

One was a fluent and elegant performance by a professor of government at Harvard, an author of books on Russian Marxism which have been translated into several languages. He had made a success out of the intellectual life as the West lives it, and he resented the radicals' moralistic attack on that life. We now always ask "Who has sinned?" instead of "Who has goofed?" he complained. (Being a man of the world, he let touches of vulgarity spice his elegance.) Mystique and education don't mix. Radicalized American universities have copied the worst feature of totalitarian regimes—that forced participation in meetings, meetings, meetings, so that no one is left to get on with his own work, or play. He looked back with nostalgia to 1945, when he entered Harvard graduate school, and when "university politics" meant non-political politics. Students then, he still thought, had "a certain sober grace and gaiety." He blamed the present disasters on the ambitions that had driven individual academics and whole universities to meddle in matters not their business, whether in national policy in Washington or in the personal therapy of their students. Back to the old guidelines of the old intellectual tradition, was his cry.

This meant only "back," I thought, and I found the professor too fluent and elegant by half. But I thought him shrewd to base his complaint on that moralization and indeed mystification of university politics. Those four to eight hour meetings on minor points *were* intolerable. At the largest, these points were symbolic—should there be recruiting or R.O.T.C. on campus?—and real issues were often slighted in favor of the symbolic. Moreover, more typically, these were smaller points, for example, should students attend faculty meetings, should they speak there, and so forth. In such discussions political enthusiasm was intensified but falsified. The campus cannot really be treated as a political microcosm, containing all the national issues on a reduced scale, because it is such a privileged enclave, with all its essential freedoms granted a priori. National issues are reflected there, nearly always, in such rose-jelly forms, and the political zeal about them is grotesquely distorted. It was the hot breath of self-righteousness one breathed at those meetings, and a good deal of conviction—of readiness for radical change—died in that unnourishing air. But the opposite readiness—to revert to the *status quo ante*—that would not be born with this author as midwife.

Nevertheless, the problems he called our attention to were real enough. And the sharpest form they took was a series of challenges to moral-political action. He discussed the student occupation of University Hall, Harvard, on April 9, 1969, and the calling in of the police to expel them, and the subsequent recriminations. Another book dealt with the 1969 November Action of M.I.T. students, who occupied the Instrumentation Laboratory there and who were also ejected by the police. This was part of a larger "action." On March 4, faculty and students had organized a research stoppage. The Union of Concerned Scientists and the Science Action Coordinating Committee demanded that all military research at the institution should be discontinued. (The Instrumentation Laboratory had got $54 million from the Department for Defense in 1969, which was a considerable part of the Institution's total budget.) The Laboratory employees opposed the students; one union filed suit against M.I.T., to prevent it from doing what the students wanted. There were Agenda Days, a Review Panel, a November Action, and finally, on May 20, the compromise solution; the Laboratory severed connection with the university, but the military research went on. It is indeed a vivid case of university radicalism, and how long ago it seems—especially as it was rehearsed in this book.

This was a case-study, one of a series written by a team at Cornell, who study the complex implications of technological developments, such as building power-stations, using birth-control techniques, promoting military research, etc. The approach was social-scientific, rigidly objective, unconsciously obfuscating. It was an approach as hostile to radicalism as the professor's, in the long run, because one feels the issues receding into museum cabinets as they are analysed and classified this way. They recede from all moral reality. "In the political context of the late 1960's, 'problems of conscience' in the scientific community led to serious disenchantment with the symbiotic relationships between science and government." In this language as much as in overheated rhetoric ideas die. The extra effort a writer must make to push through the clutter and touch the idea on the reader's behalf, that effort is not provided for in this "social-science" approach. This approach reinforces the inhibitions, the caution, the abstractions, that keep the writer safe. And to compensate for that abstraction by elegancies like titling a chapter "Ménage à Trois" is only tying ribbons on a sausage grinder. Worse, it signals a failure in one's control over tone and meaning. Case-studies like this will not help us understand our problems, however diligently researched. They will merely cover those problems over in a gentle snow of abstractions in which all moral politics will die, and radicalism above all will be just a haunting cry in the cold.

So much one could say without too much hesitation. Criticism is easy. But beyond and behind the fumblings of this particular book lay the challenge of what one did, or rather did not do, in such situations oneself, what one would and would not do when they arose again. America was a country where moral-political action *happened* and demanded one's participation. One looked back at it from the safe vantage point of England with mixed feelings.

The liveliest of these books was Arnold Beichman's *Nine Lies About America*. Some of the generally accepted lies he set out to discredit were that America is a Fascist country, that it is an insane society, that it is genocidal, that it needs a violent revolution, that the bomber Left is a moral force. Beichman had reported labor news and revolutions abroad, for the *New York Times* and the *Herald Tribune*. He was three years city editor of *P.M.*, a left-wing daily. And he had still, he assured his readers, strong criticisms to make of American society. But he was tired of hearing these lies.

His book was dedicated to his parents, "who found in America what they could not find in their land of birth." The Harvard professor also had been born outside America, and shared this sense of gratitude to it, which derived from a sense of the contrast between it and other countries—a sense he and Beichman felt that the radical young had lost. Beichman also thanked Irving Kristol, Gertrude Himmelfarb, Richard Hofstadter, Melvin Lasky, A. M. Rosenthal, and the Trillings. In other words, his was the new conservatism of the New York Jewish Left. (Was this all one really meant oneself? Was this the company one should have been keeping?)

His book had a foreword by Tom Wolfe, who found these radical lies very "entertaining," because they showed "what fools these mortals be." He distinguished the intellectual from the scholar the same way he distinguished the *artiste* from the artist. This is the kind of distinction the Harvard professor would have applauded, and like him both Wolfe and Beichman made much of logic, clarity, correct language—the machinery of the old intellectual life. Both indeed appealed to Orwell and to his criticism of radical writing. But it is not Orwell who Wolfe reminds us of, but Mencken. Wolfe romps around in his paragraphs as in his tub, splashing everyone with the exuberant fun of being Tom Wolfe. There is no real ascesis behind this conservatism.

I ended my review by saying that Beichman (and the others to some extent) appealed to Burke and to English tradition in general. He apparently had belonged to the Tuesday Luncheon Club in London, and he thanked Kingsley Amis, Robert Conquest, Anthony Hartley, and others he met there. Orwell, as we have seen, was often cited, and the British distrust of "intellectuals." Coming at such a moment of choice and hesitation, this may well announce a general turning in our direction by Americans seeking an alternative to the ideology they have just discarded. We had better bestir ourselves, if we are to have anything to offer.

I wrote that last part of my review satirically and pessimistically. With all the dangers of the American situation, and all the crudities of the American mind, I thought, it has a vitality which the British equivalents lack. Promethean or Faustian man has access to powers that no dandy can rival.

But what I came to think, when I read what I had written, was that I was identifying "America" by tracing among its many profiles a craggy one which I had selected on different principles from those I consulted in looking for "England's" profile. By what right did I take the Promethean types as central to American culture, and the dandies as central to English, and thus make the entity "America" so much larger and fiercer than the entity "England?" I had my reasons (really interesting and valid ones, I still thought) but why did I have those reasons rather than others which I saw leading other people to different interpretations? What about *socialist* England having something to offer America? What about proletarian England and the body of theory being developed by Raymond Williams to articulate proletarian experience and hopes? Why did I see such large forces in the American situation, such small ones in the British, when clearly there were closer equivalents to both—"large" forces in England, and vice versa? In the old days, the days of *Mirror for Anglo-Saxons*, I would have tried much harder to find true equivalents, and would have allowed disparities only in the case of, as evidence of, a passionate intuitive conviction. Only if I *knew* that America was to be identified with this image, England with that disparate one, would I let myself offer the pair, then. Now, I was quite complacently accepting a disparity between them, almost welcoming it. Then I said, one *must* see England and America this way. Now I said, one *may* see them this way, and this is my way. I still said "this is true," but now I mean this is *a* truth, not *the* truth. And while I still thought about both countries' political and cultural problems in a problem-solving way, I also relaxed that concern and merely observed and speculated and contemplated, allowing my imagination much more autonomy. This led to practical differences of imaginative enterprise.

Clearly one could introduce the missing element of distance into British culture by creating a dialogue, by mediating the conflict, between Chelsea and that insurgent political underworld glimpsed in industrial strikes and in radical intellectual groups. It would be possible to find in that underworld some sources of vitality like those one feels in American life. But that possibility is not a very promising one in England, at least for me to develop. It is after all already being developed, by lots of other people, with whom I am in sympathy in every way except that of participation and cooperation. My instinct is that their work will not be fruitful because their expectations are overdetermined, their imaginations are not being allowed enough freedom to be spontaneous.

Certainly recent experience teaches us that the hope of finding imaginative vitality by means of political commitment is a hope rather than a promise. The working-class writing published in the late 1930's and during the war in *New Writing* and elsewhere did not revitalize British culture. It did not create a dialogue between the Chelsea writers (the same ones were around then) and the world from which these pieces came. It did not even achieve significant literary vitality itself. The other way—to me a more promising one—to try for a new vitality is by means of what amounts to an Apollonian transcendence of such conflicts. Though this has the discrediting reputation of being the most obvious and traditional way to deal with the problem, in fact, it has not been tried. Not with intellectual and imaginative passion. There has been no sufficient effort to understand and to imagine and to put together, to realize and relate a variety. That, when it is done with passion, can be a kind of cultural vitality in itself.

And I find a lot of other elements of English life, other to me, which manifest themselves within the narrow slice of London I inhabit, which can be imaginatively embraced in that way. There is the King's Road on one side of me, and the Chelsea Pensioners on the other. Both are alien to me, but both are rich and vivid. The King's Road is of course a theater, a circus, and so has its character of feverish self-display and self-prostitution. But once one is used to that (once one accepts that a civilization like ours will have such a theater, will have its Dionysiac phases) it is remarkable how hearty, simple, and even good-natured this exhibitionism is. It isn't perversity one sees as one walks along the road, and certainly it isn't exploitation. It is a self-rejoicing proletarian dandyism, an expansion of self and a worship of life by the typical dandy means of incorporating all that is beautiful into one's own style. The towering platform soles and high heels the men wear, and even the Gibson-Girl S-curves into which those tilt their bodies, are no signs of corruption, because they convey no sense of self-degradation. These men's pride in their bodies' allure, their desirability as sexual objects, nourishes their self-respect in just the same way as muscles and fighting power would have done in the old days. The swing of those mignon hips, and even the toss of that cascade of curls has the same function as the old roll of the shoulders, and is often accompanied by just as tough and aggressive an eye. Some of the most remarkable figures are the older buccaneers of sex, marked by long and successful erotic careers, and able to distill an extra glamor even out of their aging.

All this *crêpe de chine* décolletage and costume jewelry is no worse than the starched linen and buckskin Brummel parade down St. James's between White's and Crockford's. It is certainly healthier than those top-hatted Eton parades which lie behind the dandy sensibility of the authors I have been reading. Henry Green describes walking with his elder brother, when the latter was a member of Pop, and Lord Berners describes walking with his handsome and fashionable friend, Denniston, on the Lock Up parade, and what they record were moments of the keenest delight and excitement for those who participated; the testimony of dozens of intelligent men agrees that such moments set standards and patterns for the rest of their emotional life. That is the real danger of dandyism, that it may perpetuate itself, lock the dandy into the hall of mirrors for the rest of his emotional life. That is less likely to happen on the King's Road, because of the comparative diffusion, anonymity, open-endedness. The fatal excitement of the Eton scene derived largely from its concentration, reinforcement, repetition—the multiplicity of contacts between the same people, day after day, who knew everything about each other. The King's Road, comparatively speaking, is a healthy manifestation of dandy eroticism.

The Duke of York's Headquarters are directly on the King's

Road, and the Chelsea Hospital and the new National Army Museum are just across Burton's Court, while the Guards' Barracks are just down the Chelsea Bridge Road. This is a very military part of London. But it is striking how alien in spirit this military elegance is to that of the King's Road. The army must be in any country one of the permanent centers of dandyism, since the cult of the male body, and particularly of the *young* male body, is necessarily part of its mythos. Yet when one sees young army officers on the King's Road—even in civilian clothes one recognizes them—their elegance is radically different. Proletarian dandyism is not their thing. Of course, the class affinity of the Guards officers is clearly with the upper middle-class buisnessmen who live just off, and yet infinitely remote from, the Road. But neither are the private soldiers of the Road type. They form a third race, each an ocean apart from the others as they brush past each other in the Sloane Square Tube Station. The soldiers one sees in the pubs near the Guards' barracks are country boys, who clump along in thick tweed sports coats and turtleneck sweaters, looking thick necked and stiff limbed. They are the antithesis of the wasp-thin ephebes of the Road with their feverish bodies fined down to the narrowest stiletto of pleasure and sheathed in the frailest cottons. Just as the soldiers' plump puddingy cropped heads are the antithesis of the others' flaring theater-posters of faces with hair, eyes, beards, all intensely dramatic. The skins, the flesh, the bones of the three races are alien to each other, and repudiate contact.

Of all the military manifestations, the Sunday Parade service at the Hospital is the most remarkable. It gives one the old England, Establishment, upper-class, official England. Thirty or forty pensioners parade, in blue or on great occasions scarlet, and are inspected to the roll of a drum. Then they are marched gently into the chapel—their age and frailty set off against Wren's marble, oak, and stucco grandeur. On great days trumpeters from the Life Guards tramp down the aisle, trumpeting their calls to death and glory, flashing their brass helmets and white thighs between the pews of bald and shaking heads. The officers wear spurs and white plumes in their hats, and the commander marches the length of the chapel to read the Lesson, his hand on the pommel of his sword, his spurs clanking discreetly, his head slightly bowed. He reads it very well, in a ringing but not over-emphatic voice. He appropriates the service, and Christianity, for the Empire, or the Commonwealth. The physical type of the officers is predominantly small-headed and small-featured, smooth-skinned and crisp-haired, handsome even in age. Or perhaps that is the predominant *handsome* type. There are also the heavy, red-faced types, whose faces are concentrations of command. But all have a certain air of innocence. So much of life is non-professional to them. In peace-time, so few of the issues that trouble others can seem their concern to them. The soldiers, bald or white-haired and waxed-skinned above their blue or their scarlet, look quite nun-like in their quietude. It is literally nuns one thinks of, as one watches them sit so patiently, so quietly, in their pews. The flannel of their uniforms, like that of the habit, no doubt creates something of an optical illusion, in making their faces seem so untouched, so remote, so removed. But the discipline that the uniform represents presumably *does* simplify their lives and relieve them of responsibilities.

The hymns are the standard ones, the prayers extra-patriotic, the preachers hearty and chaplainy. It is not much like religion. But it is very poignant as a national ritual, all the more now that it seems so harmless, so ineffectual, so out of touch with the rest of the national life. The atmosphere in the chapel is very much that of a garrison service in some outpost of the Empire, except on a very grand scale. Perhaps the services in the Viceroy's Chapel in New Delhi were like this. And it is doubly poignant when a regiment sends a band to the chapel, and one sees the pensioners side by side with younger men, younger soldiers.

Perhaps the most eloquent thing is the faces of the officers' wives. There are large, dignified, managerial women there, of the type of Mrs. Turton in *Passage to India*; there are one or two *charming* women—Mrs. Minivers—bright-faced, whimsical, musical, ironical; but most of them fall into two related categories, the cruelly dowdy and the harshly dashing. The dowdy ones often spend a lot of money on clothes that just don't do what clothes should—that are just imitations of clothes. The faces below those circles of straw or fur often wear a lot of make-up, which seems equally inappropriate, beside the point. They are faces strangely innocent of expression and experience. They have never achieved any of the major expressions, or any adventurous experiences. They are uninteresting human beings, drilled into a human style that was only an imitation of being human. They are much more deformed than the soldiers. The dashing ones bear the marks of age from early on and wear *smart* hats and clothes and make-up, which challenge the viewer to deny the wearer's sex-appeal. That appeal is there all right, but it is crude, naked, almost ugly, like that of a bitch in heat. There is an attractive gallantry about some of them, which combines with a sex-appeal, but it is a haggard, pathetic gallantry. These are the "grand girls" whom Evelyn Waugh writes about and Anthony Powell—the Virginia Troys and Jean Duports, and Lancaster's Maudie Littlehampton. There is a tremble to their fingers, as they adjust their dashing hats, and wait for the service to begin. Perhaps they drink heavily. But the purple cheeks of the dowdy ones give the same hint. And after the service they pay their respects to the commanding officer, and totter away on too high heels over the gravel to their cars and are driven away to cocktails.

These faces are new to me. Of course, they are the oldest platitudes of "England," to the tourist and the travelogue. But partly just for that reason, I have never been able to focus my eyes fully on them, or regard them as part of my nation. Partly because I was committed to seeing other faces and other streets and other smiles as "English"—*Saturday Night and Sunday Morning*—I couldn't see these. Now I do. That's the great difference between this book and *Mirror for Anglo-Saxons*.

This idea is more vivid in relation to English subjects, because it means a more drastic change of loyalties, away from my old ones there. In matters of American culture I had no such master as Leavis, and no such party as his to belong to and to follow the policies of. Moreover, I met in America the extraordinarily playful genius of Nabokov, whose lessons I might be said to be applying now, so he and it are related for me. I had no great changes to make in my imaginings of American culture—only to confirm my resistances to the Calvinist Left there. What I had to do was in England, was—what I had been doing—to re-imagine Leavis and Lawrence.

Of course one cannot offer just an indiscriminate cataloguing or even appreciation of everything as an imaginative policy with much cultural promise. Lots of people have gone that way before, and meager were the posies they came back with. Some flowers are just not worth picking. Everything depends on the discrimination. But the taste that guides discrimination may be more or less autonomous. The policy I am recommending allows taste a great autonomy, and relieves it from the pressure of many responsibilities I have hitherto acknowledged. If I have read the signs wrong, I shall fall into mere triviality, impressionism, aestheticism. But perhaps I have read them right.

Index

Index

Index

Index

Index

Index